DAUGHTER OF LAZARUS

Daughter of Lazarus

Albert A. Bell, Jr.

Cover Illustration:
Ken Walker

Library of Congress Catalog Number
87-72375

ISBN 0-87029-215-3

St. Meinrad, Indiana 47577

For
Bettye Jo

Because I said I would dedicate my first book to her,
and because she believed there would be a first book.

PROLOGUE

FALL, A.D. 61

"Have I done the right thing, Yesu?" Sarah wondered softly. Sitting in silence for a moment as though listening to a reply, she added, "What else could I have done?"

What else, indeed. The infant girl tugging at her breast and the young boy sleeping in the bed beside her testified to the urgency of her decision. Her situation was reducible to a simple fact: her husband was dead. The news had almost killed her. Her darling Lazarus, so handsome and strong for a man of fifty, so proud of his young children—ignoring the snide comments questioning their parentage—had left on a business trip to the province of Asia shortly after the birth of his daughter. Word had come two months ago that he had been killed in an earthquake in Laodicea.

"Dear Yesu, could you not protect him so far away from Antioch?" Sarah began to weep as the memories of those few precious years with her gentle husband welled up. "He believed you were a god," she said bitterly. "Can you not do again what he claimed you did for him once in Bethany?"

Only a few days after the news of Lazarus' death arrived, Sarah had been visited by Ariston, a Greek moneylender with whom Lazarus occasionally—though reluctantly— had dealings. She had been expecting him. He had made no secret of his desire for her, and she had rebuffed him in no uncertain terms. Now, showing documents witnessed by the city magistrates (among whom was an influential cousin), Ariston claimed that Lazarus had borrowed large sums of money from him to finance his last business trip.

"But our business is small," Sarah had objected. "My husband would never have borrowed such sums. And I doubt that you ever had that much to lend."

He held up the documents again. "These prove that I did." He stepped closer to her, and she felt the same threat she always experienced in his presence. "I will take over Lazarus' business and home to repay the debt, as the law allows me to do," he added emphatically before she could protest. "I am entitled to take you and your children as slaves and to sell you if I choose. But I will offer you the opportunity to marry me, so you can preserve your freedom and that of your children."

"What else could I have done?" she now wondered aloud. She was helpless, a Jew in a gentile city, a woman without a husband or family. Slavery of one sort or another was inevitably her fate. At least she would do what was best for her children.

Though her new husband could not change the fact that they were Lazarus' children, he had attempted to take them away from his dead rival by changing their names. Joshua's name became Jason. And the baby, Martha, would never learn the name given her in memory of Lazarus' sister. Her stepfather had renamed her in honor of his favorite mistress, Lorcis.

Tomorrow Ariston would move into this house which, though modest, was far nicer than his own. Perhaps, Sarah thought, it would be wise to hide the picture of Yesu. Her new husband, a devotee of Hermes, god of merchants and travelers—and thieves—would not understand. And perhaps she shouldn't be too angry at Yesu. Without his miraculous intervention she would never have known Lazarus at all, or borne his children.

"Don't desert us," she whispered.

BOOK I

June, A.D. 80

CHAPTER

I

Lorcis was awakened by someone prodding her in the ribs. "You, flute player," a thin, whiney voice was saying. "Wake up!" She rolled over to escape the rough treatment, but it continued. "Come on! Up you go!" A pudgy hand grabbed her arm and pulled her to a sitting position.

Her head hanging down, she opened her eyes. As she focused them she saw that her stola—the long, loose gown worn by Roman women of all classes—had worked itself up past the middle of her thighs. She was about to pull it down when Harmodius, eunuch and chief steward of her owner's household, jerked her to her feet. She steadied herself and cleared her vision enough to realize that she had been sleeping on a couch in the triclinium where her master had given a riotous dinner party the night before. Judging from the disarray of the room, the guests had enjoyed themselves thoroughly. Her only memories of the evening were disjointed, blurred, and slightly distasteful.

Harmodius shook her. "Are you awake?"

Lorcis slapped his hand away. She was no stranger to the touch of a man—or of a woman, for that matter—but this fat, oily creature was neither, and she found him repulsive.

"Yes, I'm awake," she mumbled. "What I want to know is why I'm awake." She slumped back down on the edge of the couch and yawned.

"The master says you're to go to your room and pack your things," Harmodius replied smugly.

Anxiety suddenly cleared Lorcis' head. "Pack? in the middle of the night? why?"

"Because you don't belong here anymore," Harmodius taunted her with obvious glee. "You've been sold!"

Lorcis could not have been more stunned if he'd told her she had died and was now awake in the underworld. "Sold? to whom? why?" she cried helplessly.

"Just pack and get back down here quickly," Harmodius barked. "Slaves shouldn't ask questions. Of course, you never have understood that, so I don't know why I should expect you to start now."

He had disliked the girl since the day, nine years earlier, when Encolpius had brought her back to Naples after buying her during a business trip to Antioch. Even then, at age ten, she had been willful and stubborn. He often beat her or deprived her of food or privileges. Then, at age fourteen, she became the master's favorite. Now she was clever, educated, and spirited—spoiled, Harmodius thought—qualities which made his task of managing her more difficult. She had never reported her mistreatment to Encolpius since she knew Harmodius was in a position to exact his own subtle but unpleasant revenge. The relationship between slave and steward constantly verged on warfare.

"You old biddy," Lorcis jeered as she left the triclinium. Entering the atrium—the large reception hall—she glanced up at the open skylight and realized that it was in fact morning, though very early. She knelt by the impluvium, the pool beneath the skylight where rainwater was collected, to refresh herself.

As she splashed her face, she examined it to see if there were any marks from the festivities the evening before. None were visible, but she was more aware of certain parts of her body than she liked to be. At least her blue eyes sparkled. They offset what she considered her worst feature: a slightly pointed chin. But even her chin was dear to her, for all she could remember of her mother was that she had had the same characteristic.

Running her fingers through her long black hair, which someone had unpinned and let down, she shook her head to let the tresses fall into place—and to clear the fuzziness from last night's wine. She could not recall exactly what she'd done, especially in the latter part of the evening. From the condition of her stola and the soreness of some parts of her body, she knew that things must have gotten boisterous.

Lorcis stood up, straightened her stola, and climbed the

stairs leading off the atrium to the servants' quarters. Her room was the last and smallest on the dim hall, a testimony to Harmodius' disdain for her. But she had her revenge; most of her nights were spent in the master's bedroom.

Packing wasn't difficult. Her owner, though basically a kind man by Roman standards, allowed his slaves to keep very few personal belongings. Lorcis had only one other stola, some toilet articles, and her flutes—which she now realized were still in the triclinium. The one truly personal item she possessed was a wooden medallion about three inches by four inches, with a picture of a bearded man painted on one side and some strange markings on the other. Lorcis assumed the markings were writing but did not know what language it was. Nor did she know for certain who the man was, though she dimly remembered that her mother had made some connection between him and her real father. As a child, she had pretended that the image represented her real father; as a more mature young woman, she even created a whole personality for him, a composite of all the things men in her own life had failed to be.

The medallion was her only link to her past, to a time when she had not been a slave but a child of a family living in the city of Antioch in Syria. She had no memory of her father, who had died shortly after her birth. The only male parent she had known was her stepfather, and she could no longer recall his face.

Her bedridden mother had given her the medallion at the age of five, just before Lorcis had been sold for the first time. Her mother had been quite secretive about the object. "Don't let your stepfather know you have it," she had said. "We'll hide it and pretend we're playing a game." She had inserted it into Lorcis' favorite rag doll and had sewed up the seams carefully. "Always guard it well and it will protect you," her mother had admonished her.

Looking at the medallion, loneliness welled up in her. Where was her mother? Was she still alive? Had her mother tried to find her? What about her brother? Any time she was in the marketplace, she would study the faces of the merchants, especially those from Syria, on the chance that her brother might be among them. At those times she experienced a distinct sense of her differentness, a sense of separation from the people around her, a distance that kept her from ever quite belonging among a group of people, however popular or physically desirable she might appear to be. Now she was being cast out of the one place she had convinced herself she could at least live pleasantly, even if she never felt entirely able to let down those defenses by which she protected herself from other people. That shell had been developing since her early childhood.

Her stepfather had never been financially successful. When several business ventures failed within a few years and he became desperate for money, he had sold Lorcis into slavery. One afternoon, when her mother was too sick to know what was happening, he came home with a man and simply said to Lorcis, "Go with him and do as he tells you." She could not remember her stepfather saying good-bye or touching her—not that he'd ever shown her much affection. She had tried so hard to please him—to avoid displeasing him. But he had never shown any interest in her or her brother. As her new owner led her out the door, she had watched her stepfather count coins and put them into his money pouch.

From that childhood home Lorcis had taken nothing with her except her doll—and she'd been able to keep that only because her nine-year-old brother had run after her to bring it to her. "It's very special to her," he had said meekly to the man who was regarding them suspiciously. Lorcis had hugged it tightly, fearing that the man would take it from her and feel the medallion inside. But he merely shrugged his shoulders and led her away, doll in hand.

As they had wormed their way through a particularly crowded street, the man had picked her up to keep from losing her in the throng. He smelled different from her stepfather; he was clean and perfumed.

"I know you don't understand what's happening, little one," he had said matter-of-factly, "but you'll actually be better off. You'll have plenty to eat and a clean place to sleep, and I don't imagine you'll have to work any harder for me than for that scoundrel Ariston."

The promise of enough food intrigued her. Because her brother was big enough to help in Ariston's little shop, he was fed first at every meal. She had seldom left the table with her hunger satisfied.

Lorcis lived in the household of this man, Evagrius, for five years, doing small jobs to assist the kitchen slaves. Once the novelty of a full stomach had worn off, however, she became a miserable child, unable to understand why her mother didn't come for her. Her unarticulated resentment of her situation gradually made her a rebel. Evagrius was a stern man who gave his steward a free hand in disciplining the slaves, and Lorcis often felt his cane on her legs and backside. Her instinct to fight back had always provoked even more punishment.

When she was ten Evagrius died, and his widow sold a number of slaves to reduce the size of the household. Since the steward considered her a difficult child, Lorcis had been included in the lot. Vividly, she still recalled being led onto the auction platform naked, as slaves were at public sales, with her hands tied behind her back. There had been appreciative murmurs from the buyers, for the promise of her beauty was already evident. After spirited bidding, Encolpius had paid quite a high price for her.

The trip back to Naples had been the happiest experience of Lorcis' life. Encolpius was wealthy enough to hire a boat exclusively for himself, the small group of freedmen and slaves traveling with him, and the cargo of spices and luxury goods he was bringing back to sell in his shops in Naples.

They had followed the usual pattern of breaking the journey into small island-hopping segments, from Antioch to Paphos on Cyprus, then Rhodes, from there to Crete, then to Syracuse on Sicily, and finally along the coast of southern Italy to Naples. As the only child aboard, Lorcis had received more kind attention than she had ever known. She remembered wishing that the trip would go on forever so all those people would continue to be nice to her and she would never have to work again.

Her special friend had been an elderly musician named Favonia, who taught her the rudiments of flute playing to while away the hours on the voyage. She had learned to play the *auloi,* two reed instruments held together by a leather band passing around the player's head and played simultaneously, one as a bass drone, the other carrying the melody. Lorcis had been pleased to discover that she was good at it, "a natural musician," Favonia had said.

But Lorcis derived more than just the satisfaction of doing something new and doing it well. For the first time in her young life she had a means of expressing her emotions which had known no natural outlet since she had been taken away from her mother. The slow, mournful Lydian tunes which Favonia herself loved seemed to Lorcis but an extension of the sadness in her own soul. Playing the flutes also delighted her because it brought praise from her master, something she had seldom, if ever, enjoyed.

Yes, except for the hatred of Harmodius, life in Encolpius' house had been good; she felt it was her home. She had matured here, physically and emotionally. She had learned to read and write—both Latin and Greek—and had become an accomplished musician and well-known entertainer, instead of the kitchen drudge Evagrius had fated her to be. She had first known a man here and had learned a variety of refinements on that act. For nine years Encolpius had been father, lover, teacher. Since the death of his wife five years ago, she had been virtually mistress of his house. She could not believe he would sell her.

As Lorcis came back downstairs, she heard two male voices coming from Encolpius' study, which opened off the atrium. One was the familiar voice of her master, the other that of a guest at the banquet the night before. She couldn't place a face with the second voice—there had been so many faces—but she was certain that person would be her new owner, and she didn't want to know yet who he was. Staying close to the wall of the atrium, she made her way to the triclinium to retrieve her flutes. Harmodius was there supervising half a dozen servants as they cleaned up. When he noticed Lorcis looking around, he smiled slyly.

"Storing up memories before you leave?" he asked in a deliberately loud voice.

Lorcis thought of several spiteful replies but decided to stick to her original purpose. Harmodius would not hesitate to damage or destroy something he knew to be precious to her. "I left my flutes in here," she replied with considerable restraint.

"Long, slender objects with holes in them?" Harmodius asked, giggling.

"Of course," Lorcis replied suspiciously.

"They're over here," the eunuch said, motioning to the floor behind him.

Lorcis crossed the room, her senses alert for any tricks or sudden moves. She knew that Harmodius, given one last chance to hurt or humiliate her, would snatch it.

But he did nothing until she reached down and touched the pipes. Then he quickly set his foot on the other end, holding the flutes down and pinning Lorcis' hand to the floor. She could not pull her hand free for fear of damaging the ivory flutes, which had been given to her by an admirer. Harmodius picked up a cup of stale wine from the table next to him and poured it on the flutes and on Lorcis' hand. When he finished, he stepped back squealing with laughter. "Don't you want them? You said you were looking for them."

Lorcis straightened up slowly. Harmodius was still giggling when she shook the flutes in his direction, spraying him with wine. As he jerked his hands up to wipe his face, she jabbed him in the stomach as hard as she dared with the ends of the flutes. When he doubled over, she brought her knee up to meet his face. The combination of blows, which she had observed in a recent scuffle between two slaves in the household, proved effective. Harmodius sprawled on his back on the floor, half-conscious, blood flowing freely from his nose and mouth.

Lorcis stooped down, pulled up the hem of his tunic, and wiped her flutes carefully. No one else in the room moved. Lorcis leaned down to the steward's left ear and whispered, "That doesn't even begin to pay you back. I can still feel every blow you ever landed on my body, and if I can ever find a way to get even . . . "

She broke off abruptly as Encolpius and another man entered the room in casual discussion. She quickly put her arm under Harmodius' neck. "Here, help me get him up," she said to a slave standing behind her.

Encolpius, startled, broke off his conversation. "What's happened here?"

"He slipped . . . on something wet," Lorcis replied before anyone else had a chance to answer. It was a typical slave's answer, not quite true but not entirely false either.

"His feet just went right out from under him," added Andreias, a new slave near her own age with whom Lorcis had become friendly during the previous year.

"I see," Encolpius muttered. "I hope he's not badly hurt." His philosophy in dealing with slaves was to pay as little attention as possible to them—except for the pretty female ones—as long as their work was done and order was maintained in the house. He was ready to dismiss the incident, but the man with him asked, "If he fell on his back, how did he bloody his face?"

"I believe he struck something as he fell, my lord," Andreias replied, helping Lorcis pull Harmodius upright.

The man was quiet for a moment and seemed to study something near Lorcis' knees. She glanced down to discover a bloody spot on her stola over her right knee. She turned slightly sideways so her leg became partially hidden by Harmodius' ample body.

"Yes," the man said, "I suppose there are all sorts of objects around here that could cause an injury of that sort. One should be aware of such dangers and take precautions."

His eyes met Lorcis' and held them for an instant. Then he turned to Encolpius. "Now, my friend, we need to conclude our business so I can be off to Rome."

"Yes, certainly," Encolpius nodded. "Lorcis, come with us." The two men turned and left the triclinium without waiting for her.

When Lorcis let go of Harmodius' arm he slumped to his knees, causing Andreias to stagger under the weight. She felt all eyes on her as she gathered up her bag and flutes and strode across the triclinium. She fixed her gaze on the door, however, and did not respond to the stares or to the one or two furtive waves.

When she entered the atrium, the stranger—her new master—was handing a bag of coins to Encolpius. "Fifty gold pieces was the price we agreed on, I believe," he was saying.

"Yes," Encolpius replied, opening the bag. "You don't mind if I count them, I trust."

"You'd be a fool not to," the stranger laughed. Lorcis thought the laugh an unpleasant sound, but it fit the man who made it. He was short, overweight, with a face that showed flashes of simulated charm which quickly fell back into a natural malicious expression. Lorcis remembered him from the banquet. His stories had been the coarsest, his appetite the largest.

Encolpius dumped the coins onto a small table and counted them, replacing them in the bag as he did so. When he finished, he pulled the drawstring tightly. Only then did he acknowledge Lorcis' presence.

"Well, now to deliver the merchandise," he said jauntily. "Lorcis, this is your new master, Marcus Aquilius Regulus."

Despite her inner turmoil, Lorcis bowed her head. Deference had been beaten into her so deeply that it had become instinctive. It also protected her. If she did not meet her new owner's eyes, he could not see the fear and loathing in them.

"You'll be leaving at once to go to Rome with him," Encolpius continued. "I'm sure you'll serve him with the same loyalty you've displayed toward me."

How could he be so calm? How could he talk with such detachment? Was this her home or an auction block? She would not let another man simply hand her over to someone else, as her stepfather had done, with no explanation.

"My lord," she blurted out, "could I speak with you in private for a moment?"

Encolpius jingled the bag of coins. "I'm no longer the one who gives or denies you permission, my dear." He looked at Regulus, who was watching the whole exchange from under half-closed eyelids. When Regulus nodded his consent, Encolpius looked displeased, like a man who has been caught at the last possible moment, just when he thinks he has successfully avoided something distasteful.

"All right," he said grudgingly. "Let's go into my study."

The study was a small room, windowless—as were most rooms in Roman houses—to retain heat in the winter and coolness in the summer. It contained a table and shelves holding Encolpius' small library. The scrolls were laid flat on the shelves, each with a tag identifying the contents attached to one end. Several multivolume works, such as Livy's history, were kept in small wooden buckets with lids. There were also buckets for correspondence and financial reports. An oil lamp hanging over the table provided the only illumination. Encolpius sat in the chair behind the table, forcing Lorcis to stand since there was only the one chair in the room.

"What do you wish to say to me?" he asked curtly. "And do be brief. Regulus is eager to be on his way."

Lorcis opened her mouth, but the words would not form themselves. Her pride would not let her vent the tears being prompted by the uncertainty and fear that possessed her. The worst thing that could happen to a slave had just befallen her: she had been sold by a kindly master to a man whose character she fearfully questioned. What sort of treatment would she receive at his hands? Slaves coming into Encolpius' household had told of beatings administered on the whim of a despotic master and of insubordinate slaves assigned to types of work that meant a lingering but inevitable death. What had she done to deserve being sold?

Lorcis covered her face with her hands while Encolpius remained seated, staring at the table and drumming his fingers on its surface. When she was in control of herself again, taking deep breaths to keep her voice steady, she said, "My lord, I don't understand . . . why I'm being sold. How . . ."

"Is that why you asked to talk to me," Encolpius flared, "to call me to account for selling you? Perhaps Harmodius is right. I have indulged you too much." He stood up; he was a tall man and knew his height intimidated people.

"Lorcis, you are a slave. Masters sell slaves at their own pleasure, just as they do anything else they want with them. They do not ask the slaves' permission or explain their actions to them. You're being sold because I've decided to sell you. It's as simple as that."

Lorcis had never known him to be so callous and imperious toward her.

"But how can you bring yourself to sell *me*?" she pleaded. "We have shared . . . so much over the past five years. Don't I mean anything to you? Don't you love me?" She reached out her arms to him in despair.

"Love you?" Encolpius snorted. "Do you think life is a Greek comedy, with masters falling in love with their slaves? I have *enjoyed* you, Lorcis. Since my wife died you've given me great pleasure. But so did my chestnut mare. This table," he rubbed his hand slowly over the inlaid table and Lorcis could feel that hand caressing her body, "gives me considerable pleasure, too. I love all these things, and in that sense I love you. But these things are all my possessions, to be used as I see fit and disposed of when and as I please."

Lorcis stepped back as though he had slapped her in the face. "Is that all I mean to you? How can you equate me with a horse? Has that horse slept with you and done to you all the things you've taught me to do?"

"I've ridden that mare quite often," Encolpius replied dryly, "but she's not the only horse I own. And you're not my only pretty slave. In the eyes of the law you are the same as a horse—a piece of property. You're an exquisite piece, true, and that's why you bring a very high price. But I need the money now more than I need you or the mare. The eruption of Vesuvius last summer destroyed my estate outside Pompeii and the shops I owned in Stabiae. The losses have hurt me severely so I'm selling some of my most valuable possessions. I sold the mare last week, and now I'm selling you. I regret losing both of you, but it's something I have to do."

"But, my lord . . . "

"Please, Lorcis, don't make this any more difficult than it already is . . . for both of us. You are an extraordinary young woman. I've never known anyone so sensitive, so kind." He pulled himself up to his full height, trying to regain mastery of himself and the situation.

"Please, just go." He waved his hand weakly.

Lorcis took a deep breath and steadied herself. Every nerve in her body was aching to lunge at Encolpius, to beat and scratch him. But her life, she knew, would be forfeit if she did. Besides, after what he had just said to her, she suddenly realized that she must begin to live entirely for herself from this point on.

Yes, that was how it must be. She would trust no one. Why should she? She had trusted people in the past, but no one had repaid that confidence. Her mother had been too weak to help her, her stepfather too indifferent. Now Encolpius, a man she had loved and had given herself to, was betraying her totally. Though she could not stop people like him from using her, she could keep them from betraying her if she did not trust them to begin with.

The ultimate resolution to her dilemma, she now saw, lay in getting out from under the control of other people. As long as she was a slave, she was vulnerable to this sort of cold betrayal. As she turned to leave the room, she vowed to herself that no man would ever sell her again. She would be free!

CHAPTER II

As Lorcis came out of Encolpius' study into the atrium, the rest of Regulus' entourage were gathering for the trip back to Rome. Through the open door, one could see Regulus sitting in a large litter on the edge of the narrow street. Eight brawny Nubian slaves stood ready to carry him. They were naked except for red loincloths and bronze collars and wrist fetters. A wagon loaded with the party's supplies stood behind the litter; the mules munched contentedly in their feedbags.

Regulus was reading and appeared to take little interest in the preparations other than to snap occasionally "Get a move on, Nestor!" at a middle-aged slave or freedman who was scurrying around attempting to see that everyone was present and ready to travel. There were a dozen or so persons gathered in the atrium, an equal number of men and women. Nestor seemed almost satisfied with the arrangements when he noticed Lorcis.

"Let's see, you must be the new girl, the flute player," he said, and Lorcis' first reaction was that he seemed kind. His eyes—large, black, Semitic eyes—had a sympathetic cast to them. Then she remembered her new resolve and steeled herself to distrust him and remain aloof. "I'll need to talk with you during our journey," Nestor continued, "to inform you of your duties and the general operation of our household." Lorcis nodded but said nothing.

Nestor clapped for silence, then walked out to Regulus' litter and reported that the party was ready to travel. "Very well," Regulus replied without looking up. "Proceed."

Walking to the front of the Nubians, Nestor silently made an upward gesture with his hands. Four of the huge Africans took their places and lifted the litter onto their shoulders. The other four and the remaining male slaves walked in front of the party, clearing a path through the crowds of people doing their morning marketing. The women fell in behind the litter, with Nestor bringing up the rear and watching for possible runaways. The wagon lumbered along behind him, its metal-rimmed wheels creating more than the usual noise on the paving stones.

Lorcis was unaccustomed to the confusion and press of humanity which characterized Naples, or any Roman city, at this hour of the morning. People hurried to buy their day's supply of food before the fresh goods were sold and yesterday's leftovers made their way to the front of the shelves. In Encolpius' household, she had performed her duties at night and generally slept until midmorning. Other slaves bought and prepared the food and dealt with tradesmen.

She reacted with an almost aristocratic disdain to the common folk gawking at her. Their stench nauseated her. The men whose bodies were usually close to hers were accustomed to taking long, leisurely baths before dinner and the evening's entertainment. She was thankful for the black behemoths in front of her whose mere presence caused the crowds to give way, although not without resentment. Refugees overcrowded the city since the eruption of Vesuvius. Food supplies were strained, nerves were frayed, tempers were short.

As they turned a corner, the aroma of bread baking overpowered all the unpleasant odors. This was the Street of the Bakers which led to the gate and the road to Baiae and Misenum, the resort and port cities some fifteen miles away on the route to Rome. The smell of the bread made Lorcis painfully aware that she had not had breakfast. She doubted she would be able to walk very far. Should she say something to the other slave women to see if they had brought any food with them? She was hesitant to do that because of her status in the household. She knew all too well that a new slave would be sized up for several days before the others would accept her, if they did so at all. An outsider once again, she did not want to appear to be a complainer.

She looked around for Nestor, to explain her predicament. She did not want to anger him by passing out on the trip and creating confusion. But at the moment, he was nowhere in sight.

As she was craning her neck to see if he was in front of the litter or behind the wagon, they came to the narrow city gate. Incoming traffic had to stop altogether to allow Regulus' litter to pass through. There would be no stopping for several miles once they left the city. She resigned herself to simply make the best of it.

The crowd thinned out rapidly when they got outside the city walls. The other slave women still walked in a group, deliberately excluding Lorcis. She resented the treatment but remembered doing the same thing to new arrivals in her household—her *former* household, she reminded herself. She noticed that one of the women wore a small bronze collar similar to the ones the Nubians wore. The others wore tight-fitting bracelets or anklets of the same metal.

Since she was obviously not going to have any company on this trip, she studied the sights along the road for a few minutes until she heard someone walking rapidly behind her, sandals flapping on the volcanic tufa paving stones. She turned and was surprised to see Nestor hurrying past the wagon and trying to catch up with the party. In one hand he carried a small round loaf of bread. Slowing down as he came up beside her, he took a couple of deep breaths and handed her the loaf, still warm from the oven. When he got his wind back, he said, "I realized as we passed the bakers that you probably didn't get anything to eat this morning."

"No, I didn't. Thank you," Lorcis said with a sincere smile which she rarely had occasion to use. "I'm very grateful—and very hungry." She tore off a piece and chewed it quickly. Then a second, and a third. With the most severe hunger pangs quieted, she could eat more slowly and enjoy the flavor of the bread.

Nestor was still walking beside her, watching with a pleased expression that stopped just short of a smile. Lorcis was no stranger to having men stare at her, but Nestor's gaze was different, almost paternal. She had to remind herself again that she was not going to trust anyone, least of all her new master's steward. If past experience was any guide, this man would soon be her worst enemy.

"Don't you have duties to perform?" she asked coolly.

"No," he replied, with a glance at the litter and the other slaves. "In fact, as steward, my primary responsibility right now is to get acquainted with you and to familiarize you with our household."

Lorcis shrugged indifferently and looked toward the side of the road.

"Now, Harmodius told me last night," Nestor went on, "that you are," he ticked off on his fingers, "from Antioch, have been a slave since you were five, are a talented musician, and an absolute bitch."

He included the last item so matter-of-factly that Lorcis was forced to laugh in spite of herself. The other women turned around to stare, but a gesture and hard glance from Nestor sent them back to their gossip.

"Are you a bitch?"

"Only by reputation," Lorcis admitted with a smile.

"You're not Greek either, are you, in spite of your name?"

"No," Lorcis said after another bite of bread. "My stepfather named me. I'm Syrian."

"Are you sure? How much do you know about your family?"

"I remember so little. My parents did argue a lot, most often about my brother studying with some old men in black robes. My mother wanted him to, my stepfather didn't. And I went with Mother a few times to what must have been a religious ritual of some kind. People talked in a strange language."

"Can you remember if a man held up a book for everyone to see?"

Lorcis thought for a moment. "I believe I do remember something like that. But it was so long ago."

"I'd wager you were at a synagogue," Nestor beamed. "That means you're Jewish, at least on your mother's side. And for Jews that's what counts."

Lorcis shrugged. It was an interesting clue to a piece of her past, but not one that she was pleased to have pointed out. Jews were a despised group in the Roman world; they were considered misanthropic and peculiar.

"I'm Jewish too, as you may have suspected," Nestor added with a diffident nod of his head and a tug at his prominent nose.

"But Nestor isn't a Jewish name," Lorcis observed.

"It's not my name. My name is Jacob ben Malak, but Regulus disliked the barbaric sound of it and gave me a Greek name."

"Wise old Nestor, from the *Iliad,*" Lorcis said. "It's an appropriate name for someone in your position." Encolpius had allowed her access to his library, and she had read as much as she could absorb, both from her desire to satisfy her own keen mind and because she saw it as another way to gain her master's approval. She could discuss literature with him as facilely as she could gratify him physically.

Nestor snorted derisively. "Regulus says he chose it because Homer also calls Nestor 'the much talking.' "

Lorcis sensed the poignancy behind his words. This man had lost not only his freedom and dignity but even his identity. She felt an affection for him which she could not deny.

"I'll call you Jacob," she said impulsively, "whenever I can." She was surprised to feel tears welling up in herself.

"That would mean a great deal to me," he replied, fixing her with a steady gaze that made her uncomfortable. It seemed to hold her and probe her.

"How did you become a slave, Jacob?" she asked to break his concentration on her.

"I'm supposed to be finding out about you," he smiled. "I was taken prisoner when our beloved emperor, Titus, captured Jerusalem ten years ago. My wife and daughter died in the siege. I was judged too small for forced labor and would have been put to death in the arena, a fate I was happy to accept. But a traitor named Josephus, who had surrendered to the Romans earlier, recognized me and told them I was a businessman and quite skilled in managing accounts and people. One of the officers, a man named Pliny, took me as part of his spoils and sold me to Regulus when we got back to Rome."

Lorcis was surprised to hear a name she knew. "Pliny? The same man who was killed in the eruption last summer?"

"Yes. Did you know him?"

"Encolpius was a friend of his. We were at his villa during the eruption." She started to say something about young Pliny, the nephew of the elder Pliny, giving her the ivory flutes which she was carrying in her bag, but she decided against it. It was a long and highly personal story; she still did not know Jacob that well.

"If you know Pliny's family," Jacob was saying, "you'll be interested to know that we're staying at their villa tonight. The younger Pliny has taken over the estate."

Lorcis was more pleased than Jacob guessed. Even as she mulled over that piece of good news, however, she still wanted to know about her new environment. "Tell me something about

Regulus," she said. "How does he treat you? What should I know about him?"

Jacob touched her arm and slowed down so that they dropped another couple of steps behind the other slave women. The clatter of the wagon masked anything they might say, but he spoke softly nonetheless. "Regulus is one of the most famous lawyers in Rome, and probably the richest."

"He must be pretty good, then," Lorcis said.

Jacob chuckled. "Such naiveté, so charming in the young." He tore off a chunk of bread from the loaf which Lorcis had stopped eating but was still carrying. "Lawyers," he said, "are neither good nor bad. They are either poor or rich."

"Well, what sort of cases does Regulus handle that he's made so much money?"

"He deals exclusively with inheritances."

"Is there a lot of money to be made from cases like that?" Lorcis asked in surprise.

"Oh, you are a provincial, aren't you," Jacob chuckled. "In Rome you must listen carefully to every word that is said, and to the words that aren't said. I said nothing about inheritance *cases*. I said Regulus deals with inheritances."

Lorcis' face betrayed her confusion.

"Our master," Jacob went on, "is what we in Rome call—behind his back, of course—a legacy hunter. He flatters rich old people, especially the childless, and persuades them to leave him something in their wills. He has even married a couple of toothless old crones who, he knew, would hardly live past the wedding night."

"And he actually makes a living that way?"

"He is one of the wealthiest men in Rome. His fortune is almost incalculable. And I should know, because he expects me to keep track of it." He leaned over and whispered close to Lorcis' ear, "He is also one of the vilest, greediest, most vicious men I have ever known. Be careful, my child."

For the rest of the morning the party walked west on the road overlooking the Bay of Naples. Jacob was frequently called to the side of Regulus' litter to confer on some matter, and the other slave women continued to shun Lorcis. To help her ignore their attitude, she pretended an intense interest in the countryside.

The mention of Pliny had brought to mind the last time she

had traveled this road, almost a year earlier. At that time the view on either side had been spectacular, with the bay opening up on her left and the golden fields nearly ready for harvest on the right. Now the bay was blue and tranquil again, but the countryside had not recovered from the destruction that Vesuvius wrought. Large patches of gray ash covered the ground, especially in open, unplowed fields. In the city, the debris from the eruption had been cleaned up quickly and damaged buildings had been repaired or torn down. But in the country the earth had to cleanse herself. Her mechanisms for destruction were quick and effective, but her restorative powers seemed to work at a snail's pace.

The visible reminders of the eruption conjured up for Lorcis the whole terrible experience. In mid-August, Encolpius had been invited to spend a week at the seaside villa of his friend Pliny in Misenum. Pliny, who was in command of the fleet stationed in the bay, had known Encolpius since the two had done military service together as young men. Leaving Harmodius in charge of the household, Encolpius had taken Lorcis and two other slaves to attend to his personal needs during the visit.

Also at the villa then were Pliny's widowed sister, Plinia, and her seventeen-year-old son. When Plinia's husband died, the childless Pliny had adopted his young nephew and given him his own name. On the afternoon of August twenty-fourth, the two Plinys, Encolpius, and Plinia had been sitting on a terrace reading and listening to Lorcis play her flutes. Plinia was the first to notice a large cloud beginning to rise from one of the mountains on the southeastern side of the bay. From that distance, they had not been able to tell which mountain. The cloud looked like one of the pine trees which lined the roads of southern Italy, with a long bare trunk and all the branches in a flat mass at the top.

The elder Pliny, a scientist and investigator of natural phenomena (and the author of an encyclopedia) wanted to take a closer look. He ordered boats to be made ready. His nephew declined an invitation to accompany him, preferring to continue his reading. Lorcis was pleased when the young man decided to remain at the village. Only a year older than young Pliny, she found him very attractive, though bookish and aloof. Encolpius, however, decided to go with Pliny.

After the men left, there was little to do at the villa. Young Pliny spent the afternoon reading and making notes, then bathed before eating supper with his mother. Lorcis spent her time entertaining and then went to bed early. During the night the house was shaken by violent earth tremors. Such shocks were not particularly unusual in that part of Italy, but these had been stronger and more numerous than any that even the oldest servants could recall.

Young Pliny and his mother finally gathered all the members of the household on the terrace because the danger of the house falling on them at any moment was becoming all too real. Lorcis was terrified and could not believe it when Pliny asked a servant to get him a book and told Lorcis to play her flutes. She realized later that he was trying to calm everyone by his own appearance of serenity, and she admired him greatly for his courage. They later learned that his uncle had tried to do the same thing when he arrived at a friend's villa in Stabiae, one of the three towns closest to Vesuvius. The elder Pliny had followed the normal pattern of bath, dinner, and bed as though nothing was happening.

By morning, young Pliny decided they should all leave town; the house and neighboring buildings were swaying visibly. Some smaller structures had already collapsed and cracks were starting to appear in even the best-constructed walls. The sunlight was almost obliterated by the cloud of ash, and in the distance they could see flames belching from Vesuvius.

The seven people left in the house took the road north out of town. Once in the street, however, it made little difference where they went or how fast they walked; the panic-stricken crowd simply swept them along. Had they tried to stop or turn around, they would have been crushed. Children cried, women shrieked, and men shouted, trying to keep their families together.

Lorcis recalled hearing Plinia shout to her son that she could not keep up with him. The woman begged—even ordered—him to go on without her. She did not want to be the cause of his death. She had lived a full life, she said, while he still had his life ahead of him. But Pliny wouldn't listen to her. He had grabbed one of her arms and told Lorcis, who was trying to keep as close to them as possible, to take hold of the other.

"But what about my flutes?" Lorcis asked, no more rational than anyone else at that time.

"Damn your flutes!" Pliny cried. "Get hold of her arm!"

Lorcis had tried to hold the flutes in one hand while grasping Plinia's arm with her other hand, but she was not strong enough to support the heavier, older woman with only one hand. Pliny suddenly yanked the flutes away from her and threw them to the side of the road where they sank in the ash.

"Hold her arm, I told you!"

Lorcis had then grasped Plinia's right arm firmly with both hands. Between them she and Pliny kept her on her feet for a couple of miles.

When they reached a point well north of the city, Pliny suggested they leave the road. People were being knocked down and trampled in the mad rush, and it became obvious that his mother could not go much farther even with their help.

They found a roadside shrine and fountain and sat down on the north side of it so the stone structure could shield them from the press of the crowd. Pliny positioned himself between his mother and Lorcis and held them both in his arms. The other slaves had long been separated from them.

The already faint sunlight was gradually blotted out entirely by a heavier cloud of ash. The darkness became total, deeper than a moonless night. It was as though a lamp had been snuffed out in a windowless room. Only Pliny's arm around Lorcis' shoulder told her that he was still there. In return, she had put her arms around him and held him tight. People stumbling by on the road moaned about the end of the world or cursed the gods for deserting them. Like them, Lorcis felt sure they were all going to die. She had even felt a heavy numbness settle over her body, and tears made tracks down her sooty cheeks.

"Get up!" Pliny suddenly yelled. "Both of you!" Lorcis dabbed at her eyes with her hand, not fully comprehending what he had said. "Come on, get up," he commanded a second time, pulling both women to their feet. Then Lorcis realized that they were slowly being buried alive by the ash from the volcano.

They spent the rest of the day huddled beside the fountain, standing up frequently to shake the ash off themselves. In the late afternoon, pale sunlight barely filtered through the oppressive cloud. The road had finally cleared of crowds and the tremors became infrequent enough that the three felt they could try to return home. Pliny had been confident that his uncle would return to the villa as soon as he was able and he did not want to alarm him by their absence.

The journey home had taken the rest of the day; walking through the soft ash was more difficult than walking in sand along a beach. They sometimes stumbled over articles which people had dropped in their flight. Several times they barely avoided tripping over bodies—both animal and human.

The landscape had become virtually unrecognizable, with several inches of ash everywhere and drifts of two or more feet on the southern and eastern sides of buildings and walls. Pliny commented that the town looked like a village near the Alps which he saw once after a heavy snowfall. They encountered occasional travelers who told conflicting tales of conditions at various points around the bay.

Shortly after nightfall, which was barely distinguishable from the preceding day, the three reached the villa and found it habitable. The atrium and the garden, lacking roofs, were full of ash, but the interior rooms in the front of the house were usable. Quickly, Lorcis lit all the lamps she could find. The horrible blackness frightened her almost as much as the shaking of the earth and the deadly ash raining from the heavens.

Leaving Plinia in the triclinium, the least affected room of the house, Pliny and Lorcis looked over the back part of the villa, which surrounded the garden. They soon discovered that they would not be able to use those bedrooms because of the ash piled against the doors that opened outward toward the garden. Even if they had been able to clear enough ash to get into the rooms, they may have been trapped there by the next morning since the ash continued to fall, although at a slower rate. They returned to the triclinium and cleared off several couches so the three of them could sleep there that night. In the kitchen they found enough bread, cheese, fruit, and wine for a satisfactory meal. They all craved a bath, but the pools in the atrium and the garden were both full of ash and the municipal water system also seemed to be clogged. They could get no water from the pipes in the villa.

None of them slept for more than brief periods that night. Lorcis heard Plinia snoring a time or two, but never for very long. Morning on the twenty-sixth had at least brought light, though it was still a very pale light, filtered through the cloud of ash that seemed destined to hang over them eternally. At midday Encolpius returned with one of the three boats. The others, he said, were still picking up survivors on the other side of the bay.

The news was bad, worse than they had feared. The elder Pliny had died, overcome by poisonous fumes near Stabiae. He had long suffered from respiratory problems, so the volcanic gases had affected him more quickly than anyone else in the party. But their personal tragedy was only part of a larger catastrophe. Stabiae was gone—along with Pompeii and Herculaneum—obliterated from the face of the earth as easily and utterly as drawings erased from a child's school slate.

Encolpius brought Pliny's body back with him. His nephew, legally of age for only a year, then became master of the villa and in possession of a vast fortune. His grief for his uncle and adoptive father was restrained, as befitted a Roman nobleman, yet genuine, Lorcis felt.

The afternoon of the twenty-sixth, Encolpius left for Naples to check on his own property. He would return on the twenty-ninth for Pliny's funeral. Lorcis remained at Misenum to assist Pliny and his mother, since all their slaves were gone. During the following three days, however, many of them returned, primarily because they could find nothing to eat in the immediate area and had no means of going anywhere else. Pliny greeted them as members of his family, blaming no one for running away. By the time of his uncle's funeral, only two slaves were unaccounted for and Pliny presumed they were dead. Lorcis credited this line of thought to either the young man's innate good nature or his inexperience as a master. She was sure they had managed to get away from the bay area, as most slaves would do if given the chance. She had often pondered making a break herself, but the punishment for a captured runaway was death. Besides, a woman had little chance of surviving long on her own in this society.

Encolpius returned by boat for his friend's funeral. The road from Naples remained too difficult for travel, although the emperor had sent troops to maintain order and gangs of state-owned slaves to clear the roads. Naples itself had not been heavily damaged, and Lorcis was relieved to learn that Encolpius' house was virtually unscathed. She regretted, though, that a stray brick had not found its way onto Harmodius' greasy head.

Encolpius reported that large numbers of runaway slaves were creating problems around Naples. The masters of some of them had been killed in the eruption; other slaves had seized on the confusion as an opportunity to escape. The memory of Spartacus' revolt, which had begun on the slopes of Vesuvius a hundred and fifty years earlier, inspired some of them. It also prompted the government to crucify captured slaves, as Spartacus and his followers had been executed, if their owners could not be found. Even some owners whose slaves were returned followed that example. Encolpius boasted that he had ordered three of his own slaves crucified as an object lesson.

"An object lesson of what?" Pliny had protested. "Your own cruelty?"

As Lorcis was preparing to leave with Encolpius on the thirtieth of August, Pliny came to her room. He stood at the door with one hand behind his back as though concealing something. In that moment, she thought how much older he seemed than he had just a week before, though there was something of the mischievous boy about him still.

"I've missed your flute playing these last few days," he admitted meekly, "and then I remembered why you haven't been able to play. I don't recall what happened on the road, but I know I behaved wretchedly. I would like to apologize."

"You don't have to do that," Lorcis said.

"No, I must apologize," Pliny insisted as he stepped into the small room. Pulling his hand from behind his back with a flourish, he held out to her a long slender package. She untied the string, opened the cloth, and gasped when she found a set of flutes carved from ivory.

"I sent to Naples for them," he said proudly. "Look, they're even inscribed: 'A gift for Lorcis.' I was afraid you'd be gone before they arrived."

Lorcis was overwhelmed. "My lord, I cannot accept something so fine."

Pliny put his hands gently on her arms. "You helped save my mother's life. And the way you held me when we were sitting by the fountain gave me courage and comfort at a time when I badly needed both."

Lorcis pulled back from him and laughed. "I thought you were comforting me."

"The details don't matter," Pliny replied. "The fact is, you made me behave as a man. No gift I can give you will ever repay that."

CHAPTER III

The memory of those days faded and Lorcis touched the ivory flutes now packed in the bag slung over her shoulder. She regretted that Pliny had never heard her play them and was pleased that she might now have a chance to entertain him.

The sun was directly overhead and the barren landscape seemed to redouble the heat which it reflected back at the travelers. Lorcis recognized a grove of trees and a fountain ahead of them as marking the halfway point between Naples and Misenum. Regulus called Nestor and gave orders for the party to rest and have lunch in the grove.

The Nubians deposited Regulus' litter in the most shaded area of the grove. They then sat in a circle around the litter, facing outward. The female slaves sat on one side of the litter and the remaining males on the other. Lorcis continued to feel that the other women wanted no part of her company so she started for the men's side. She knew she could always get a friendly reception among a group of men. But one of the Nubians grabbed her ankle as she went by, shook his head, and pointed to the women's side.

"Let go of me!" Lorcis demanded. "I'll sit where I please." She tried to pull her foot free from the huge black hand, but the African tightened his grip, stood up, and flipped her to the ground. Then, in spite of her kicking, wriggling, and screaming, he picked her up as though she were a child. Regulus drew back a curtain on his litter and looked out in time to see the African throw Lorcis over his shoulder and flip her stola up. As he turned to face the litter, Regulus laconically held up his hand with the thumb turned down, the gesture used in the arena to signal the fate of a defeated gladiator.

The Nubian threw Lorcis on the ground so hard it knocked the wind out of her. As she gasped for breath she saw with horror that he was removing his loincloth. Before she could move, he was on top of her, pinning both her arms to the ground over her head with one of his massive hands. Lorcis managed to get one hand free and clawed at his back, trying to tear his flesh as much as he was tearing her insides—but he brushed her off like a fly. Lorcis feared she would be crushed if she didn't die from the pain first.

As soon as he finished and got up, Lorcis rolled over, readying herself to spring up onto the giant's back. But Jacob, who had been seeing to the arrangements at the food wagon, returned just as the drama was ending. Stepping between Lorcis and the Nubian, he held out his hands and gestured for her to stay where she was. Her chest heaved as she remained crouched like a lioness. He held her eyes for a long moment before she crumbled to the ground, her arms covering her face.

Regulus applauded. "Well done, Nestor!" Jacob turned and nodded but did not speak. "A scene worthy of the arena!" Regulus rhapsodized. "A beautiful young animal, full of spirit, vanquished by a lumbering giant, then calmed by the steel nerves and cool eye of her trainer. Magnificent!" He held his handkerchief to his brow. "Keep her under control, Nestor, but don't break her spirit."

"Yes, my lord," Jacob replied evenly. He was tempted to attack Regulus right then, but thought better of it. Besides, his chances of getting through the Nubians and killing the man were remote. "Would you like lunch now?" was all he said.

"Oh yes, good Nestor," Regulus chortled. "I do find travel so tiring—and now all this excitement! Have the men break out the food. Thais will serve me. Procne and Xanthippe will tend to the rest of you."

"Yes, my lord."

Lunch was served quickly and eaten with little conversation. Regulus closed the curtains on three sides of his litter, leaving open only the end facing into the grove. Thais walked around to that end, removed her stola, knelt, and crawled into the litter.

Lorcis made her way slowly to the women's side. At first

she refused the food which was offered to her, but Xanthippe urged her to eat. "We still have a long walk ahead of us," she said gently. Lorcis took a few figs, some cheese, bread, and wine. With her back turned to the rest of the slaves she ate in silence and was surprised when Xanthippe, after distributing food to the others, sat down beside her.

"Do you mind?" Xanthippe asked.

Lorcis shook her head but did not reply.

Xanthippe, a large-boned blonde woman in her early thirties, put her arm around Lorcis' shoulder and said, "Go on. It's all right." Growing up without a mother, Lorcis had never had a woman with whom she could share her fears or her joys. By her tender gesture, Xanthippe initiated a bond between them that could only grow stronger.

Lorcis put her head on the woman's shoulder and sobbed. Xanthippe kissed her on the forehead and ran her fingers through the young woman's dirty hair.

When she was able to speak again, Lorcis asked, "What's going on? Why didn't that ape just tell me I had to sit over here?"

"He can't tell you," Xanthippe said. "None of them can."

"Don't they speak Greek or Latin?"

"They don't speak at all. Those collars not only mark them as slaves, but they also cover the scars where their vocal cords were cut."

"Oh my god!" Lorcis said softly. Her rage was not mollified, but she did cast a sympathetic glance at them. "The poor brutes."

"Not only that," Xanthippe went on, "they can't hear either. Eardrums punctured."

Lorcis was horrified. "Why? What good are they to him?"

"Plenty," Xanthippe replied. "You know how strong they are. Nobody could get to that litter now at any price, yet they can't hear anything that goes on or tell anything he does, even if they see it. You'll soon learn how important it is in Rome to have servants who can't hear what a master says or tell anyone what he does."

"What hold does he have over them? Any one of them could crush him in an instant."

"The story is that he bought them from a slave dealer just before they were castrated. They're grateful to him for that, of course, and for the women and fine food he supplies them. They live like kings."

Their conversation was interrupted by a loud giggle from Thais. The litter rocked briefly and a foot protruded from one of the curtained sides. Regulus chuckled and the foot was pulled back in.

"This is incredible," Lorcis said. Even the most hedonistic, dissolute men in Encolpius' circle would have found such behavior shocking.

"No, it's just Regulus," Xanthippe sighed. "And you still don't know why he separates the men and the women."

"You mean it gets worse?" Lorcis asked in disbelief.

"Oh yes," Xanthippe assured her. "You see, Regulus doesn't believe in free and easy association between slaves of the opposite sex."

"But that sort of thing goes on in any household," said Lorcis, recalling occasional experiences of her own in Encolpius' house.

"Well, in Regulus' house the men have to pay him for the privilege."

"You mean he's a pimp for his female slaves?"

Xanthippe leaned closer and whispered, "Regulus would pimp for his grandmother if she were still alive."

Lorcis could not believe that Encolpius had sold her to a man like this—or that Pliny could be a friend of such a person. She wanted to ask more questions, but her opportunity was cut short when Thais emerged from the litter, dressed, and took a seat with the other women. Her face was flushed, her hair disheveled. She was smiling, but it was a forced, nervous smile.

Regulus opened all the curtains on his litter and tapped one of the Nubians on the shoulder. When the man turned around, Regulus handed him a gold chamberpot and motioned for him to take it away and empty it. He then got out of the litter, stretched, and took a position between the male and female slaves.

"All right, men," he said, clapping his hands once and rubbing them together. "If you care for any company for your midday rest, we will begin the bidding. Xanthippe, my dear, you look especially lovely today. Come here."

With a look of disgust that only Lorcis could see, Xanthippe rose and straightened her stola. By the time she turned to face Regulus and the male slaves she was smiling. She walked seductively over to where Regulus was standing.

"Now," Regulus said to the men, "Xanthippe's charms are well known to all of you, so I need not waste words describing them. Who'll start the bidding at five sesterces?"

No one responded.

"Four?" Regulus asked hopefully.

Still no response.

"Perhaps you do need to be reminded of her charms. Show the men your long, slender legs, my dear."

Xanthippe pulled her stola up around her waist. From the back, Lorcis could see that she did have a magnificent figure.

"Come now, gentlemen," Regulus urged, "who will bid four sesterces for all this happiness?"

Still none of the men responded. Several of the Nubians were obviously interested, but Lorcis guessed that they were not allowed to bid.

"My lord," one of the slaves spoke up, "if I may presume to suggest, you would get a more favorable response if the new flute player were the first one on the block."

Lorcis's heart almost stopped.

"I see," Regulus leered. "Saving your money for the choice merchandise, eh? Shrewd, but the auctioneer has reserved that item for his own personal use. Now, who will bid four sesterces for Xanthippe?"

One of the men raised his hand, and the bid quickly went up to nine sesterces. When Xanthippe had been "sold" at that price, the buyer paid the money to Jacob and led Xanthippe off into another part of the grove. Three other women were auctioned off in the same way. Two men had dropped off to sleep by then, and Regulus glared at them, debating whether to wake them up and force them to bid. Then he glanced around at Lorcis and decided to forget the slaves and gratify himself.

"Now, flute player," he smiled sickeningly, "I would like to become more intimately acquainted with your talents. Come here." He beckoned limply with one hand.

Lorcis picked up her bag and walked with Regulus through the circle of Nubians. As Regulus closed the curtains on the litter, Lorcis knelt down and prepared to enter. Regulus grabbed her by the hair and pulled hard, snapping her neck back. "Now, now, my dear," he said in a mock scolding voice, "you've forgotten something."

Lorcis was afraid that her failure to follow another rule unknown to her was about to result in another drastic punishment. "Remember Thais," Regulus hinted, releasing his grip on her. She removed her stola, then entered the litter.

Regulus stretched out on his back with the upper part of his body propped up on pillows. Lorcis sat beside him, her legs folded beneath her. "Play me something, a favorite of yours, perhaps," he said.

As Lorcis played a tune, he ran his hands over her body, touching her in ways that even yesterday would have excited her intensely. But all she could think about now was that he had raped her only a few minutes before, just as surely as if he himself had thrown her to the ground.

She still could hardly believe it had happened. She had been treated roughly before, but always with an element of playfulness. Never had she experienced the sheer brutality to which Regulus had subjected her. She was now so repulsed by him that his touch gave her cold chills—and Regulus mistook her shudders for pleasure.

"You have other talents, I understand," he said, putting his hand behind her neck and pulling her down to him.

When she had finally satisfied him he said, "You are indeed going to be worth the price. Let me put you on notice that I am very fond of flute playing. You may expect to entertain me quite often." He sighed and lay back on the pillows. "That will be all for now. Tell Nestor that we'll resume travel in an hour." He was almost asleep by the time Lorcis got out of the litter.

Dressing and walking quickly over to the fountain, she spat and rinsed her mouth out several times, then splashed some of the cool water on her face and neck. Oh, how she longed for a bath! She knew, however, some of the dirtiness she felt could never be washed off.

Jacob approached her and put his arm around her shoulder. "I am so sorry," he said. "I should have told you about keeping away from the men. Everything that happened to you is my fault."

"But you're not the one who got raped," Lorcis snapped, pulling away from him.

"Come sit with me," Jacob offered.

Lorcis stepped further away. "I don't blame you for what happened, but right now I just want to be left alone for a while."

She found a spot out of sight from the litter and curled up on the ground, but sleep was impossible. Even her physical exhaustion could not overcome the anguish and revulsion which swept over her as she relived the last few moments. Like any female slave, she had no choice but to submit to the sexual advances of her master or his friends, but she had never found physical intimacy, in any of its seemingly infinite variations, objectionable—until now.

She was almost in tears when a hand touched her shoulder. She jerked around, fearing another demand on her, but it was Xanthippe with a cup in her hand.

"Drink this," she said. "I mixed it especially for you."

"What is it?"

"It's a potion that will relax you. I've studied herbs and medicines since I was a child. Believe me, this will help."

Distrusting her, Lorcis hesitated. But what reason would Xanthippe have to harm her? She took the cup and drained it. The bitter liquid made her gag, but at least it killed the awful taste of Regulus. Almost at once she noticed a numbness creeping over her. Xanthippe patted her shoulder. "You'll sleep a little while now."

For Lorcis, the rest of the trip to Misenum passed like a dream from which she could not awaken. Xanthippe's potion had enabled her to sleep soundly for an hour or so, but it had also left her in a daze. Everything, in fact, now combined to heighten her sense of unreality. The landscape was gray and featureless, and the strange people around her acted as if everything that had happened that morning was normal. Although Lorcis found it all hard to believe, the pain between her legs was all too genuine and convinced her with every step that the nightmare was, indeed, reality.

Putting her arm around Lorcis' shoulder and pulling her into the group, Xanthippe urged her to walk with the other women. "You can't dwell on it," she whispered. "It's past. It'll be gone as soon as you stop thinking about it."

Thais, Procne, and the rest chattered endlessly about people Lorcis would meet in Rome, about who was sleeping with whose wife or husband, and about Regulus' splendid house on the Caelian Hill. They teased Xanthippe about her latest love affair with a writer named Gorgias. All the talk and unfamiliar names added to the air of unreality which Lorcis felt. Her old life seemed immeasurably more than just a few hours and a few miles behind her.

Her spirits were cheered when they entered Misenum late that afternoon and Jacob led the Nubians to Pliny's villa. At least this was a place she knew and Pliny was a person she could trust to be kind.

She had hoped to see Pliny as soon as they arrived. Merely by being there—a person from her past life, her real life—he would seem to rescue her from the horror into which she had been cast. But the slaves were taken upstairs immediately while only Regulus went to the garden to greet his host.

The slaves were given decent sleeping quarters, two to a room, and immediately Lorcis lay down on a low couch, totally exhausted. She had been emotionally devastated as well as physically strained beyond her endurance. She was no more accustomed to walking long distances than Regulus was.

"How far is it to Rome?" she asked wearily. "A million miles? I don't think I can make it."

"It's only about two hundred miles," replied Xanthippe, who had chosen to be her roommate, "but you won't have to walk it. We'll take a ship tomorrow." She turned around and started to say something to console Lorcis further, but the younger girl was already asleep. Xanthippe put a light cover over her, stroked her hair gently, then went to the room next door to talk with the other women.

CHAPTER IV

Pliny was by no means happy to see Regulus coming into the garden. The man was wealthy and a valuable political ally—but a dangerous enemy. Under Nero's regime he had been an informer, distorting the most casual, innocuous remarks he overheard at dinner parties or bribed out of slaves into threats of treason; he would then report them to the crazed emperor. Two men speculating on who the next emperor might be, for example, would find themselves arrested on charges of plotting to kill the emperor. Those mentioned as possible successors might also be arrested. All would be executed or banished to remote corners of the empire. Their wealth would be confiscated, some of it given to Regulus as a reward for helping to thwart the "conspiracy." Such had been the origins of his own enormous wealth.

Pliny found the man thoroughly repugnant, but Regulus' position in society was much stronger than Pliny's, so the young man had to honor the older one's request to visit overnight. He knew that Regulus was simply hoping to recruit a new ally.

Pliny was learning quickly that being an adult in Roman society was largely a matter of pretending: pretending to be happy to see someone whom he despised; pretending to enjoy exotic foods at loud banquets night after night when he would prefer bread, cheese, and wine in the quiet of his own dining room; pretending to be interested in the latest gossip about which slave or freedman had the most power in the emperor's household this week, when he merely wanted to talk about literature with his friend Tacitus.

Yet, he had to protect himself. Although his uncle's wealth and influence gave him an enviable foundation on which to build his own career, Roman society would not automatically grant him entrance. He could not remain static. Those who did not actively promote their own careers quickly lost all power and influence, regardless of reputation or wealth. Young Pliny had to either fall back or move forward, building his own network of friends and allies regardless of how he actually felt about the people.

He rose from his reading to greet a man who symbolized this sycophantic, self-indulgent way of life with his whole being. "Regulus, my friend, welcome." Pliny forced himself to smile as he extended both hands to clasp Regulus'.

"Thank you, friend Pliny. Your lovely home is a veritable oasis. Traveling in this area is so unpleasant since the eruption. I'm beginning to wonder if that accursed ash is ever going to wash away."

"It's doubly unfortunate," Pliny replied, "that we've had so little rain this year. But we do have the baths. Shall we wash away at least a bit of the ash while dinner is being prepared?"

"A most welcome offer, my young friend." Regulus clasped Pliny around the shoulder as they headed for the bath, located in the middle of the villa.

Pliny motioned for two male slaves to accompany them, but Regulus jerked his head toward a female slave cutting flowers in the garden. "She would make a lovely bath attendant if you don't mind indulging a guest."

"That is a host's responsibility," Pliny replied noncommitally, even though his innate humanity objected. The young woman would be forced to perform the disagreeable task of helping Regulus undress, oiling and scraping his fat body, and finally massaging him. But in the name of hospitality it had to be done, so he called the girl to come with them.

"You've done quite a bit of redecorating since the last time I was here," Regulus noted. "Of course, that was almost four years ago." Neither of them mentioned, though both of them knew, that the elder Pliny had despised him and that Regulus had been in the house only as part of a group of senators inspecting the naval installation on the bay.

"Most of the work has been done in the last year," Pliny replied, wriggling loose from Regulus' grasp to point to different things. "The house was damaged by the tremors accompanying the eruption. Several of the mosaic floors were ruined beyond repair. The frescoes in most of the bedrooms had to be redone also."

"The new style is charming," Regulus purred, "as nice as anything I've seen in Rome." At the same time he was forming in his mind the words and phrases he would use to ridicule this "provincial graffiti" when he returned to Rome.

They reached the bath. In a public bath there were four rooms: a dressing room, a cold room, a warm room, and a hot room where the bath was completed. In most private baths, as in Pliny's, the dressing room and the cold room were combined, as were the warm and hot rooms. The temperature was moderate when the bathers entered, but the slaves operating the furnace under the floor heaped on the wood, gradually turning the warm room into a steam bath. Pliny and Regulus stepped out of their sandals and removed their tunics, which the slaves folded and placed on a shelf. On one side of the room was a shallow pool filled with cool water where they would rinse off and cool down before dressing.

But the bath began in the adjoining caldarium, with its waist-deep pool surrounded by six stone benches. The furnace provided hot water as well as warm air to heat the room through ducts in the walls and floor.

The two men soaked in the warm water while Regulus talked about the fire which had swept Rome two months earlier, the worst in the city since Nero's fire fifteen years ago. Emperor Titus had handled the crisis well, providing relief for the victims out of his own funds. But people were beginning to ask themselves whether the gods really favored his rule. He had taken power only two months before the eruption of Vesuvius, so his short reign had been plagued by major disasters. It was considered especially ominous that Vesuvius had never been known to erupt before.

"People are talking," Regulus said, "and I've tried to warn the emperor, but he's just like his father. He won't listen to those of us who have his own welfare at heart."

Pliny rejoiced inwardly that Titus was levelheaded enough to spurn rascals like Regulus, but he knew better than to say anything—even in veiled sarcasm. You never know, he told himself, whose ear will catch your words or what form your words will have by this time tomorrow. "Perhaps it's just as well that I haven't been in Rome in several months," was all he said, not sure he conveyed quite the neutrality he intended.

"Ah, lad, Rome is the only place there is," Regulus exulted. "Whenever I have to go away from the exciting, exasperating place, I try to console myself by thinking of my departure as the beginning of the journey back to the city."

When they were ready to bathe, they called the slaves to the edge of the pool. Each slave brought a small jar of perfumed olive oil which they smeared over the men's bodies to soak up the dirt. They then scraped the skin with strigils, small curved pieces of metal, to remove the oil and dirt.

After rinsing off, the two men got out of the pool and lay down on neighboring stone benches. Because Pliny indicated that he did not want a massage, his attendant covered him with a towel and retired to a corner of the room.

Regulus, however, lay down on his back and ordered his attendant to give him a *thorough* massage. The girl looked at Pliny in dismay, but all he could do was nod his head in disgust. He then began to study the mosaic of Neptune and sea creatures on the far wall of the room as though he had never seen it before.

"There's nothing like a bath and a massage," Regulus sighed, "to ease the weariness of a long journey."

Without turning his head, Pliny said, "Your servants must have suffered from the trip as much as you did. After we're done, why don't we allow them to bathe also." He hoped this suggestion might encourage Regulus to finish more quickly.

But Regulus raised himself on his elbows. "Why wait? Why not let them bathe now?"

"Now? While we're still here?" Although he treated his slaves humanely, Pliny was enough of a traditionalist to be dismayed by this suggested breach of etiquette.

"Yes," Regulus chortled. "It would provide some excellent amusement to watch my boys and girls bathe one another. And it's not as if I'm going to bring in the Nubians, too." He snapped his fingers at Pliny's attendant, who left to summon his servants.

"Men and women bathe together?" Pliny protested. "Aren't you going a bit too far, even as a guest?"

"You certainly haven't been in Rome in a long time, have you, my friend," Regulus laughed. "Mixed bathing is all the rage there now. Domitian started it at the dedication of Titus' new baths."

"The emperor's brother?" Pliny gasped.

"Come now—don't be such a provincial. Besides, I've got a new girl you'll enjoy seeing. I just purchased her this morning from a fellow in Naples for fifty gold pieces. Of course, she'll earn that back in her first month in Rome."

Regulus' slaves soon entered the caldarium, most of them shuffling and shivering, not yet fully awake. Despite their familiarity, even intimacy, with one another, they were ill-at-ease to find themselves so coldly stripped and herded together. None more so than Jacob.

"My children," Regulus said in an unctuous tone, "our gracious host has taken thought for your welfare and mine. He invites you to wash away the grime of your travels. There aren't enough attendants to care for all of you, so you will need to wash one another. Nestor, you tend to the new girl. I don't want these other brutes to get their hands on her—not yet. The rest of you pair off, male with female, as your fancy strikes you."

The other six couples jumped into the pool and gradually began to enjoy themselves. Jacob and Lorcis were the last to get into the water and spent several minutes washing one another's backs. They tried to stay on the side of the pool away from Regulus, but he soon called out, "Nestor, bring that girl over here."

Lorcis fought back tears; she did not want Pliny to see her humiliated. When she had left him a year before, they had been equals, regardless of their legal status.

She and Jacob waded through the crowd of glistening, naked bodies to stand before Regulus and Pliny. Lorcis' head was down so she did not see Pliny's initial shock of recognition. She did hear the catch in his voice, though, as he said, "Why, that's Encolpius' flute player, isn't it?"

"She was until this morning," Regulus replied. "How do you know her?" He sensed that there might be something here that would give him a hold on Pliny, a bit of information that he might file away for future use.

Pliny explained briefly about Encolpius' visit at the time of the eruption, omitting anything that Regulus might have hoped to hear. "I'm pleased to see you again, Lorcis," he said with restraint. "If you aren't too tired, I hope you can play your flutes for us at dinner."

Lorcis raised her head and smiled weakly at him. Before she could say anything, however, Regulus interrupted. "Nestor, you and Lorcis haven't finished your baths yet. Please continue."

When Jacob turned around to let Lorcis wash his back, Regulus sneered, "The rest of your body is dirty, too, old man. Turn around."

Jacob did as he was told. He and Lorcis began to wash each other gingerly. He concentrated on her shoulders and arms until Regulus snarled, "Wash all of her, old man. I want her clean. And you, Lorcis, don't miss any part of his wrinkled old hide. Slowly, the other slaves gathered in a semicircle around them and watched—a couple of them fondling one another.

Pliny viewed the scene to this point with his fists clenched so tightly that his fingernails were cutting into his flesh. He vehemently objected to the abuse or degradation of any human being, but he was powerless to prevent Regulus from doing as he pleased with his own slaves. His affection for Lorcis only intensified his hatred of Regulus, which grew stronger each moment the man remained in his house. Unable to do anything else, he wrapped his towel around his waist, got up abruptly, and announced, "It's time for dinner." He left, but Regulus did not follow him.

Dinner was a very uncomfortable affair for Pliny. He loathed Regulus now, yet dared say nothing. All the while, Regulus seemed unaware of his host's attitude, or chose to ignore it. He chattered on about Titus' building program, especially the new amphitheater. His house on the Caelian Hill overlooked the site, so he had been able to follow the construction closely. Titus had also completed the demolition of Nero's Golden House, which his father Vespasian had initiated. So many people were offended by that reminder of the late emperor's excessive life-style that no ruler since had dared live in it. The amphitheater itself sat where Nero had dug out a lake for his estate.

"The statue of Nero that stood in the vestibule—it's at least a hundred feet high—has been moved to a spot in front of the new amphitheater," Regulus concluded. "They knocked off Nero's head, put another one on, and they're calling it the Apollo Colossus now. Some people are already referring to the amphitheater as the Colosseum. Titus doesn't like that at all. He wants it to be the Flavian Amphitheater in honor of his family.

Throughout the dinner Lorcis played her flutes quietly, sitting between the couches on which Pliny and Regulus reclined. As the evening progressed and Regulus became drunker, she edged toward Pliny's couch.

Regulus ate with the same excessiveness he displayed in everything. He downed several roast suckling pigs, three generous helpings of fish in wine sauce, and a large quantity of fruit, cheese, and bread, washing it all down with a fine wine. When he finally excused himself to go to the bathroom, Lorcis was leaning against Pliny's couch but did not look up. Pliny touched her hair lightly, uncertain of what privileges he enjoyed in his relationship with her.

"I'm so happy to see you again," he said.

"I'd rather have gone the rest of my life without seeing you again," Lorcis said softly, "than to have had you see me in the bath."

"I don't think any less of you because of that. You did what you were forced to do. A slave isn't responsible for things done on the command of her master," he said with an extra element of sadness in his voice, thinking of the slave girl forced to massage Regulus that afternoon. "Sometimes a master isn't entirely able to control what he does in a particular situation. But it was Regulus who degraded himself in that incident. I had thought I might try to cultivate him as a political ally, but I can't stoop so low. I don't care how rich or powerful he is, I despise him and will oppose him whenever I can."

Before anything else could be said, Regulus returned. Pliny had the uncomfortable feeling he might have been listening outside the door for a moment before he came back into the room. The dinner ended not long afterward. Regulus said he wanted to get an early start the next day, and Pliny did not want him to stay any longer than absolutely necessary.

Lorcis climbed the stairs to her room and was walking down the hall when she met Jacob. They both stopped, but neither spoke for an instant. Finally, Jacob mumbled something about Lorcis getting plenty of rest for the trip. Then he turned to go into his room.

"Jacob, wait," Lorcis whispered. "I must talk to you."

"The incident is finished," he replied. "The less said about it, the better."

"No," Lorcis insisted. "I want to say I'm sorry. I would give anything if that had never happened."

Jacob sighed the eternal sigh of the slave, the Jew, of all people who know subjection as a way of life. "My child, it is the lot of a slave to do whatever his or her master wishes, be it counting money, playing flutes, or enduring humiliation in front of others. Now, get some sleep."

Lorcis reached out to embrace him, but he drew back. "I can't, not now," he said, then scurried into his room.

CHAPTER V

Except for a brief afternoon squall, the two-day boat ride from Misenum to Rome's port city of Ostia on the mouth of the Tiber River was uneventful. Lorcis had a chance to talk with the other slave women, especially Xanthippe and Thais, the most outspoken of the group. She was eager to see Rome for the first time, but also apprehensive about her life in Regulus' household. She heard endless stories about his cruelty and deviousness, told in whispers and with constant glancing around. From what she could gather, his wife was well mated to him.

The thing that impressed her most deeply was the other women's acceptance of such things as the norm. Their life stories were not much different from Lorcis', but she felt she was the only one of the group who perceived any injustice in her situation. The others were satisfied as long as their physical needs were met.

"But haven't you ever wanted to be free?" Lorcis asked earnestly.

"Free to do what?" Thais snapped back.

"Whatever you want to do," Lorcis replied. "To live where you want to, do whatever work you want, make love to only one man if you want to—and how you want to."

"Oh, freedom," Thais snorted. "We pass by the shops and homes of free people every day. Usually their shops are their homes. They're dirty little hovels, with six or eight children playing by the door while their parents work themselves to an early grave just trying to put food on the table."

"If you can call it food," Xanthippe chimed in. "Porridge, barley bread, half-rotten fruit and vegetables. Our cats and dogs eat better than most of those free people."

"But what about the abuse and humiliation we're subjected to?" Lorcis objected.

"Haven't you ever seen a drunken shopkeeper slap his wife around?" Thais replied. "Regulus may have his fun with us, but he has money invested in each of us, and he's not going to damage his investment."

Nivea had been silent until now. "Freedom is an illusion, Lorcis," she put in. "Unlike the rest of you I wasn't enslaved until I was a teenager, so I can remember being free. The men I knew then expected no less of me than Regulus does, but they had no intention of paying for it. If I had married one of them, he wouldn't have been able to offer me as much as Regulus does. We have a pleasant enough life, as long as we keep on Regulus' good side. He makes fewer demands on us than a husband does and provides us much more comfort than any husband could. What more can you ask?"

Lorcis shook her head in disagreement, yet she did not know exactly what more she was seeking. Her present life left her unsatisfied, but what did she have to compare it with?

"You're upset," Xanthippe said, "because of what's happened to you. You've been sold; that's one of the hazards of a slave's life. But you've been sold to a man who has everything you could possibly want. You'll live in a house that is the envy of almost everyone in Rome, and all you have to do is play the flute occasionally."

"And pretend that you enjoy Regulus' company once in a while," Thais said. The others laughed.

Lorcis reddened but said nothing. Their arguments made sense on the surface, but she could not accept what they were saying. She wanted to be free, free to—to do what? She didn't know. She couldn't remember having been free, so she didn't know what free people did. But the rebellious spirit that had gotten her into trouble from the day she had first been sold had risen to the surface. She would be free or die in the attempt.

They reached Ostia midafternoon on the second day of their voyage. The walk from the port to Rome itself passed quickly for Lorcis because of the excitement of seeing new places. Even when they were still a half mile from the city gate the road became lined with apartment houses like those in Naples, only larger. Called insulae, or islands, they were five or six stories high, and each covered an entire city block. The first floor of each was taken up by shops; the rest of the building consisted of small apartments. Rents were so high that a family of six or seven often tried to live in one or two rooms. Because there were no bath facilities in the apartments, residents flocked to the gigantic public baths maintained by the emperor. They emptied their chamberpots in the same way they disposed of their food scraps: by dumping them out the windows.

As the party drew closer to the gate Lorcis was overwhelmed by the stench. Naples had not exactly been aromatic, but she had never experienced an odor so fetid as that of Rome. There had been no rain in several days, and refuse lay all over the streets, trampled on by pedestrians, played in by children, scavenged by dogs and other animals. Regulus covered his mouth and nose with a scented handkerchief, a new fashion among the rich.

Marking the unofficial boundary of the city was the pyramidal tomb of Cestius, an official of Augustus' day and an admirer of Egyptian antiquities. At the time of the tomb's construction ninety years earlier, it had been almost half a mile outside the city. Now buildings were packed around it as densely as anywhere inside the walls.

Their supply wagon, which had been cumbersomely loaded and unloaded for the sea voyage, had to remain outside the gate. Congestion in the city's streets was so bad that vehicular traffic had long been prohibited within the walls during the day. As they entered the gate several of the male slaves moved to the rear of the party to keep the crowd from crushing them from that side. The Nubians gleefully shoved aside anyone who did not yield ground quickly enough.

Once inside the gate Lorcis looked eagerly from side to side, taking in all she could of this immense city. For its admirers, all roads truly led to Rome; when Romans used the word urbs, "the city," they meant only Rome. But there were those who gladly took those same roads in the opposite direction, sacrificing the glamor and excitement of life in the teeming—or festering—metropolis for the quiet and security of some provincial town. Until a few days ago Rome had been for Lorcis the capital of the world but as unreal as the moon. Now it was to be her home, whether she wished it to be or not.

Apartment houses crowded together on either side of the street. Narrow, unpaved side streets wound off from the Ostian Way at irregular intervals. The buildings were so tall and the streets so narrow that pedestrians were in perpetual shade, even in the middle of the street. The side streets were so dark and narrow that Lorcis could not see more than a few yards down any of them. There seemed to be activity down these alleys, but she had no desire to learn what sorts of things were transpiring.

The shopkeepers on the first floor of the apartment houses spread their merchandise on the sidewalks in front of their shops, forcing passersby to walk in the filthy street, which was scarcely fifteen feet wide. Their incessant hawking of their goods became louder as Regulus' litter progressed up the street.

Soon Lorcis heard a steady murmur which became louder as they neared the heart of the city. It grew to a roar long before they actually came within sight of the Circus Maximus. Chariot races were being run that afternoon, and two hundred thousand voices were frantically cheering for their favorites. Outside the massive race course partisans of the different teams—blue, green, red, and white—were placing or collecting on bets. Here and there fights broke out over the results of a close race or a losing bettor's inability to pay.

As they turned onto the Street of Scaurus, which would take them up the Caelian Hill to Regulus' house, the crowds thinned out. They passed block after block of tenements on the lower slope. After they passed the temple of the deified Claudius, erected by Nero in honor of his predecessor and adoptive father whom he had poisoned, they came to a district of wealthy homes. From the outside none of these dwellings was impressive. The blank walls which faced the street were unadorned except for graffiti scribbled by passersby. Only the joints where two walls came together distinguished one home from the next. Space was at a premium in Rome, so all buildings butted up to the ones next to them, usually sharing a wall. This was why fires spread so rapidly and caused such devastation.

The party stopped in front of a large brass-studded oak door, on which Jacob knocked heavily. It was quickly opened by a servant. The party waited until Regulus got out of his litter and went inside before filing into the house.

Lorcis had been steeling herself not to be overly impressed

with the house. After all, Encolpius was a wealthy man, and his house contained some fine furnishings. Nevertheless, she was not prepared for the elegance of Regulus' house. It bespoke unlimited wealth, the scope of which she could not comprehend. Had she been dropped here without knowing the owner, she would have thought herself in the emperor's palace.

The atrium was the largest she had ever seen, about half the size of Encolpius' entire house. The mosaic on the floor was made of colored marble chips instead of the usual tile or glass pieces. Silk tapestries hung on the walls while Greek statues, many of them quite old, adorned the atrium and the hall connecting it with the main part of the house. Prominently displayed in one corner was a gold bust of Regulus. Lorcis did not get to see the rest of the house because the slaves were then sent upstairs to their quarters.

Jacob showed Lorcis to her room. Not surprisingly, Regulus' magnificence did not extend to the slaves' rooms. Hers was as small and dingy as the one had been at Encolpius' house, but at least she would not have to share it with anyone as she had sometimes had to do in Naples.

"I hope you'll be comfortable here," Jacob said. "Now, one more thing," he added apologetically. "I'm afraid I must inspect your belongings."

"Why? I have practically nothing." She knew Jacob was going to find her medallion, and for reasons unclear to her, she did not want him to see it. When the doll in which she had hidden it for years had fallen apart, she'd simply wrapped it in a piece of cloth. Through the years she had paid little attention to the thing but had developed the habit of keeping it secret.

"Regulus demands to know what each new arrival in the household brings with him or her," Jacob explained patiently. "I keep an inventory. Then he checks periodically to see how much each slave has added to his or her little pile. Legally, of course, Regulus owns anything his slaves have, but in practice he takes only half. Another example of his generosity."

"But do his slaves really make much money?" Lorcis asked. In Encolpius' house she had not heard of slaves having any source of income except for stealing from their master.

"Most of the slaves work outside the house in their free time," Jacob replied. "Some of the girls make a fair amount of money. I think Regulus plans for you to do the same."

Lorcis closed her eyes and shook her head in disbelief as she opened her bag and dumped the meager contents out on the bed. She had learned early that a female slave's body was not her own to control, but as Encolpius' favorite she had only limited experience with other men. Encolpius shared her only on rare occasions. Her promiscuity on the last night in his house had been unusual, and she realized now that he had encouraged it only because he had already agreed to sell her. Now to be told that she was expected to become a prostitute and to turn over half her earnings to that bloated pimp!

Her train of thought was broken by Jacob's hand on her arm. He held her medallion and was asking where she had gotten it.

"Where? Oh, my mother," she replied vaguely. "My mother gave it to me. Why?"

"Do you know where she got it?"

"I was very young. All I can remember is that she told me I should guard it carefully. Why are you so interested in it?" No one else had ever seen the medallion, and it made her nervous to have someone else handling it.

"Do you know who this man is?" Jacob asked, growing more and more excited.

"No. There are some marks on the back, but I don't know what they mean."

"It's Aramaic, my native language," Jacob said.

"Can you read it?" Lorcis asked with a spark of interest. "I've always wanted to know what it says."

"I can read it, but I can hardly believe what it says." Jacob drew a deep breath. "It says, 'I, Lazarus, drew this picture of Yeshua bar-Yusif, who raised me from the dead, so that my children might know him. May I be forgiven my transgression of Torah.' "

"Lazarus? That was my father's name," Lorcis said. "My real father, that is." But that was all she understood. "What's Torah?"

"That's the Jewish law. One part of it forbids the making of images of any living thing. Lazarus took a great risk in drawing this picture, but he had good reason."

"Do you expect me to believe someone raised him from the dead?" Lorcis stifled a laugh out of respect for Jacob.

"Whether you believe it or not, it happened," Jacob replied confidently.

"Who was Yeshua bar-Yusif?" Lorcis asked, stumbling over the strange names. "How could he raise a dead man?"

Jacob's countenance seemed to take on a radiance unlike anything Lorcis had ever seen on anyone's face. "He could do it because he is the son of God!"

"Which god?" she asked without much surprise.

"There is only one God," Jacob replied.

"Oh, yes, so you Jews believe."

"You should say 'we Jews,' my child."

"I'm not a Jew," Lorcis protested. "I'm a Syrian."

"Your mother was a Jew, and as I told you, that makes you a Jew. Now we know that your father was Lazarus of Bethany, near Jerusalem. He was a Jew. So you are, entirely and inescapably, a Jew."

"Well, whatever I am, what's so important about this Yeshua? Why do you call him the son of God?"

"That's what he is." Jacob held the medallion tightly and said nothing for a moment. Then he spoke slowly, never taking his eyes off the medallion. "It's a story that one cannot easily tell in just a few words. For centuries the Jews have been expecting a messiah—a deliverer—to overthrow their enemies and lead them out of their troubles. At least, that's what they thought he would do. Then, some years ago, Yeshua, a rabbi from Nazareth, came along preaching that God's deliverance is near—within their own hearts. He healed the sick, cast out demons, and worked other wonders—many people believed he was the messiah. But certain Jewish leaders feared his teaching and handed him over for crucifixion to Pontius Pilate, the Roman governor of Judaea.

"He was crucified on a Friday and, because of Sabbath laws, his body was hurriedly placed in a tomb without the full burial preparations. Then a strange thing happened: when some of the women among his followers returned to the tomb after the Sabbath to complete the anointing, the body wasn't there!"

"Someone had stolen it?" Lorcis asked, intrigued in spite of herself.

"No, no, my child. He was alive again!" Jacob's face fairly glowed as he spoke.

"Alive again? Do you expect me to believe that? Once you're dead, you're dead. Maybe they took him off the cross before he was actually dead."

"Oh, no," Jacob replied. "I assure you, when Roman soldiers crucify someone, they make sure he's dead. And no one stole the body. His disciples found the linen cloth that had wrapped him lying undisturbed right where they had put him. It was as though the body had vanished out of it. But the real proof that he was alive again was that people saw him, talked to him, ate with him, touched him. He was alive!"

"Maybe so, maybe not," Lorcis shrugged. "I wasn't there. Were you? Have you seen him?"

Jacob shook his head slowly. "Ever the sceptic, aren't you." He ran his hand lovingly over the face on the medallion, outlining the features. "No, I didn't see him after his resurrection, but I have my own reasons for believing in him. You see, he healed me from a dreadful disease when I was nine. I had had convulsions and seizures since I was an infant. Sometimes I would even hurt myself during these attacks. It was as though there was some evil spirit in me, trying to destroy me. My father had taken me to doctors from Antioch to Alexandria, but nothing helped. Finally we decided to seek out Yeshua, who had a reputation for healing the sick. One day we found some of Yeshua's disciples in a crowd, but Yeshua was gone and they couldn't help me. My father was in despair until at last Yeshua himself came down from a mountain where he'd been praying. He put his hands on my head and ordered the evil spirit to come out of me.

"I felt as though the spirit were being ripped out of me, that it was trying to hold on as something tore at it. I cried out with pain and collapsed as though I were dead. But when I opened my eyes Yeshua was leaning over me, peering at my face. That was the first thing I saw when I was in my right mind—his face close to mine, gazing intently at me. I have seen that face in my mind every day for the past fifty years. And this," he held up the medallion, "is that face, the face of Christ."

"Christ?" Lorcis echoed. "This Yeshua you're talking about is called Christ?"

"That's what the Greeks call him. It means the same thing as messiah, the anointed one. They also call him Jesus."

"And his followers are called Christians?"

"Yes," Jacob said. "You've heard about Christians then?"

"Just stories about secret meetings and strange rituals. And about their plots to overthrow the government."

"Ah, yes," Jacob sighed. "The usual lies."

"How do you know they're lies?" Lorcis asked, although by now she guessed the truth.

"I am a Christian," Jacob replied proudly.

"That's a dangerous admission to make. How do you know I won't tell Regulus just to get on his good side?"

Jacob smiled serenely. "It wouldn't matter to me if you did, but I think you know already that Regulus has no good side. Besides, I have a feeling about you."

"What sort of feeling?"

"I can't quite define it yet. It's still just a feeling."

They talked for a few minutes about the new religion. Lorcis was interested if for no other reason than that she had been carrying around a picture of its founder for most of her life. Jacob needed no prompting to describe the teachings of Jesus. He stressed those about loving others, even one's enemies.

"Am I to love Regulus?" Lorcis asked bitterly.

"Yes, you are," Jacob answered. "God loves him."

Lorcis started to object, but Jacob hushed her with a gesture and went on. "God wants him to be a different man, of course, a better man, but he loves him even now."

"Then I want no part of your god," Lorcis snapped. "He demands too much."

"That's true," Jacob conceded, patting her knee, "but he'll give you the strength to do whatever he requires."

"Do *you* love Regulus?" Lorcis demanded.

"I do," Jacob answered, "but not in a sense you could understand right now."

"You're talking nonsense."

"It only seems so because you're trying to understand with your head, not with your heart." He stood up to go. "I hope we can talk again. You have more reason to be interested in Jesus than you know. You owe him your life."

Lorcis sat up. "What on earth are you talking about?"

"Your father Lazarus died. But Jesus, who was his friend, stood in front of his tomb and called out his name. Lazarus walked out. He wasn't married at the time of his death. He married later—and became your father. You wouldn't be alive if it were not for the power of God displayed through Christ."

"Then I wouldn't be a slave," Lorcis shot back. "I wouldn't have been raped by the Nubian. Yes, I have a lot to thank Jesus for!"

"Perhaps you won't always be a slave," Jacob said quietly. "God often works in ways we don't understand." He gathered up his papers. "The peace of God be with you," he whispered. As he opened the door he added in a normal tone, "The servants will eat dinner in about half an hour."

That night, Lorcis could not sleep. Her conversation with Jacob disturbed her more than she wanted to admit to herself. The revelation about her father: what could she say about it? How could she comprehend a dead person living again, even fathering a child?

She had no particular religious convictions because she had never seen any real evidence that the Roman and Greek gods had any power over people's lives. She had never known an instance in her life when a god or goddess had helped or hindered; fate seemed to rule. People lived, and things happened to them at random. She had watched Encolpius and his wife pray and sacrifice for the healing of their only child—and then watched that child die within hours. Bad people like Regulus got rich; good people like Jacob lost their families and were enslaved. People seemed to just muddle along until it was time for them to die.

But Jesus had healed Jacob; this fact seemed indisputable. If what Jacob said was true, Jesus seemed to be able to change the unchangeable. Fate, left to itself, would have prevented her from ever being born. The very fact of her existence might be a testimony to a power greater than fate.

She dozed off still resisting the idea. If she did not want another person controlling her destiny, she was far more unwilling to have some unseen, unknowable deity toying with her life.

CHAPTER VI

While Lorcis was eating breakfast the next morning, Regulus' wife sent for her. A slave girl of eleven or twelve brought the message and led Lorcis to the mistress's room, or rather her rooms, which constituted an entire wing on the west end of the house.

Regulus' wife reclined on a couch while a maid fixed her blonde hair in the current style—with curls piled on top and toward the front of her head. Achieving the effect required a wire frame inserted under the hair and numerous extra pieces of hair, usually supplied from the heads of slaves. It took infinite patience on the part of the lady and the hairdresser to set this elaborate coiffure. Once it was in place the lady could move her head only with great deliberation. The time it required and the restrictions it placed on movement marked its wearer as a great lady of leisure.

On Regulus' wife the style was completely inappropriate. She was a small woman in her mid-forties, and her face was thin, almost gaunt. She seemed to be hiding under her hairdo, peeping out to see if it were safe to emerge.

"Come in, my dear," she called pleasantly as Lorcis followed the girl into the room. She dismissed the hairdresser with a slight wave. "I am Sempronia, wife of Regulus. Welcome to our house."

"Thank you, my lady," Lorcis replied, bowing her head, then straightening up to glance around the elegant room. She was surprised to see standing beside a table to Sempronia's left another person, clad only in a loincloth of senatorial purple. This person's back was turned and Lorcis could not be sure whether it was a man or a woman. The legs and buttocks seemed to be those of a woman, but the back was slender and straight like a man's. The person's hair was cut manishly short.

Sempronia followed the direction of Lorcis' gaze. She smiled languidly, turned her head in that direction, and said, "Gallia, dear, perhaps you'd better put it away—for now, anyway."

Gallia pouted prettily but removed the loincloth and wrapped something from the table up in it. She walked slowly across the room, like a priestess carrying a sacred object, to a small niche in the wall. Every Roman house contained at least one of these niches, usually set aside as a shrine to the household gods, the lares. A fresco painted on the back wall of this niche depicted several women engaged in sexual activities with one another. Gallia opened a gold box in the niche, reverently deposited her treasure in it, and replaced the lid. She then strolled back across the room and picked up a man's tunic and a woman's blonde wig which were lying on a couch.

Sempronia watched her appreciatively, then turned back to Lorcis. "You'll soon learn, my dear, that I tolerate my husband's life-style because he makes no objection to mine. It is an eminently convenient arrangement. Occasionally we even combine the two," she said, elevating her chin slightly, "just for the novelty of it. One can get bored with anything after awhile."

Gallia, now dressed and wigged, sat at the foot of Sempronia's couch and rubbed her mistress's leg as she talked.

"But enough of that," Sempronia went on. "That's not why I sent for you, not this time. Nestor tells me that you have only two dresses to your name and that neither of them is fit for a dustcloth."

Lorcis looked down at her stola, her best one, and touched it with both hands.

"Come here, child," Sempronia said, with the slightest gesture of her hand. When Lorcis moved close to the couch, Sempronia touched the stola with the tips of two fingers as she might handle a baby's dirty diaper. "Oh, this will never do. We can't have one of our slaves going around dressed like a plebeian. What will people say? Go on, take it off, right now!"

Gallia leaned forward expectantly as Lorcis reluctantly removed her stola but held it in front of her, covering as much of her body as she could. Gallia yanked it away from her and tossed it to the servant child. "Daphne, go burn this," she said imperiously. Lorcis recognized the tone of a former slave now in a position to give orders and relishing it.

"While you're out," Sempronia added, "get a dress from Nivea. I think she's about the same size."

Daphne started to run out of the room, but Sempronia called after her. "You needn't be in such a rush." She looked Lorcis over carefully, then said, "Wait a moment, Daphne." The child stopped at the door.

"Lorcis, it seems you've not been fettered yet. Nestor should have seen to that last night. We must take care of it at once." She looked at Gallia. "Where shall we put it?"

"I think it should be on her wrist," Gallia said.

Sempronia mulled that over, then turned back to Lorcis. "That seems appropriate," she said. "Every time you play your flutes you'll be reminded of your status in this household. Daphne, tell Nestor to have a wrist fetter prepared for Lorcis."

"Yes, my lady," the child said with a bow and left the room.

"Now . . ." Sempronia said, leaning back on her couch.

"Excuse me, my lady," Lorcis stammered, "but I don't understand, about the fetter, I mean."

"Oh, it's a simple thing," Sempronia said with a slight laugh. "Some owners brand their slaves, but we prefer that ours not be disfigured, so we place a tight-fitting bronze band on the throat, wrist, or ankle. It bears the slave's name and the fact of our ownership."

"But I've never been marked before," Lorcis protested, "and I've never tried to run away."

"You've never lived in Rome before," Sempronia retorted. "In a fairly small town like Naples everyone knows who is a slave and who's free. But in Rome a slave could simply disappear into the crowd without some kind of mark."

"It's an attractive piece of jewelry," Gallia interjected, "and it can be removed, as mine was when I was freed, thanks to my lady's generosity."

Lorcis seethed over this new degradation. Over the last few days, in new circumstances, among different people, she had found that she could distance herself from her situation for a few precious moments now and then. In her own mind she could be free. Now, a permanent, chafing reminder of someone else's control over her was to be placed on her body. Her owner's name would be inscribed on her. They might as well brand it across her forehead. But she knew she would gain nothing by protesting further.

"Now," Sempronia said again, "I've already heard stories about the beauty and talent of our new flute player. My first impression is that the reports are no exaggeration. Come closer." She studied Lorcis through a lorgnette—a large, cut ruby placed on a long, thin gold handle. With her other hand, she stroked Lorcis' breasts. "A bit barrel-chested, don't you think?" Gallia nodded.

Continuing her examination, Sempronia ran her hand down Lorcis' stomach and thighs; the young woman flinched involuntarily. Sempronia kept her eyes on Lorcis' face but only said, "Turn around." Lorcis did so. "Oh, buttocks as nice and round as any we've ever encountered." Gallia reached out and pinched her. "Turn back around now," Sempronia commanded.

Lorcis crossed her hands in front of her, but Sempronia tapped her wrist with her lorgnette. "Keep them by your sides," she said.

She touched the lorgnette to her cheek and held Gallia's hand while she talked to Lorcis. "My husband will not require your services every night, and since what is his is also mine, I'll be calling on you from time to time. Have you ever been with another woman?"

"A few times," Lorcis replied.

"How did you react to the experience?" Sempronia asked.

"It can be quite pleasurable," Lorcis said, blushing slightly.

"Oh, indeed it can," Sempronia smiled. "Indeed it can." She looked knowingly at Gallia.

The door opened and Daphne returned with a new stola.

"Here, try this on," Sempronia said.

The new stola, light blue with a dark blue border, was the loveliest thing Lorcis had ever worn and fit her perfectly.

"Well, it isn't much," Sempronia fretted, "but I suppose it will do until we can have something made for her."

She turned to Gallia. "Shall we send her on to Nestor for her bracelet? You've already worn me out this morning."

Both women laughed and Gallia said, "I think we can save her for another day." She looked at Lorcis with a smile that was really a threat.

Book II

August, A.D. 80 - June, A.D. 81

CHAPTER VII

After two months in Rome Lorcis could hardly remember Naples. Everything in the capital was bigger, noisier, more expensive, more wicked—more exciting. True to her resolve to rely on herself, she had made few friends among the members of Regulus' household aside from Jacob and Xanthippe. The steward seemed to regard her as a daughter, and in Xanthippe she found an older woman in whom she could confide—a pleasure she had never known before.

Her routine in the household had quickly been established. Regulus, as influential as he was, received dinner invitations daily from people obligated to him or hoping to ingratiate themselves with him. He ate at home no more than twice a week. On those nights Lorcis entertained the guests on her flutes. Regulus also owned or hired other entertainers, however, so the amount of time Lorcis actually spent performing was less than it had been in the house of Encolpius.

On nights when he did not dine at home, Regulus often hired Lorcis out to his friends. Sometimes they wanted her for her musical abilities, but the report of her other talents spread quickly through Regulus' circle. The first few men she was with found her frightened and vulnerable, not as crass as the slave women and prostitutes they were accustomed to consorting with. Yet, she knew what was expected of her and was adept at whatever the men wanted. One of them dubbed her "an experienced virgin," and the sobriquet stuck.

Lorcis was paid for her work in both their bedrooms and their dining rooms, although she would have preferred not to receive any money for the former. Taking money confirmed what Regulus was doing to her; it made her a whore in her own eyes. She thought it ironic that the men she satisfied sexually paid so eagerly for that few minutes of effort when she did not want to be paid, but the men for whose parties she entertained often begrudged her the money she'd earned for several hours' work.

She was sometimes tempted to refuse the money for her sexual efforts, or to throw it away on her way home, but she knew Regulus was aware of how much she was getting and would hold her accountable for half. She also recognized that money was the key to power in this power-mad city. Would she someday be able to purchase her own freedom? Regardless, every coin placed in her hand was a step toward some ill-defined goal and raised her above every other person of her class who had not gotten that coin.

On nights when Regulus made no demands on her, Sempronia frequently sent for her. She and her friends had smaller parties, no more than a dozen women at a time. They generally read poetry, sometimes Sappho's, sometimes their own.

Lorcis was more frightened of these women than of the men she encountered. Underlying the women's sexual play she felt an element of brutality stronger than any she had ever experienced at the hands of a man—except for the Nubian. The women seemed bored, jaded even, and sought ever new ways of amusing themselves. She had been horrified one night to see them tie up a slave girl and stick pins in her especially large breasts.

They never inflicted bodily injury on Lorcis, however, because Regulus would quickly detect it. Instead, they abused her in more devious, degrading ways. They were particularly fond of tying her up in positions that left her vulnerable to their explorations, whether they actually did anything to her or not. Gallia, with her slender hips and almost nonexistent breasts, seemed especially jealous of Lorcis' body.

Her days were largely her own. The number of slaves in the house was large enough that none had to do double duties. Most had only limited, specialized tasks. Regulus considered it a proof of his wealth that he had so many slaves there was not enough work to keep them busy. Lorcis was often called to Regulus' bedroom in the late morning or early afternoon to gratify him. After that she could do as she liked until the evening. Now that she wore the bronze bracelet declaring her a slave of Regulus, she was free—the irony of the word!—to leave the house, as long as she obtained permission from Jacob and returned by the appointed time.

Some days she went to the Forum, the business center of Rome. Originally there had been only one Forum, but as the city had grown, Julius Caesar, then Augustus, and most recently Vespasian had built new forums adjacent to the ancient one. But unless they needed to specify a meeting place, most Romans still spoke of going to the Forum.

In the heart of the city Lorcis could browse in the various shops or listen to court cases, which were tried in the open air if the weather permitted. If nothing else, she could sit under the shady colonnade of the large basilicas that surrounded parts of the Forum and simply watch the people.

What a show! The city attracted people from all over the Mediterranean basin—and that was good or bad, depending on one's perspective. The crusty old historian Sallust had likened Rome to a sewer into which the world's ordure flowed unchecked. Lorcis would watch with fascination as Spaniards, Egyptians, Gauls, and Mauretanians rubbed elbows with Romulus' descendants—and nearly elbowed them out.

Many of these people, like Lorcis herself, had come to Rome as slaves. Upon being emancipated by their masters, they received citizenship and were legally the equals of men like Regulus and Pliny.

Lorcis would ask herself if it were unrealistic to want that for herself. Mindful of the other slave women's comments about the disadvantages of freedom, she watched these people's behavior closely. There was, she had to admit, an element of truth to the disparaging remarks Thais and the others had made. She sometimes saw obviously ill people struggling to carry on at their jobs. Doctors hurried by to attend the rich, but the sick shopkeeper could not afford to call them in. She saw women buying day-old meat that would have to be slathered with thick, salty garum sauce to mask its almost rancid taste.

But freedom didn't have to mean squalor, she blithely assured herself. One just had to work hard enough to make a living. Free people didn't appreciate what they had, she concluded. She was sure she would be happy to work as long as she was doing something of her own choice.

Not that the free life was all work. There were pleasures like browsing in a bookshop. Her favorite one was located on a side street off Augustus' forum and owned by a Jew named Apelles. She had discovered it one afternoon by following a group of Jews.

The Jews fascinated her, not only because of what Jacob had told her about her own heritage, but because they seemed to be the one group of people in Rome who were indifferent to the world around them. They chose, for example, not to work every seventh day, so they didn't. To Lorcis that was the ultimate in freedom. Some Romans even adopted the Jewish custom. Knowing they couldn't get supplies on the day called Sabbath from a Jewish merchant, they would stock up ahead or close on that day.

Apelles kept a stock of books that drew Lorcis back again and again. He had the most complete selection of the Alexandrian poets she had ever seen—and they were her favorites. She read them for the beauty of the words and the rhythms of the lines. Often she devised tunes for them which she would play on her flutes. She had discovered that Thais had a lovely singing voice, so the two of them sometimes performed at Regulus' dinners.

In the back of the bookstore she also discovered a shelf of works about the Jews. Historical books had never appealed to her, but she purchased and poured over ethnographers like Hecataeus, eager to learn as much as she could about these enigmatic people—her people, apparently.

Her greatest find on Apelles' dusty shelves was a copy of a book by Josephus concerning the war which the Jews had fought against the Romans a decade earlier. She did not have enough money in her bag to buy it the day she saw it, and she held her breath as she hurried into the shop the next day. To her great relief, it was still there. Old Apelles eyed her curiously as she toted all seven scrolls up to the table by the door where he sat.

"That's a bit more weighty than your usual diet of poets, miss," he said.

Lorcis was flustered. She had never dreamed he was paying enough attention to recognize her or to recall what sort of books she usually bought.

"Well . . . I know someone who was involved in the war," she stammered. "I just want to know more about it."

"No personal interest though?" the bookseller asked.

"No. Why should I have any personal interest? I wasn't involved in it."

"Oh, I just thought you might. But since you don't, I don't suppose you'd have any interest in any other books about—or by—Jews."

"Well, this is all I can afford right now," Lorcis said, wanting very much to know what kinds of other books he might have but afraid to identify herself too closely with this outcast group.

On her next outing she decided to avoid Apelles' shop—it was not wise to let anyone in Rome know too much about one's private life and interests. Someone would eventually find a way to turn the information against you.

Instead, Lorcis went to another bookstore several blocks away from Apelles'. There she noticed a new name among the poets and picked up a little scroll entitled *On the Spectacles* by Marcus Valerius Martial. She had read only a few lines of the first poem when she became aware of a man standing beside her. She moved over slightly so he could reach the shelves in front of her, but he showed no interest in selecting a book. She glanced up at him and realized he was staring at her.

"Are you going to buy that one?" he asked.

Lorcis was flustered. She thought he must work in the shop, had recognized her as a slave, and was politely asking her to put the book back. She started to roll up the papyrus scroll.

"No, I . . . I don't think I will," she stammered.

The man appeared absolutely crushed. He slammed his right fist into his left palm. "Oh, damn!" he said. Lorcis jerked involuntarily. "You're the first person who's even looked at it, and I was so hoping you'd buy it," he said, almost pleading with her.

"What difference does it make to you whether I buy this particular book?" Lorcis asked.

"I wrote it," Martial answered.

Lorcis couldn't help but laugh at his pathetic expression. "Do you always stand around in bookstores badgering people to buy your books?" she chuckled.

"Oh, no, of course not!" Martial replied, drawing himself up. "This is my first one—my first book, I mean. The copyists just finished it yesterday." He lowered his voice and spoke as though he were confiding in an old friend. "The owner didn't much want to take it, but I reminded him that it is in honor of the emperor and his new amphitheater, and it would show a glaring lack of patriotism to refuse to carry it. Now I'm trying to sell as many copies as I can so he'll be willing to take my next book. So please, won't you buy a copy?"

Lorcis tried unsuccessfully to hide her amusement. "It would be unpatriotic not to, wouldn't it?" she stated with a smile.

"A good point!" Martial crowed, clapping his hands. "Perhaps I should stand in front of the shop and remind people of that." He walked out of the shop in a flat-footed comic fashion Lorcis recognized as copied from the stage. She laughed and shook her head in disbelief. Then she got her coin bag out and paid for the book.

As Lorcis left, Martial was standing by the door of the shop anxiously eyeing the shelf where his book was kept. She showed him the book, smiled, and said, "This had better be good."

"I assure you, my lady, you will be well pleased," he replied with a quick bow.

At the sound of the phrase "my lady" Lorcis covered her slave bracelet surreptitiously with her other hand. The phrase was properly used only by servants addressing their superiors. She didn't know if Martial was mocking her or had genuinely mistaken her for a free woman.

She had walked almost a block when someone grabbed her elbow. She was frightened at first but smiled in relief when she turned and recognized Martial. "You haven't written another book already, have you?" she teased.

"No," he smiled. "I do write fast, but not that fast. I was watching you walk away when it suddenly dawned on me that you were the first person to buy my first book, and I don't know your name or where you live or anything about you."

Lorcis studied him for a moment. There was something intense and unsettling about this young man with the dark hair and the fiery eyes.

"I am Lorcis," she replied uneasily. "I am . . . I live in the house of Marcus Regulus." She'd started to tell him that she was a slave, but he hadn't asked, had he? "Do you know his house?"

"Who in Rome does not know the house of Regulus?" Martial was obviously impressed. "Are you going there now?"

Lorcis nodded.

"May I walk with you?"

She nodded again, adding a smile this time.

As they walked, they exchanged information about their

backgrounds. Lorcis continued to be vague about her exact status, hoping Martial would assume she was a free woman or a professional entertainer, even a courtesan—anything but a slave. Roman morals were flexible, but no self-respecting Roman man would engage in anything more than a casual, physical relationship with a slave woman.

Martial was from Spain. He and his parents had come to Rome late in Nero's reign. Feeling the obligation to support his aging parents, he had tried a career in law, with little success. Within the past year, his father, then his mother, had died. Now that he had only himself to look after, he was trying to establish himself as a poet. He was looking for a patron to support him, as Maecenas had done for Vergil. His new book would hopefully convince some rich man that here was a talent worthy of help, and one who could glorify his patron in the process.

As they passed a taberna, Martial invited Lorcis to eat with him. She longed to accept but knew the hour was late and if she arrived home after the appointed time there would be trouble. "I'm sorry," she said, "but I have duties to perform at Regulus' house."

"Duties?" Martial echoed, his suspicions apparent. "Do you work for Regulus?"

"No. That is . . . I am . . . a slave, a flute player."

"I see," Martial said, pursing his lips—then smiling. "Well, no matter. You're a beautiful woman with excellent literary tastes. I could ask no more. Are you sure you don't have time to dine with me?"

"No. Regulus is very strict about his slaves being at home when we're supposed to be. He would have his ruffians out looking for me within minutes if I were late."

She looked into the crowded little eating place with its smoky oil lamps and boisterous customers. One part of her knew that eating in there could not be called dining, but another part of her ached to be able to walk in there, sit down, and spend as much time with her new friend as she would like.

"If I were free, like you . . ." she started to say, but the burden of the thought crushed any other words that tried to make their way out of her mouth.

Martial seemed to understand what she was feeling. He put his arm around her shoulder, and neither spoke for a while as they continued up the Caelian Hill.

When they had passed the Temple of Claudius and were approaching Regulus' house Martial said, "How ironic! You want to be free to leave all of this, yet you are so fortunate. You know where you'll sleep tonight and for as many nights as you can see into the future. You know you'll be well-fed, clothed, cared for if you become ill. But you long to be free like me. Do you even fathom what that would be like?"

"I often dream about it," Lorcis replied.

"Freedom isn't a dream," Martial sneered, "it's a nightmare. Let me tell you about freedom. I'll go home tonight to my sweltering room on the third floor of a firetrap. While you're having a supper prepared by a gourmet cook from the choicest items in the market, I'll be eating whatever scraps I could afford to buy at the end of the day. Meat doesn't keep well in Rome in the summers, incidentally, but you don't have to worry about that. Instead of soft music and scintillating conversation, I have to listen to the drunken neighbors and their screeching children. I have enough money to last me another week or so. After that, if I don't find some way of putting a few coins in my pouch, I don't know where I'll be living or what I'll be eating. You want to be free like me, and I'm looking for a patron—a master, if you like—to take care of me the way Regulus takes care of you."

"Takes care of me!" Lorcis almost shrieked. "Surely you know how Roman aristocrats take care of their female slaves. Are you suggesting I should be content with that?"

"But look at your dress, your hair," Martial countered. "And you don't look like you're going hungry. I even mistook you for a free woman, and one of some standing at that."

Lorcis shook her head. "I've had this argument with too many people. Why does everyone think that material things are all that matter in life? I know it sounds crazy, but the freedom to starve or wear rags is exactly what I want."

By now they were standing at Regulus' door. Before she knocked, Lorcis said, "You talk about being willing to give up your freedom. Suppose Regulus came to the door and said, 'You may come into my house and enjoy my wealth, but once you enter, you cannot go out again until I say so.' Would you go in?" She pounded on the massive door. "Would you?" she echoed plaintively. She wanted desperately for him to understand her situation. Though she hardly knew him, she felt a new hope in his presence.

Martial stared at the door but made no reply as the doorkeeper opened it. Lorcis, passing through the door, looked back at him, her eyes begging him to do something to save her. The myth of Eurydice flashed through her mind, the young woman being drawn down into the underworld as her lover, the poet Orpheus, watched helplessly. Martial started to reach out to her, but the slave pushed her on inside and closed and bolted the door.

Martial stood in front of the door for a long time, running his hands over it, touching the hinges and the large brass handle as though trying to decide how best to dismantle it.

CHAPTER VIII

The conversation with Martial upset Lorcis. She felt a closeness to him that surprised her, but his desire to live the sycophantic life-style that she despised disappointed her. For several days she could not bring herself to read his book. One evening when she was unable to sleep, she flipped through the small pile of books she had acquired since her arrival. She could not find one that suited her mood. She wanted something new and thought of Martial's book still in the bag she'd been carrying the day she bought it. Lorcis drew it out, unrolled it, and began to read.

The first few poems were heavily patriotic, glorifying Emperor Titus and his regime. She skimmed them, hoping the rest were different. They were, but not in the way she had anticipated. One described a prisoner tied to a stake in the arena and mauled by an angry bear. Another mocked a man who had been tied up in a net and tossed around by a bull until he was gored to death. Other poems vividly described the tortures endured by unfortunates as the crowds jeered at them and screamed for their blood.

Lorcis could not finish it. She had suffered and been humiliated in front of others enough to have no stomach for such entertainment. She also had an innate abhorrence of the mistreatment of others and a sympathy for those so treated. She had never understood where her sympathies came from; perhaps it was her Jewishness. From the other slave women she had heard of the brutal things that happened in the amphitheater and had avoided going there. Now, she felt betrayed by Martial for parading these horrors before her eyes. He was a good poet; he made his reader feel everything he described. She wanted to tell him, though, that she hated his poems and to ask him why he wrote about such things.

But she didn't know where he lived. On the third floor of a firetrap, he had said, but that could describe half the apartment buildings in Rome. She had no way of contacting him. Perhaps she could check at the bookshop. He might be there again, or the owner might know where to find him.

The next morning, as she was preparing to return to the bookshop, Xanthippe and Nivea walked by her room. Seeing the door open, they stuck their heads in.

"Getting ready to go to the amphitheater?" Xanthippe asked.

"No," Lorcis replied, a bit too sharply. Then, to smooth her friend's obviously ruffled feelings, she added, "I have to go to a bookshop."

"But this is the day we all go to the amphitheater," Nivea said, almost as a taunt. She and Lorcis had not become friends, primarily, Lorcis thought, because she had worn Nivea's blue stola at a banquet and it had been ruined by one of the guests in his drunken lurching after Lorcis.

"I would just prefer not to go," Lorcis answered coolly. "What's so special about today that we all have to go?"

Xanthippe and Nivea looked at each other in disbelief. "Don't you remember that today is the day Regulus is giving the games? It's part of his responsibility as aedile and part of his re-election campaign. The whole household has been talking about it for days."

Lorcis looked at the floor dejectedly. She did recall the subject coming up in conversations with the other servants, but she had paid no attention to the date. Now she had no choice but to go. She walked out of her room with the air of one sentenced to death in the arena rather than one on her way to enjoy the spectacle.

They joined the other slaves in the atrium and left the house in a group. As they made their way down the sloping street to the amphitheater, the other slaves commented on Lorcis' lack of enthusiasm for the show. "That silly old bookshop can't be that important," Nivea laughed. "Besides, it'll be there tomorrow, and the spectacle won't."

Lorcis didn't want to make herself appear odd, but she finally admitted that she did not relish watching people hacking at one another or being torn apart by animals.

"But it's so exciting!" Thais protested. "The struggle, the tension! And those gladiators' bodies!" The other women giggled.

Xanthippe was perceptive enough to sense that Lorcis was deeply disturbed. She placed a hand on Thais' arm to silence her. "There are some things you may enjoy," she told Lorcis. "I understand there'll be reenactments of some famous stories from Greek myth. Surely you can't object to something like that."

"Well," Lorcis replied doubtfully, "maybe I'll watch those performances and then turn my head during the rest."

"Oh, the first time a gladiator is hit and the crowd roars, your head will snap around," Nivea prophesied. "I'll bet on it."

While she was speaking they turned a corner and the Flavian Amphitheater came into view. Even from a distance it was colossal. The stone structure stood 160 feet high. When shows or games were being held, an enormous multicolored awning was stretched over it to shade the crowd. They passed groups of sailors hauling the vast expanse of canvas into position, fastening their lines to stones which ringed the amphitheater.

It was early, and the groups of people milling around waiting to be admitted were small when Regulus' party reached the amphitheater's main gate. Regulus and his entourage were ushered in and shown to the section of seats reserved for the producer of the show. Regulus left to attend to last-minute details while Jacob saw to the seating of the group. Sempronia and Gallia were in the center of the box, up front, while surrounding seats were reserved for Regulus' most intimate friends. The freedmen and slaves of the household sat to the rear of the area. Although she was close to the arena floor, Lorcis realized that she could hide her head behind the slaves sitting in front of her and not have to watch anything she didn't want to see.

Gradually, the seats began to fill up. Barriers marked off seats reserved—in front, of course—for members of the aristocratic senatorial class. The next range of seats was for the knights, people with money but without a family member or ancestor among the senators. The highest seats, as well as a standing area at the very top, were for the rest of the populace. Lorcis shook her head ruefully as she imagined the poor wretches in the highest seats who probably envied her because she was sitting so close to the action. She would gladly yield her seat to any of them.

When the ticket holders all had their seats, the guards at the entrances stepped aside and people were allowed to find whatever vacant seats or standing room was available in the upper rows. There was a mad scramble as hundreds of people fought for the few remaining spaces. Lorcis saw people knocking each other over, even walking on those who fell, to find a place to stand. She wondered what attraction suffering must have for people. She almost wished she could share their enthusiasm so she wouldn't feel like such an outsider, a foreigner.

With the seats filled to overflowing, Lorcis' attention turned to the arena itself. It was an oval, two hundred eighty-five by one hundred seventy-five feet. Fountains around the edge sprayed perfumed water into the air to mask the increasingly oppressive smell of sixty thousand or more closely packed human beings. The spectators sat about fifteen feet above the arena, remaining a safe distance from the animals. Spikes protruding from the wall provided an extra barrier against frightened or wounded animals leaping into the seats.

The animals were kept in pens beneath the floor of the arena. Occasionally their noises could be heard over the murmur of the crowd. As the day grew warmer their stench became increasingly noticeable. They would be brought into the arena by gates at various points in the walls or through trap doors in the floor of the arena. Few, if any, would walk out.

One of the household slaves sitting in front of Lorcis volunteered the information that more than five thousand animals from all over the world would be used in that day's spectacle. Some species, he had heard, were becoming scarce in areas close to Italy, driving up the price of the animals as they became more difficult to procure and ship.

Before he could explain further, a trumpet sounded, signaling the arrival of the emperor and his party. They occupied the section of seats next to Regulus' party, so Lorcis was close enough to see Titus. She could not make out the details of his face, but he seemed a dignified if not really handsome man. At forty years of age and several years away from active military duty, he was growing paunchy but had obviously been quite muscular in his youth. The surprising thing about him, to Lorcis, was that he was much shorter than she had imagined an emperor would be. He did not seem self-conscious about his height, however, and did not resort to the thick-soled sandals worn by some of Regulus' more diminutive friends. Most of the people in the imperial party slouched anyway, so sensitive were they to anything that might displease their "lord and master"—their phrase, not Titus'.

With the emperor present, the games could begin. Another trumpet fanfare heralded the raising of the main entrance gate, to Lorcis' left, and the beginning of the procession which officially opened the spectacle. A band of musicians led the way, followed by images of the gods adorned with wreaths and carried on large wagons accompanied by their priests and priestesses. Next, Regulus entered, riding in a chariot drawn by two stags—animals very difficult to break to harness. Behind him walked a number of his friends and hangers-on carrying placards reminding the crowd that his munificence was responsible for their pleasure that day and urging them to reelect him. The post of aedile was largely honorific, but it was one of the few offices still filled by election. The senate and the emperor chose all the other public magistrates.

While the procession wound slowly around the edge of the arena, Regulus smiled and waved to the crowd. But they were indifferent. Some even jeered and shouted at him to keep moving so the show could begin; they would wait to see how good the games were before deciding their vote. The applause was loudest when Regulus finally completed his circuit and disappeared through the main gate.

While he made his way back to his seat, the procession of performers took place—creating a much more enthusiastic reaction from the crowd. The gladiators led the parade, grouped according to the types of equipment they used. Regulus had spared no expense in hiring the most exotic fighters available. The Samnites, men with regular shields, swords, and helmets, came first. Next marched the retiarii, or net men, who attempted to entangle their opponents in a fishing net weighted with small pieces of lead so it could be cast quickly and accurately. A trapped opponent would then be killed with the trident which these men also carried.

Other gladiators were dressed in their various national costumes: large blond Germans with their two-handed swords and leather britches, swarthy Parthians with their baggy silk pants and curved scimitars. There were Ethiopians, Scythians, and Mauretanians, representatives of every part of the empire. The most sensational, however, were three Scots who, according to their tribal custom, had stripped naked and dyed themselves blue before going into battle. Rome had only recently consolidated her conquest of Britain far enough north to take Scottish prisoners, so these were the first ever to appear in the capital. The jaded crowd sent up a mad cry of approval all around the arena.

"Let Cornelius Priscus top this," Regulus muttered to Sempronia as he sat back down after acknowledging the applause. He was beginning to think he might finally be outdoing his opponent. He hoped so; the campaign was proving costly. Priscus was every bit as determined as himself to win and, though not as wealthy, was willing to run himself into debt to impress the crowds.

The post itself was immaterial; it actually cost him money to fulfill the responsibilities that went with it. But, like any Roman aristocrat, he craved prestige—*gloria*—and with the emperor controlling all other political and military appointments, this office was the only possibility. He watched the combatants critically, believing his prestige rode on their brawny shoulders.

Some of the gladiators wore no clothing except a loin cloth. As they marched they flexed their muscles and showed off their bodies, glistening with olive oil. The spectators watched carefully to see what condition the fighters were in, then checked their programs to see which pairs were matched. Odds were given, bets made, and the noise level of the crowd rose appreciably.

Behind the gladiators came some of the beasts to be used that day. Lions and other great cats strained at leashes held tightly by muscular bestiarii, animal trainers and fighters. A dwarf rode in a small chariot pulled somewhat erratically by two ostriches. Behind him lumbered several elephants with their mahouts swaying in elaborate seats. In a cage pulled by zebras lolled a hippopotamus.

Alongside the procession walked a number of girls scantily dressed as the hunting goddess Diana and her band of wood nymphs. They carried small bows and shot blunt toy arrows into the crowd. Each arrow carried a lottery ticket which could be redeemed during the day. Because it was rumored that some of the prizes were quite large, a scramble occurred wherever one of these arrows landed, even among the senatorial seats. Speculators often offered cash on the spot for the unopened tickets.

As the procession passed their box, Lorcis remarked that it must cost a lot to feed all the animals, especially the cats. One of the male slaves sitting in front of her snorted back, "The meat for the cats is the cheapest of all. It doesn't cost anything!"

"Where does Regulus get free meat?" Lorcis asked in amazement. Romans ate meat only infrequently because of its scarcity and high price.

"Don't you know?" the male slave replied. "They feed the victims to the cats."

Lorcis recoiled in horror. "You mean the animals that are killed in the arena?" she asked hopefully.

"I mean anything or *anybody* that's killed," the man sneered.

Lorcis felt queasy in the pit of her stomach at the thought of human beings, having already faced the degradation of torture and death in the arena, being tossed into an animal's cage to serve as food. "Why would they do such a cruel thing?" she cried.

"What's cruel about it?" another slave countered. "They're dead. What do they know?"

"Well, they're usually dead," the first slave pointed out. "A friend of mine tells me people don't always die in the arena. Sometimes they just pass out from the shock. It must be a rude awakening to find a lion munching on your leg." The slaves sitting around him laughed.

"That's horrible!" Lorcis gasped.

"It's just practical," the first slave snapped. "It solves two big problems: what to do with the victims after the show and how to get a large enough supply of meat for the cats without bankrupting the government or the people who provide the shows. It also gives the cats a taste for human blood. They're not natural man-eaters, you know."

Lorcis leaned back against the cool marble wall which separated their box from the surrounding seats. A wave of nausea was starting deep inside her and she forced herself to fight it back; she didn't even see the procession of performers clear the arena.

Finally, the show was ready to begin. Regulus stood and waved to the crowd, drawing a mixture of cheers and boos; his opponent, Priscus, had seen to it that a fair number of his supporters were in the stands. Regulus raised a large white piece of cloth and shouted, "Let the games begin!"

As he dropped the cloth, trumpets blared, the entrance gate opened again, and hundreds of animals were turned loose in the arena to fight and kill one another. Those reluctant to leave the gate area were prodded with sharp sticks or firebrands. Then, maddened by pain, they rushed upon the first creature they came to, regardless of its size, and attacked. If the noise of the crowd stunned an animal into immobility, men with small darts or stones were positioned around the edge of the arena behind a protective wall and would rouse it into a fighting rage. Many spectators bet on pairs of fighting animals, and groans or cheers would go up around the arena as a bear finished off a tiger, or a wolf bit a chunk out of a fox's neck.

When Regulus judged that the animals' fury was spent and the crowd's enthusiasm was waning, he signaled for the hunters to finish off any of the beasts that remained alive. A dozen men and women moved into the arena and began shooting arrows into the small knots of animals that huddled together near the wall at various points. The crowd did not entirely lose interest in this routine mopping up because animals had been known to perk up occasionally and attack one of the unsuspecting hunters. On this day, however, the business was completed without incident. Slaves moved in to drag the carcasses out the gate to Lorcis' right while others smoothed the floor of the arena with rakes and spread fresh sand over the particularly bloody spots.

When the entrance gate opened again the crowd expected more animals or some preliminary gladiatorial bouts. Instead, there was a creaking of machinery as an elaborate stage set representing a king's palace in Greece was hauled out. A herald announced that the king had decreed that his daughter, Atalanta, would marry the first man to beat her in a foot race. Those interested in challenging her were invited to assemble before the palace. The crowd murmured and groaned at having to sit through a reenactment of this tired old myth. Several young men, however, emerged from various side gates in the arena and took their places before the palace. A young girl then came out of the palace to stand beside the herald.

"Who will be the first to run against the lovely Atalanta?" the herald called. None of the men moved. Then Atalanta stepped into clear view of the audience. "It seems we need to arouse some interest," she said as she took off her stola, to the great delight of the crowd. She was about eighteen, with light brown hair and a trim figure.

"She's not any older than I am," Lorcis thought. "She could be me." And, against her will, she found herself absorbed in the spectacle.

As Atalanta walked provocatively in front of the young men, one of them stepped forward, unable entirely to hide his reluctance. He was a criminal, under a death sentence, but he had not been told exactly how or when it would be carried out. As he removed his tunic for the race, a soldier set up a spear in the sand twenty-five yards or so from the palace steps. The young man stood nervously next to Atalanta.

Raising his hand, the herald casually announced, "Oh, did I forget to mention that any man who fails to outrace Atalanta forfeits his life?" The crowd roared at the offhand way he included this crucial element in the story.

Nevertheless, the young man took his position to begin the race. When the herald started to give the signal, Atalanta raised her hand to stop him. She walked around the young man, as if examining him, especially the evidence of his masculinity. Her contemptuous expression made it clear she wasn't satisfied. The crowd laughed as she lined up next to him.

At the starter's signal, they dashed for the upright spear. The young man who had had little sleep or food for several days was, of course, no match for Atalanta—a fleet runner in her own right.

Two soldiers waiting at the finish line quickly seized the loser and a third swiftly decapitated him and placed the head on a sharp stick, which he then set up in the sand. The crowd applauded, though only politely. This was all predictable; it was supposed to happen in the story. Where was the novelty?

As a similar fate befell the next three challengers, the crowd murmured restlessly. The fifth stepped forward looking frail, almost effeminate. Atalanta walked around him with a mincing step, then brought her knee up sharply into his groin; the crowd moaned and laughed. Before the man could recover, the herald signaled the start of the race. Atalanta won easily.

When the soldiers started to behead the loser, Atalanta laid her hand on the executioner's sword arm. The crowd groaned in disappointment, then leaned forward expectantly as Atalanta took the sword and emasculated the young man. The applause was deafening as the unfortunate youth thrashed on the sand.

The sixth man, named Hippomenes in the myth, then stepped forward, grinning. When he removed his tunic to reveal that he would measure up to Atalanta's standards, the young girl rolled her eyes and made various signs of amazement and delight. The crowd loved it. Even Lorcis could not suppress a chuckle.

As she lined up for the race, Atalanta's smile made it evident that this race would end differently. She hardly exerted herself at all, allowing Hippomenes to beat her convincingly.

The herald announced that the marriage would take place immediately. The couple were attired in wedding clothes by one set of slaves and pantomimed a quick ceremony as other slaves dragged the bodies of the losers away. Lorcis watched in horror, knowing where they would take the bodies.

Leaving the palace, the newlyweds walked toward the other end of the arena, kissing and fondling each other all the way. Halfway across, they came to another stage set representing a temple, which had been wheeled out during the wedding. They removed their clothes and made love on the front steps. The audience knew that, according to the story, the couple would be punished for violating a temple; the plot called for them to be turned into a pair of lions. It would be a difficult feat to get the two into costumes of some sort in the middle of the arena. Anticipation began to build around the stands.

After finishing their lovemaking, the couple continued their journey, but before they had gone more than a dozen yards the urge overtook them again. Once more they hurriedly undressed. Just as they had assumed an animal-like position, a cymbal clashed and an enormous cloud of smoke bellowed from the earth around them. When the air cleared, the crowd saw a pair of lions mating in the same spot and in the same position the couple had just been in. Even Lorcis had to admire the cleverness of the engineers who built the trap doors and elevators beneath the floor of the arena and the skill of the animal trainers who had gotten the lions into position with such precise timing.

The crowd stood roaring and clapping—but the scene was not over. The king and a party of noblemen in hunting gear rode in, chased the lions around the arena, and finally cornered and killed them on the steps of the temple. The female was shot with an arrow in the throat; and the male took a spear in the belly as he tried to attack one of the hunters.

The crowd was throwing flowers and cheering madly at this apparent climax of the familiar story when another cloud of smoke belched out of the temple and obscured the steps entirely. Immediately, the crowd fell silent at this unexpected development.

Then, gradually, the smoke cleared. Enthralled, the crowd saw Atalanta lying in the sand with an arrow through her throat and Hippomenes with a spear still quivering in his stomach.

Lorcis did not hear the crowd's hysterical applause. She clutched at her own throat, gasped, and went rigid.

"They were a handsome couple," Sempronia observed to Regulus. "It's a shame they couldn't have been forewarned of the conclusion of their little drama."

"Yes," Regulus nodded with a smile "but it would have dampened the spontaneity of their performances, don't you think? As it is, they've won the election for me, and they'll live on in the memory of all these thousands of people."

"For a week, at least," Sempronia replied sardonically.

It was several minutes before Xanthippe and Nivea noticed that Lorcis had passed out. Xanthippe called to Jacob, but he could not hear her over the crowd. She elbowed her way through the other slaves until she could get next to Jacob who was standing like everyone else but was looking down at his feet.

"Something's wrong with Lorcis!" she shouted in his ear.

Immediately, they worked their way back through the slaves to Lorcis' seat where she sat slumped against the wall of the box, her hands still clutching her throat. Except that her eyes were open, she did not appear to be conscious.

"Make room!" Jacob ordered, pushing away those closest to her. "Let her lie down." The other slaves, intent on the arena, paid scant attention to him. It took him several minutes of calling Lorcis' name and patting her cheeks to get a response from her. Then she just moaned and repeated "No! No!"

"Stay with her," Jacob said to Xanthippe. With the crowd settling down while the carnage and the scenery were removed, Jacob was able to get to Regulus' seat without undue difficulty.

"My lord, pardon the intrusion," he began.

Regulus was feeling beneficent in the glow of his triumph. "It's quite all right, Nestor," he beamed. "What is it?"

"Lorcis, the flute player, has been taken ill, sir. I think I should take her home at once."

Regulus glanced around in Lorcis' direction and saw Xanthippe and Nivea worriedly standing over her. "By all means, get her out of here," he snapped. He peeped anxiously at the emperor's box. "I don't want people thinking there's sickness in my household. Get her on her feet and walk her out."

"Yes, my lord. I'll do my best," Jacob replied.

He returned to Lorcis' seat. "Lorcis," he said, putting his hands on her cheeks and holding his face close to hers. "This is Jacob. We're going home now, my child. Everything's going to be all right."

"Can you stand up?" he asked.

She nodded and slowly rose to her feet.

"Good girl," Jacob cooed. "Now, let me hold on to your arm—and we're going to walk out of here."

While they made their way out of the box, trumpets blared and the crowd cheered as the first pairs of gladiators marched into the arena. Jacob felt Lorcis tense. "Don't listen to them," he said, gripping her elbow more firmly. "Just listen to me and concentrate on getting out of here."

Lorcis managed to get down the steps and through the maze of passages leading to the entrance before she broke down. Throwing her arms around Jacob's neck, she sobbed uncontrollably. Jacob could make out only bits of what she was saying: "Horrible . . . that girl . . . so alive . . . the arrow . . . people laughing . . . cheering." Jacob held her tightly until the crying lessened. She was still sobbing quietly and dabbing at her eyes as he turned her away from the amphitheater toward Regulus' house.

By the time they walked a few blocks Lorcis had regained a semblance of control. "Let's get something to drink," Jacob suggested when they passed a taberna. "It'll do you good to sit down for a few minutes." Lorcis agreed.

Jacob bought two cups of wine and they found a table. The surly owner produced a reasonably clean cloth and made an effort to wipe off some of the grease and the scraps imbedded in it. "At least get the top layer," Jacob prodded.

They sat quietly for a few moments, engulfed by the chatter of the other customers and the smoke of lamps filled with cheap oil. Shakily, Lorcis ran her hands over her eyes.

"Still seeing that scene in the arena, aren't you," Jacob said, patting her arm tenderly.

"It's just the smoke," Lorcis replied quickly, "just the smoke."

"You're not the first person to react that way," Jacob assured her. "People throw up every day at the games. Others go temporarily crazy and attack people around them. Some people have even died in the stands from the excitement."

"How do you react?" Lorcis asked.

"I just hope I'll be brave when my time comes," he replied softly.

Lorcis was caught off guard by this completely unexpected answer. "What makes you think you'll die that way?"

"I feel that's what God intended to happen to me when Jerusalem fell, but Josephus got in the way. It was he, not Pliny or Regulus, who was responsible for me becoming a slave. My death in the arena has been postponed for a while, and perhaps for a purpose, but it will happen eventually. God's plans always work out in his time, not ours."

"Don't you want to try to avoid it?" Lorcis asked incredulously.

"Why should I?" Jacob shrugged. "I will die some time, in some way."

"I'm afraid to die," Lorcis shivered. "Aren't you?"

"No. I look forward to it. Death is the way I will obtain my freedom."

Lorcis shook her head. It was as though Jacob were speaking a foreign language. "No. Not for me. I'm going to get my freedom while I can still enjoy it."

"Oh? How are you going to get it?" Jacob asked.

That simple question remained so large an obstacle that Lorcis could not begin to imagine how to overcome it. Runaway slaves were almost always caught, and the punishment was severe. Even if she succeeded in escaping, what sort of life would she have, hiding in some provincial town, living under another name in constant fear of detection?

"Maybe I'll buy my freedom," she said defiantly. "Regulus' friends pay me well. I've already saved a good bit of money."

"True, the law says you can purchase your freedom," Jacob said thoughtfully, "but it also allows masters to set the price that their slaves pay for manumission. You know Regulus would set your price so high you'd have to have sex with half the men in Rome to get the money."

Lorcis looked down at the table and did not reply.

"Even if you obtained your freedom," Jacob went on, "what would you do with it?"

"I'd get even!" Lorcis said through clenched teeth. "With Encolpius, with Regulus, with Sempronia, with every damned one of them!"

"And how would you do that?"

"I'd become famous and rich," Lorcis said airily. "Other girls have done it."

"In other words, you'd become one of them."

Lorcis was stopped short. She felt the truth of Jacob's words as surely as she had felt the arrow in her throat a few minutes earlier.

"What can I do?" she asked in despair.

"I've found that the only way to escape slavery," Jacob replied, "is to decide within myself that it doesn't matter."

"How can a slave simply decide that slavery doesn't matter?" Lorcis demanded. "Do all Christians talk such nonsense?"

"Calm down, my child," Jacob said, taking her hands in both of his. "People do listen to other people's conversations." When Lorcis relaxed a bit he went on. "You'll soon realize that there is no such thing as freedom." He paused to let that idea sink in, but Lorcis just pulled her hands away.

"Everyone keeps telling me that," she said, too loudly. Other patrons looked around at them. She lowered her voice, but her tone was still angry, not so much at Jacob as at the whole world, which seemed designed solely to oppress her. "Then why are some people called slaves and some free? Freedom is the most important thing there is. You either have it or you don't."

"No one really has it," Jacob replied, shaking his head. "Some men are called slaves because another person tells them what to do and has power over their bodies. But men who call themselves free have their own masters. Some fawn on the rich for handouts, groveling and debasing themselves in a way that even slaves find offensive." Lorcis thought of Martial. "Others are slaves to their own desires for possessions. They force themselves to work not at jobs they enjoy but at whatever they think will make them the most money the quickest."

"But Regulus is free," Lorcis objected.

"Only in appearance. His every action is determined by his desire for more money or by what he thinks his peers expect of him. He never says 'I want to do this and not that.' It's always 'What will the emperor or Fundanus or someone else think if I do one thing and not the other?' From what I've seen of the world, I would say that only Caesar has the possibility of being free in the sense that you're defining the word."

Lorcis' spirits sank. Jacob, her trusted friend, was destroying the one hope that had kept her determination alive since Encolpius had sold her.

"You were free most of your life," she finally continued. "Did you feel this way about slavery then?"

"No," Jacob admitted. "I have never had occasion to think about it, just as you had probably never considered what you would do if you were sold to someone else. But I now realize that my true status has changed little since those days. I am free in Christ, as I always have been, and I will join him some day. I had once hoped it would be soon so I could be reunited with my wife and daughter. But now I feel I have some purpose to serve in your life and in mine, so I am content to tarry here awhile."

He put his hands on the table and stood up abruptly. "And now we have tarried here too long. You must go home, and I must return to the arena to 'enjoy' the rest of the show."

CHAPTER IX

When Lorcis finally had an opportunity to get to the bookshop several days later, the owner gave her directions to Martial's home. She recognized from his description that she would have to pass through the worst section of Rome to get there—and then there was no guarantee that Martial would be home.

"He spends most of his time trying to land invitations to dinner, I believe," the bookseller pointed out. "And since his book has become popular he's finding that easier."

Would she ever see him again? She couldn't spend every day at the bookshop waiting for him, and the chances that their paths might cross again in a city the size of Rome seemed remote. She kept reminding herself that she wanted to see him because she was angry at him, but she also kept seeing his smile and feeling his arm around her as they walked up the Caelian Hill.

The next night, as she was playing her flutes for Regulus and Sempronia at dinner, Regulus said to Jacob, "Oh, Nestor, I invited that fellow Martial to dinner on Thursday. He's been damnably persistent in his attentions to me the past couple of weeks. But everybody's quite taken with him and his silly poems so I suppose I'm fortunate. Add his name to the list. Just see to it that he's placed as far from me as possible." Jacob nodded. Lorcis suddenly burst into a cheerful tune on her flutes which drew a raised eyebrow from Sempronia.

On Thursday she fixed her hair more carefully than she had in weeks, borrowed one of Xanthippe's most beautiful stolas, painted her nails, and spent almost an hour on her make-up. Finally she polished her flutes and went down to the triclinium. She would begin playing as soon as the first guests arrived.

Regulus' triclinium was one of the largest in Rome outside the imperial palace. It could accommodate eighty diners, though Thursday night it was set for only fifty, leaving room in the center of the floor for dancers and other entertainers. The floor itself was an elaborate mosaic depicting farm scenes, hunting and fishing scenes, and still lifes of various kinds of foods. The frescoes on the walls showed famous banquets and simple meals. On one wall was a representation of Dido's banquet for Aeneas, described by Vergil in the *Aeneid.* On another wall Philemon and Baucis were depicted offering a humble meal to a disguised Jupiter and Mercury. No matter how much they served, the bowls remained full. On the third wall Ulysses was shown dining in the fantastic palace of the Phaeaceans, while on the fourth wall the guests could contemplate Socrates eating with his circle of disciples, including Plato.

In front of the wall with the Socrates fresco the floor was raised a few inches, forming a dais. Here were placed couches for Regulus and honored guests. The other guests knew their standing in Regulus' eyes by their distance from that dais.

The couches were placed in groups of three, at right angles to each other, with a table for each group of three couches. The couches occupied three sides of the table, leaving the fourth side open for slaves to serve and clear the food. Each couch had three sections, and each section could be occupied by a single person or a couple. Thus each couch could accommodate from three to six persons; altogether, nine to eighteen persons could eat from each table.

It was late afternoon when guests began arriving. Because the streets of Rome were so dangerous at night, it was customary to begin a dinner before dark so everyone could finish and get home before it got too late.

Each arrival was greeted by a servant called the nomenclator, the name-caller. His job was to recall the names of everyone Regulus knew and walk with him through the streets to remind him of those names when his master encountered people. As he announced the guests, Jacob led them to their places in the triclinium.

From her corner of the room Lorcis could watch each guest

arrive. Most of the men came with women younger than themselves. Some of these men were married to other women, but no one objected to their present companions. After all, their wives were undoubtedly out with their lovers. Lorcis wondered how many marriages in Rome were like Regulus'.

A few men came by themselves, accompanied only by three or four slaves whose responsibility would be to insure that their owner got home safely. Lorcis knew that she would probably be "attending" one of these men before the evening was over, especially since Regulus was currying favor with anyone who could help him in the upcoming election. "If you want him to vote for you, *you* sleep with him," she often thought, wishing she had the courage to say it.

Finally the nomenclator called out "Marcus Valerius Martial." Lorcis fumbled with her fingering as she waited for him to come in. Would he have someone with him? For that matter, he might be married. Until that very moment, such a possibility hadn't occurred to her.

But Martial entered the triclinium alone, and Jacob showed him to a couch in the corner of the room farthest away from Regulus' place, what the Romans considered the "lowest" couch in the room. Martial had obviously been expecting this snub and gave no sign that he noticed the snickering of some of the other guests, to whom status was all-important.

He took a cup of wine from Xanthippe and looked around the room until he found Lorcis. She raised her eyes intending only to glance at him, but he grabbed her with his dark eyes and for a moment she could not look back down. He saluted her surreptitiously with his cup and mouthed, "Good evening, my lady." Then someone on the other side of the room spoke too loudly, someone else laughed raucously, and everyone's attention turned that way.

Martial's table companions had arrived. The man reclining next to and "above" him was an elderly freedman, a former slave of Regulus' who had made a considerable fortune for himself. He was wealthier than many of the other guests, but his status would never change in the eyes of Rome's aristocracy; his money could buy him everything except respectability. The others were poor aristocrats whose family fortunes had been frittered away but who still retained a name that assured them at least entry to the homes of the wealthy and powerful.

Once all the guests had arrived, Regulus made his grand entrance. All the guests applauded as he made his way through them, nodding, patting an arm here, kissing a cheek at another table. Taking his place on his couch, he said with a grand gesture of his arm, "Welcome, my friends. I trust you are all comfortable." Following a murmur of agreement, Regulus pointed to a man who was leaning on the ample bosom of the young woman on the couch beside him. "I see Rufinus has brought his own cushions. I'll be happy to fluff them up for you, my friend." The room rocked with laughter.

"Now, if you're all as hungry as I am, we'll do justice to the superb meal my cook has prepared for us. At least it had damn well better be superb, considering what the rascal says he paid for the food. Shall we begin?" He clapped his hands and the slaves began serving the meal.

The first course consisted of several small items designed to whet the appetite. There were sheep's livers soaked in mead, eggs, and milk, then stewed in wine sauce and sprinkled with pepper. Another tray held onions cooked in thyme, honey, vinegar, date wine, and olive oil. A third was filled with stuffed dormice. The favorite delicacy, however, was snails sprinkled with milk and flour, then roasted alive.

Playing quietly in her corner, Lorcis was able to observe the behavior of the guests more closely than any of them would have liked. What she herself did or did not do, and with whom she did it, were of course dictated by her master, but her own standards of behavior were shaped by her intense desire to be her own person and to control her own body. She did not believe she would ever comport herself as wantonly as the women around her were doing.

Strict Roman tradition called for a woman at a meal to sit on a chair or on the end of her husband's couch. In smaller provincial towns the custom was still observed, but in Rome it had long been fashionable for women to recline alongside their male companions.

Lorcis had once read a poem by Ovid about men and women engaging in sexual activity during dinner, and she had seen a lot of intimate fondling between couples at the dinners where she had entertained. But for the first time that she was aware of, a man and a woman were actually engaged in intercourse just a few feet away from her while everyone else ate unconcernedly.

This particular couple had come into the triclinium practically draped all over each other. Lorcis assumed they had followed the normal pattern of bathing together earlier in the afternoon and had found the experience particularly stimulating. The woman's long gown covered their activity for the most part, but the movements of their bodies and their rapid breathing left no doubt about what they were doing.

When they finished, the woman rolled over and her glazed eyes met Lorcis' for a moment without really seeing her. "You stupid slut," Lorcis thought. "You're free. You don't have to do that." Momentarily, Jacob's observations about the general lack of freedom in their society haunted her.

While the servants were refilling wine cups, one of the men eating with Regulus signaled for quiet. When he had everyone's attention he said, "I'm certain we will all long remember the games which our friend Regulus presented last week, especially the Atalanta play which sent the crowd into such raptures."

There was a round of applause.

"It was a truly noble gesture to sacrifice a handsome couple like that for the sake of art."

Martial suddenly blurted out, "No one but Regulus would have done it!" Everyone applauded again. Lorcis was angry at him for saying such a thing until she studied his face and perceived that it had been an insult. No one else seemed to notice. Or perhaps they all did, and were endorsing Martial's feelings with their applause. She found herself hopelessly confused sometimes trying to determine what people in Rome meant by what they said.

The man continued, "It seems to me that someone like that last young man would be missed. After all, beautiful young women are easy enough to come by, but such a well-endowed youth is a rarity. After a diligent search, however, I have found a worthy successor, and I would like now to present him to Regulus as a token of my esteem."

He motioned to the slaves standing at the foot of his couch and one of them stepped forward. His tunic was a bit longer than normal, for reasons which became obvious when Fundanus raised the front of it. A gasp spread around the triclinium.

Regulus laughed. "You've earned my undying gratitude, Fundanus," he said, "for such a magnificent gift. He'll be a welcome addition to my household, perhaps even to my stable."

The servants then brought in a more substantial course. In the center of a large tray was an ostrich cooked in a sauce of pepper, mint, cumin, onion, celery seeds, honey, vinegar, and raisin wine. Around the edge of the tray were sows' wombs and udders stuffed with pepper and caraway. On a second tray was a delicacy consisting of fine white bread with the crust removed, soaked in milk and eggs, fried in oil and covered with honey. Since the Romans used no table utensils, all food had to be cut to bite size before it was served. After the ostrich had been shown around the room, it was placed on a table before Regulus, carved up, and put on platters to be set before the guests.

Along with the main course came the first full-scale entertainment. Lorcis got up to make room for the musicians who accompanied a troupe of dancers Regulus had hired. She worked her way through the slaves standing behind their masters' couches until she found room in the corner where Martial was eating. Since he was on a couch next to the wall and had no slaves, she was able to get close to him with no difficulty.

Martial waited until the dancers began their routine before he turned and motioned for Lorcis to come sit on his couch. She did not dare do that without Regulus' permission, but noticing he was occupied, she quickly sat on the floor close to Martial.

"I'm pleased to see you again, my lady," he smiled.

"Please don't call me that," Lorcis replied. "You're just making fun of me."

"No, I'm not, I assure you. You've been the mistress of my every thought these past two weeks. I've been trying to see you, but it's awkward to explain to a man that you're interested in one of his slave girls, so I finally buttered up old Regulus so much he had to invite me to dinner just to shut me up." He leaned down so no one else could hear. "But I don't care about the food, or about him. I just wanted to see you again."

Lorcis looked up at him and smiled. "I confess I've been trying to find you, too. I went back to the bookshop and would have come to your room if I could've been sure you were there."

"Don't try to make that trip alone," Martial said seriously, putting his hand on her shoulder. "It's much too dangerous. The only reason I'm safe there is because the thieves know I'm as poor as they are."

"Why don't you move?" Lorcis asked.

"One of the privileges of freedom," he replied, "is paying

for the place where you live. I can barely afford that slum as it is."

It became difficult to talk as the music grew louder and the dancing more frantic. The leading dancer, a woman in her mid-twenties, wore a brightly colored but diaphanous costume, with an abundance of bells and fake jewelry attached to it. She whirled, clashing small cymbals together, then stopped in the middle of the floor and fell to her knees.

The leading male dancer suddenly sprang over one of the couches and touched down in front of her. To everyone's shock he whipped out a short sword from under his robes and began to threaten the woman with it. With gestures and facial expressions she pleaded with him while the musicians supported her with plaintive wails from their instruments.

Suddenly the woman took the sword from the man, threw her head back, opened her mouth, and put the tip of the sword down her throat. Everyone gasped as she proceeded to swallow the sword, inch by inch, until the hilt touched her lips. Then she took her hand off the handle and held out both arms as the musicians played furiously and the guests applauded enthusiastically.

Slowly, the woman removed the sword and tossed it to her partner, who caught it, whirled it around his head, and then brought it down full force on a thick stick held by two other dancers. The wood split with a sharp crack. The guests were delighted, and the dancers scurried off to a thunderous ovation.

Regulus raised a fat hand to silence the guests. "By a remarkable coincidence," he announced, "we have sausages on the menu—sausages served on skewers, as a matter of fact." A mixture of groans and laughter swelled around the room. "In honor of the astounding performance we've just witnessed, I have asked the cook to change the order of the courses slightly, so the sausages will be brought in momentarily."

Even as he finished speaking and reclined back on his couch again, the first tray of sausages appeared. For the next few minutes there was great hilarity and a good deal of gagging.

When the novelty wore off, the next course was brought in: fish with oysters cooked in pepper, egg yolks, vinegar, olive oil, wine, and honey; sardines in a sauce made of mint, onion, honey, vinegar and sprinkled with chopped boiled eggs.

While the food was served a team of acrobats took their places in the center of the floor. With everyone else distracted,

Martial and Lorcis were free to converse for a few minutes.

"Is this your first step toward becoming a slave of Regulus?" Lorcis asked.

"I don't know," Martial replied, "but it is the first decent meal I've had in three days."

Lorcis started to say something else, but Martial put a finger to her lips. "You happen to have some self-respect and a sense of decency. I don't," he said bluntly. "Why waste the few precious minutes we have together arguing about it? It doesn't matter who is slave and who is free. The only difference between us that does matter is that I am a man and you are a woman—a beautiful, charming woman whom I am eager to get to know. Can't we be content with that?"

"I want more, so much more," Lorcis replied earnestly. "But I suppose we can start there," she smiled—a genuine smile, the quick and radiant one she used so seldom.

The acrobats weren't particularly good, and Regulus realized that his guests were growing impatient. How could he get rid of the fools? To order them off would be to admit that he had chosen poor entertainment. Then, noticing Fundanus fumbling with a slippery oyster that had gotten away from him, Regulus had an inspiration. He picked up an oyster from his own plate and let it intentionally slip out onto the floor near the acrobats. When Fundanus noticed what Regulus had done and saw the wicked gleam in the man's eye, he joined in the mischief by tossing another piece of slick fish in the same area. The acrobats were too involved to notice what was happening until one of them, trying to balance two others on his shoulders, stepped on an oyster. His fall left him senseless on the floor and one of the other men with a broken arm. The audience applauded and laughed as though it had been the troupe's best trick. Regulus then seized the opportunity to order the whole group out.

Conversation buzzed loudly until someone near the front of the room said, "Oh, that's good! You really must share it." He turned to face the dais and said, "Regulus, my kind host, Fidentinus has just recited the most delightful epigram in honor of your narrow escape when that portico collapsed last week. Shall we have him share it with us?"

"By all means," Regulus replied regally. Though he had no taste whatever for poetry, he was never reluctant to hear his own praises sung. No one but himself was aware that the portico had fallen because he had been driving his chariot too fast and had bumped against one of the central pillars. He'd been alone at the time and had circulated among his friends a story about his miraculous escape. It would be interesting to have it celebrated in a poem, even a poem written by someone he did not particularly like. "Please honor us, Fidentinus," he said with a wave of his hand.

Fidentinus, unaware of Martial's presence since he had arrived after the poet, sat up on his couch, took a swallow of wine, cleared his throat, and recited a poem which Martial had composed and recited while walking with Fidentinus several days earlier. Fidentinus had even asked him to repeat it, allegedly because he appreciated it so much, but in fact so he could memorize it for just this occasion:

This portico
which scatters its long ruins in a cloud of dust,
is absolved at least from even greater blame.
For Regulus had just passed
under that roof and out again
when, suddenly, overcome by its own weight
and no longer fearing its master's safety,
it caved in, but harmlessly.
Who can now deny, Regulus,
that you are the darling of the gods,
for whose sake a disaster was without victims?

Everyone applauded dutifully, but Martial spoke up as they settled back down to eating. "My lord Regulus," he called. Fidentinus blanched as soon as he recognized the voice.

Regulus raised his eyes and craned his neck, like a man looking at some unrecognized object he can hardly see in the distance. "Yes, friend Martial," he said. "Have you some comment about the poem? You are a poet, aren't you," he added uncertainly, to remind the upstart that he was on the very fringe of the company in more ways than just in the seating arrangement.

"Yes, my lord," Martial replied cheerfully, "and Fidentinus' effort has proved inspirational. May I share my newest poem with you, composed even as I listened to this veritable muse?"

Lorcis looked up at him, startled. She did not believe he could have composed a poem so quickly, merely upon hearing another man recite. She was also uncomfortable that he was drawing attention to himself and to the fact that she was sitting with him without Regulus' permission.

"Go ahead," Regulus said without enthusiasm.

"Thank you, my lord," Martial said, standing up quickly. Without introduction he began:

The poem you recite, Fidentinus, is mine.
But since you do it so badly,
I'll ever so gladly
Let it be reckoned as thine.

After a brief stunned silence, Regulus guffawed and burst into applause. The other guests immediately joined in. "Like dogs," Lorcis thought, "barking whenever the leader of the pack does, whether they know what they're yelping about or not."

Martial acknowledged the applause, then reclined on his couch again. He was about to say something to Lorcis when Regulus called her to the front to play. As she gathered up her flutes and stood up to go, Martial said, "I'll be at the bookshop by the Forum tomorrow morning."

Lorcis winked. "I could use some new reading matter—something by a rising young poet, perhaps."

Though she wanted to get back to Martial's corner again, she was unable to do so. Regulus ordered her to socialize with one of the guests who had come by himself. She reclined on the couch beside him and steeled herself to submit to a lot of groping and fondling, but the man passed out before he could do much of anything. Lorcis was surprised when she realized he was unconscious because he hadn't drunk more than a Roman artistocrat would normally consume under such circumstances; nor had he gotten progressively more drowsy or groggy. He had just slumped over suddenly, unconscious.

The next morning Lorcis mentioned the incident and her surprise to Xanthippe, who laughed quietly. "I put something in his drink," she confessed. "My herbs and potions come in handy for all sorts of things."

Xanthippe was modest. In fact, she had studied this ancient version of pharmacology as a child in her previous owner's household. An elderly Egyptian slave who served as the family's doctor had taken a liking to her and had made her his assistant.

He passed on to her his lore and eventually his books. Other slaves in Regulus' household were suspicious of her powers, and rumors circulated that she had enchanted her current lover, Gorgias, by means of a love potion.

"Why did you do it?" Lorcis asked, amazed by her boldness but touched by her bravery.

"Because you're my friend," Xanthippe answered with sudden seriousness. "I've been with Titanius before, and it's not an experience I want any friend of mine subjected to."

Lorcis smiled and squeezed Xanthippe's hand. "I don't think anyone has ever done anything for me simply out of friendship," she said. "Thank you. I'll return the favor if I ever can."

"No," Xanthippe said. "If you start keeping track and doing things in return, it's not friendship. I want us to be friends, not debtors."

CHAPTER X

It was late morning before Lorcis was finally able to get out of the house. She rushed to the Forum and down the little side street to the bookshop to find Martial still waiting for her. He was leaning against the wall beside the door, glancing anxiously up and down the street. She had been so afraid he would leave.

"My, wealthy households do sleep late, don't they," he greeted her with mock seriousness.

"If Regulus had slept late, I'd have been here on time," Lorcis replied.

"Why? What happened?"

"Oh, he had a new stunt he wanted me to try on him. Something one of Fundanus' slave girls does to him. They were discussing it at the dinner last night."

"Are you all right?" Martial asked, holding her arms tenderly.

"Yes," Lorcis replied, though she was growing agitated. "All I did was gag and throw up all over him." She laughed, but Martial could hear the frantic edge in her voice. "It was almost worth it, though, just for that."

Martial started to console her, but Lorcis cut him off. "It's over," she said, "and will be forgotten as soon as we stop talking about it." She took a deep breath and closed her eyes.

When she opened them she smiled and quipped in a playful tone of voice, "Now, are there any books by any new young poets for sale here?"

"No, just those tired old tomes of Vergil, Ovid, and that

bunch of hacks," Martial replied, picking up on her mood.

"Well, I'm disappointed," Lorcis said. "I was not at all pleased with a recent purchase of mine. I think the author has talent, but I'm eager to see some other type of poetry from him."

"I see," Martial said, nodding his head slowly. "I should perhaps explain that until he is financially secure, a new poet must sometimes write about things that he knows will sell, regardless of his personal feelings."

"Just like a prostitute," Lorcis observed, not without a touch of sarcasm.

"The analogy is . . . uncomfortable," Martial said with his head down, "but to the point."

"Well, perhaps I must look for some other poet to fill my time and win my heart," Lorcis said with a mock sigh.

"My lady," Martial bowed, "I can arrange a private recitation of some new poems by Rome's newest poet. These poems are so new that they haven't been published. In fact, some of them haven't even been written yet."

Lorcis laughed, genuinely. "And where will this recitation be held?"

"In the home of the poet, on the Quirinal Hill."

"That's a rather long walk. I have to be back before sundown."

"The poet reads quite rapidly," Martial said, pantomiming a man unrolling a scroll and reading it in great haste.

"Well, let's get started, then," Lorcis said, taking Martial by the hand.

The parts of the city through which they walked were a study in extremes. The wealthy were inordinately rich, like Regulus, and the poor were inescapably mired in their poverty. Yet there were few clearly defined rich or poor neighborhoods. All over the city, private homes sat next to tenement houses. Whenever an apartment building burned—which happened frequently—or became so dilapidated that its owner had it torn down, it was likely to be replaced by the home of an aristocrat. Only in the Subura, at the foot of the Quirinal Hill, in the city's northeast sector, was the poverty unrelieved. Many of Rome's homeless drifted there, living off the garbage in the streets and preying on those who had to pass through the area on their way to or from the Forum and the more purely residential portions on the outskirts of the city.

Lorcis quickly saw why Martial had warned her not to attempt the trip by herself. Men laughing in doorways and dark side streets eyed her and seemed to assess their chances against Martial. Even when they began to climb the Quirinal itself, the improvement in the quality of the buildings and residents was only relative.

When they came to the main door of a rundown apartment house near the top of the hill, Martial motioned for Lorcis to enter and then directed her to the stairs. They hastily climbed three flights of wooden steps littered with rotting food scraps, broken household items, and human waste. With little success, Lorcis tried to hide her revulsion.

Noticing, Martial apologized. "I'm sorry it's not as clean as you're accustomed to, my lady. Squalor is one of the privileges of freedom, you see."

Martial explained that his room was in the middle of the hall, overlooking the courtyard of the building. "It's actually much more pleasant than being on the street side," he pointed out. "People tend to throw things on public property more quickly than on their own. And the children need some place to play." As they climbed the steep stairs, Lorcis glimpsed the courtyard through a small window and noticed it was, in fact, reasonably well kept.

Martial opened his door. "Behold, the poet's retreat!" he said, bowing elaborately and stepping aside for Lorcis to enter.

Slowly, almost cautiously she walked in. It was a small room, hardly twice the size of her own cubbyhole. There was a bed, a small table with a pitcher and bowl, and another larger table covered with scraps of papyrus, a pen, some wax tablets, and other writing paraphernalia. In one corner of the room was a pile of scrolls. As she looked around, Lorcis was aware of noises from other apartments and of smells, both pleasant and revolting, drifting through the window—almost it seemed, through the walls. She said nothing.

"I see it's even worse than what you expected," Martial said sadly. "Would you like to leave?" He had dropped their playful tone entirely.

"No," Lorcis replied quickly but uncertainly. "No. It's . . . fine." She tried to recover their light mood. "When does the reading begin?"

"If my lady will take the seat of honor, the poet will be ready momentarily." He took her arm and escorted her to the bed.

Wondering how many other women had occupied this place of honor, Lorcis pushed aside the several changes of clothes draped at random over the bed and made herself a place to sit. Martial rummaged through the papers on the table, pulling out an occasional piece, glancing over it quickly, and either tossing it back or holding it in his left hand. When he had a small sheaf of pages gathered, he turned to face Lorcis.

"Book One of the Epigrams of Marcus Valerius Martial," he intoned, "or at least some poems that will soon be part of Book One." He cleared his throat and shuffled his feet. "I plan this letter to be the first thing in the book, as a greeting and a warning to the reader: *I hope that I will not offend anyone by my poems. To jest at someone does not imply a lack of respect. I will not apologize for the frankness of my language, for it is the nature of epigrams to speak in the plainest fashion. Catullus set the example a hundred and fifty years ago, and since then Marsus, Pedo, Gaetulicus, and others have written in this genre—anyone, in short, whose books are still read all the way through. If you are a prude you'd better stop with this page, or even with the title.*"

He peered at Lorcis over the top of the sheaf of papers. "Shall I continue?"

"By all means," she replied with a laugh. "I'm certainly no prude."

"That's what I was hoping," he grinned good-naturedly. "Here's a short one to begin with."

If memory serves, Aelia, you had four teeth.
One cough dislodged two; another cough, two more.
Now you can hack away all day, free from any
further concern about your choppers.

Lorcis did not know the particular woman Martial had in mind, but she had seen enough elderly noblewomen with serious dental problems that she had to laugh ruefully at the poem. Martial seemed pleased.

"This is one of my personal favorites," he admitted.

Diaulus used to be a doctor.
Now he's an undertaker.
His clients haven't noticed the change.

He read a dozen more poems, satirizing the mores and foibles of the people he and Lorcis associated with every day.

When he finished, she applauded. "Your work is truly fine. It's witty, sometimes downright cruel. The technique is superb. The only poet I can think of who could be compared to you is Catullus. And I think your work is in some ways better than his."

Martial looked crushed. "Only in some ways? By the gods, what a devastating critic you are!"

Lorcis was afraid she had provoked him. Poets could be so temperamental. But he just sighed and said, "You're right, of course. I believe I can be a great poet, but I still need something. Some inspiration besides hunger."

When he walked over to the bed and stood in front of her, his hand made a hesitant move toward her. She did not encourage him, however. Instead, she searched his eyes. "You're a strange man, Martial. I've never known anyone so intense, so devoted to something."

"Intense?" Martial echoed. "Yes, I would call myself intense. Of course, I may appear so merely by comparison with those parasites you normally associate with—men who have no purpose in life other than to live luxuriously on wealth they have inherited or married or stolen."

"What about you? You fall all over yourself flattering those same parasites, trying to beg support from them. What are you?" Lorcis asked, feeling almost as if she were defending men she despised.

"I only ask myself that question when it's dark," Martial replied somberly, "and when I'm drunk."

"How do you answer it?"

He sat down next to her on the bed. "I usually mutter something grand about being a poet, an artist," he said with a wry smile. "Not that I don't take that seriously. I feel that I produce something worthwhile, just as any artist or craftsman does. But there's more to it than that. I *have* to write poetry. I've tried not writing, but then I can't sleep and I'm miserable. I don't care how I live, even if I have to prostitute myself, as long as I have a few hours every day to write. I'm an artist, and I feel I should be paid for the products of my art. But people who buy statues or paintings, even mediocre ones, aren't willing to pay for poems. Poems aren't as impressive, I guess, since you can't set them up in your garden or your atrium. But it's a mark of distinction to have a pet poet reading poems with your name in them. So I flatter the wealthy and cadge meals so I can keep writing."

"How long do you think you can play that game?" Lorcis asked anxiously. "Won't it eventually affect your outlook on life, your attitude toward people?"

"Oh, it already has," he readily admitted. "I told you I have no self-respect. I'm an utter cynic, incapable of believing that anyone is genuinely good or sincere."

"How can you live like that?" Lorcis cried with genuine dismay. In spite of her own experience with life she still clung to a stubborn hope that there were enough people in the world like Jacob and Xanthippe and Pliny to make existence bearable and worthwhile.

"For me, life is a game," Martial replied. "If I lose, I starve to death. If I win, I'll find someone to read my poetry."

This philosophical turn in the conversation made Lorcis uncomfortable. If he revealed his deepest feelings to her, he might expect her to return that confidence—and she was not yet ready to share her inner self with him—or any man.

"How do you decide what you're going to write about?" she asked. "I've often wondered about that with poets."

"I write about what I see—people usually. Sometimes because they make me angry, sometimes because I love them."

With that, he took Lorcis' hand and pulled her toward him, obviously intending to kiss her—the very situation she had hoped to avoid. All her life she had been trained to submit to men's advances. For the first time, she found herself attracted to a man, but she surprised both of them by pulling away. "Do you think you can use me, too? I'm not your slave!" she said angrily.

"No, you're not," Martial snapped in return. "In fact, I'm the only man in Rome with whom you're free. You don't have to make love to me, or kiss me, or even sit here with me." He got up, crossed the room in two steps, and opened the door. "You may leave." He stepped aside.

Lorcis stood up, took half a step, halted, and stated sincerely, "I seem never to be able to make myself clear to you."

"Try saying what you mean," Martial shot back.

"All right, I will! I don't want to make love to you because you are the first man I've ever really *wanted* to make love to."

Martial laughed wryly. "That's not as clear to me as it may

be to you. Can you tell me what you mean when you say what you mean?"

Lorcis looked at the floor, then back at Martial. "All my life my body has belonged to some man. Even though I was genuinely fond of Encolpius, I always knew that I could not refuse to sleep with him, no matter how I felt, physically or emotionally. I doubt that a man can fully appreciate that, just because you experience sex so differently from the way a woman does. But try to imagine not being able to say no—ever!" Her voice broke as the memory of so many unpleasant experiences flooded her. She stopped and glanced up at the ceiling while getting control of herself.

"And now it's much worse. Regulus has made me a whore. I don't even know the names of half the men I've been with since I got here. I'm rented out like a sedan chair that you can hire on any street corner." She could no longer stop the tears, and Martial took her in his arms. "Then I met you. I think I really do love you, and because I do, I don't want to make love to you right now."

Martial released her and threw his hands into the air. "So that's my fate!" he lamented to the ceiling and the neighbors. "Because she loves me she can't make love to me! How can I make you hate me?" he inquired with a smile.

Lorcis smiled back. "Please understand. If I make love to you now, so soon, before I really know you, you will be like any other man I've ever slept with. I want us to know each other, to care for each other." She moved close to him and touched his cheek. "You've given me my freedom; please give me a little time."

He kissed her hand. "I have given you your freedom—and you, my lady, have enslaved me." She did not resist his kiss.

CHAPTER XI

The late summer heat in the city drove most aristocrats to their estates in the country. Regulus' household spent the month of August at his villa in the Po Valley, where the Italian peninsula joins the mainland of Europe. Lorcis enjoyed the place—its vast gardens, shaded walkways and secluded niches where one could sit undisturbed for most of an afternoon. While Regulus hunted or visited friends, Lorcis spent her time in the secluded niches reading or playing her flutes. She missed Martial but consoled herself by reasoning that the separation would test their budding relationship. If he still wanted to see her when she returned, then she had gained something precious: the genuine love of a man she loved. If he were no longer interested, she had still gained a considerable measure of self-respect when she refused to sleep with him.

When the nights grew cool in early September, the household returned to Rome. The day after their arrival Jacob came to Lorcis' room. "It seems a young man has been here to see you," he said, barely suppressing a smile. "He left a note."

She tried to take the folded piece of papyrus slowly, but she could feel herself actually grabbing it. As she examined the wax seal, Jacob left quietly. The design impressed on the wax was a scroll with "M. Val. Mart." around it. She would have saved the seal—it was the first sealed letter she had received from a man—but she had to break it to get the letter open.

Valerius Martial to his lady, greetings.

I am pleased to learn that you have brought your house-

hold back from the countryside. If you can find the time in your busy schedule, I would like to meet you at Vatinius' elegant eating establishment on the south side of the Forum at midday tomorrow. I will reserve a table for you as long as my bladder holds out.

Lorcis knew that Vatinius' was actually one of the grimiest tabernas around the Forum, but for that reason it was also one of the cheapest. What mattered, though, was that Martial wanted to see her! *I would meet him in a sewer,* she thought as she kissed the letter.

Vatinius' taberna was barely a step above a sewer; the floor appeared to be swept only when some drunken customer was dragged out. For a minute after she walked in, Lorcis wasn't able to breathe. When she did have to draw a breath, her lungs tried to expel the foul air faster than she could draw it in.

Sitting down, she tried to concentrate on being with Martial again. He was obviously overjoyed to see her. He had great news: he had moved to a new apartment only a few blocks from Regulus' house. Of course, it meant he had less money to eat on each week, but he was willing to endure that privation. "I've been saving all week to bring you here," he said proudly. "Come on, eat up!"

In spite of a heavy sauce, Lorcis could tell that the fish Martial had ordered and was eating so ravenously had been out of the water much longer than the time needed for the trip from the coast to Rome. She could not bring herself to take a second bite of her own meal. They deserved something better and Lorcis knew she had enough coins in her purse to buy them both a decent lunch somewhere else.

Not wanting to embarrass Martial, she reached across the table and stopped his hand before it reached his mouth again. "It is the responsibility of a great lady like myself," she said, removing several coins from her bag, "to feed her slave well—especially if she expects to get untiring service out of him later in the afternoon."

Martial's eyes widened and the corners of his mouth turned up as the full implication of her statement sank in. Lorcis slipped him the coins under the table, as much to keep the other customers from seeing how much she had as to spare Martial's feelings.

Dropping the coins into his own purse, Martial called the owner to their table.

The surly Vatinius lowered over them. "You want anything else?" he shouted over the clamor, typical of a place like this.

"No," Martial replied, standing up. "In fact, I don't want this garbage you've served us." He swept everything off the table onto the floor. "That's where this stuff belongs!"

He grabbed Lorcis' hand as they ran out of the taberna. Elbowing and squeezing their way through the crowd, the two quickly outdistanced old Vatinius, who could not afford to get too far from his taberna for fear the other customers, too, would leave without paying.

Martial suggested that they find another taberna, but Lorcis knew they were all filthy hovels, tolerable only if one were not accustomed to anything better. She suggested they get some things to take to Martial's room and eat there. They bought a roasted chicken, bread, a flask of wine, some lettuce and mushrooms and hurried to Martial's new apartment. The building was cleaner only because it was somewhat newer, but the room was no great improvement over his old one.

That afternoon—for the first time in her life—Lorcis made love to a man because she wanted to. She was surprised at how different even the physical sensation was from what she had experienced before, though Martial did nothing unfamiliar to her. Like all Roman men she'd known, he was primarily concerned with his own gratification. He kissed and touched her because it pleased him. But her response was genuine and eager. He did not attempt to dominate her and that resulted in a sense of emotional satisfaction and intense waves of pleasure for her which she had only rarely enjoyed before.

Afterwards, she lay snuggled in his arms, relishing a warmth and closeness as meaningful to her as their sexual intimacy. No man had ever before allowed her to do that. For the first time she felt that a man was not "finished" with her.

During the next two weeks they had more opportunities to be together than they would have dreamed possible. Regulus was involved in a court case and had little time for dinner parties. He did call on Lorcis in the mornings to "soothe his nerves," but much of her time was her own.

One afternoon she and Martial went to the Forum to hear Regulus give his climactic speech in the case. Lorcis was surprised to find that he was a rather effective orator: his voice was dramatic and well controlled, his gestures were excessive but well timed. Because she did not understand the legal issue involved, Lorcis paid little attention to the content of his speech. The crowd was obviously impressed, though, and many of the hundred and one jurors nodded their heads in agreement.

At the end of his speech, Regulus wrapped his toga around himself with a flourish and sat down. His opponent then stood facing the jury with his back to the crowd. He looked small and young, especially by comparison with Regulus. When the crowd quieted down, he began to speak.

With his first words, Lorcis recognized the voice. It was Pliny! She wished he would turn around, but he focused his entire attention on the jury, relying on the justice of his arguments to win the case. Lawyers like Regulus used their florid rhetoric to arouse crowd reactions, hoping to sway the jurors, who voted by standing on one side of the court or the other. Because it was a public vote, the jurors were susceptible to pressure from the onlookers who booed or cheered to demonstrate their sentiments. It was a cheap tactic but surprisingly effective, since jurors who stood against popular opinion were sometimes known to meet with mishaps on their way home.

Pliny was speaking forthrightly, however, like someone reborn from the simpler, early days of the republic. It was not intended as a tactic, but it was effective. The jurors forgot that they were listening to an eighteen year old pleading his first case in court.

After both men finished speaking, the presiding officer of the court, the iudex, asked all jurors favoring the prosecution—Regulus' side—to stand in a designated area; those favoring the defense were directed to stand in another spot. When the milling around ceased and a few last second changes of vote were made, Pliny had won by a two-to-one majority.

Lorcis wished she could get close enough to congratulate him, but his clients and friends thronged around him as he walked off. Just as well, she realized. Regulus would not appreciate her making such a gesture.

She caught a glimpse of Pliny's face as he turned to speak to someone, but seeing him again did not awaken in her any of the feelings she had expected. She warmly remembered her experience with him and guessed that some of his determination in this case stemmed from the humiliation that Regulus had forced on her and Jacob in the baths at his villa a few months earlier. She wished him well, but she felt her future lay with Martial.

"Speaking of laying with Martial," she said in her poet's ear as she took his arm and pulled him out of the Forum, toward his apartment house.

"What?" he asked.

CHAPTER XII

One cool morning in mid-October Lorcis woke up feeling sick at her stomach. She had entertained at a banquet the night before and had eaten more than usual, but she seemed to be hungrier lately. Still, it was unlike her to feel so uncomfortable the morning after a banquet, almost as though she was going to throw up. "But that's exactly what I'm going to do," she told herself, groping under the bed for the chamber pot.

She was lying back down when Xanthippe, whose room was next door, opened the door without knocking. "I heard some awful noises. Are you all right?" she asked, answering her own question when she saw the mess in and around the chamber pot.

"I think I overate last night," Lorcis moaned.

Xanthippe felt her forehead. "You don't seem warm. How do you feel?"

"Much better. I don't think I'm really sick. Everything seems to be localized here." She patted her stomach.

"Hmmm," was all Xanthippe said.

"Just let me rest a few minutes and I'll be fine." Lorcis assured her.

"Has anything like this ever happened to you before?" Xanthippe asked.

"No."

"Hmmm."

Xanthippe went out to get a wet towel and returned to sit with Lorcis until the girl felt like getting up. Lorcis wobbled at first but was soon back to some semblance of her normal self.

The next morning Lorcis again woke up feeling sick at her stomach. She had eaten nothing unusual and no large quantities of anything the day before, so she was at a loss to explain the problem this time. She lay very still for a few minutes, hoping the sensation would pass—but in vain. This time, there was not as much in the chamber pot, but Xanthippe was there as soon as Lorcis finished throwing up; she brought a towel and a wet cloth with her.

"Looks like this is going to be a regular thing," Xanthippe joked, wiping up the mess on the floor.

"Oh, gods, I hope not," Lorcis groaned, appreciating the cold cloth on her face. "I thought we were friends. What makes you say a thing like that?"

"Just a hunch," Xanthippe replied. "Can I ask you a few questions that might help us get to the bottom of this?"

"Sure," Lorcis replied, "anything to stop . . . " She leaned over the chamber pot again.

"I didn't say stop it; I said understand it," Xanthippe emphasized while she finished mopping up. "When was your last monthly?"

Lorcis was totally unprepared for that question. "My last monthly? What does that . . .?"

"Just answer the question," Xanthippe said, dropping the soiled towel into the chamber pot and putting the whole mess out in the hall.

Lorcis did some quick figuring. "It was a week before we came back to Rome."

"So that's six weeks," Xanthippe calculated. "Are your monthlies regular, four weeks apart?"

"They always have been."

"Now, you and Martial have been, shall we say, getting together frequently since the first of September, haven't you?"

"Well, yes. I haven't tried to hide that from you," Lorcis said testily.

"No, you haven't. It's been a delight to see you so happy. But that sort of happiness sometimes has consequences, and I think this is one of those times." She sat down and held Lorcis' hand. "My dear, sweet Lorcis, I do believe you are going to have a baby."

Lorcis felt as though someone had told her she was growing a second head. "A baby—are you sure?"

Xanthippe ticked off the evidence on her fingers. "Missed monthly, frequent sexual activity, sick in the mornings—it all adds up."

"But I've never been pregnant before!" Lorcis said, knowing this fact was irrelevant but unable to think of any more appropriate response.

"Well, I don't mean to be indelicate," Xanthippe replied, "but just think how much of your sexual activity has been—abnormal. I know something about the sexual preferences of Roman aristocrats. A lot of what they like to do will not make a girl pregnant."

"I know, I know," Lorcis said, blushing a bit. "Are you sure?"

"We've been through that. I'm as sure as I've ever been. But you're in luck. It's not every pregnant girl who has a midwife next door."

Lorcis didn't say anything.

"What are you thinking?" Xanthippe asked. "You don't seem very happy."

"I'm not sure I should be," Lorcis replied in a subdued voice. "I love Martial, and it pleases me that I'm bearing his child. But what sort of life will my child have growing up the child of a slave?"

"You've got a point," Xanthippe admitted, patting her hand. "Your child will be Regulus' property, regardless of who the father is. You're sure it's Martial?"

"Of course!" Lorcis snapped.

"I didn't mean that," Xanthippe said soothingly. "It's just that I know Regulus and several of his friends have used you since we got back."

"All they're interested in is the latest variation that some Egyptian or Greek whore has invented," Lorcis sneered. "It's no wonder people in Rome seldom have children."

"So," Xanthippe said cheerily, "you and Martial are going to have a baby!" She hugged Lorcis.

"No," Lorcis said, "I'm going to have a baby which Martial may never get to see because it will belong to Regulus." She suddenly sat up, her eyes wide with horror. "What if Regulus decides to sell my baby? or to sell me? I'd never see my baby again!" Her longing for her own mother welled up as it did at unexpected moments.

"Settle down," Xanthippe said. "Remember your condition. Besides, you have no control over the future. For right now we've just got to take care of you and this baby." She hugged Lorcis again. "I'm so happy for you I can't bear it!" she said, even while she thought about how difficult the situation actually was. She was concerned, too, over Lorcis' attitude; from her long experience in such matters, she knew that unhappy mothers often had difficult pregnancies.

The morning sickness continued for several more weeks, then stopped as suddenly as it began. Lorcis adjusted to the idea that she was going to have a baby and was content once she could begin her day without throwing up.

She wasn't even thinking about her condition while she and Xanthippe were bathing one afternoon when she noticed Xanthippe studying her.

"What are you thinking about?" Lorcis asked.

"We're going to have to tell Regulus." Xanthippe replied matter-of-factly.

"Tell him what?"

"About the baby."

"I just assumed he would find out. A baby is pretty hard to hide."

"You'd be surprised," Xanthippe told her. "It all depends on the mother's duties in the house. I've seen kitchen women get pregnant, have the baby, and give it to a friend or relative outside the house to care for, all without the master knowing what was happening. Unfortunately, since your duties place you in frequent intimate contact with Regulus, we're going to have to tell him before he finds out."

"Why?"

"Oh, he would be far angrier about being deceived than he will be about your being pregnant." she said confidently. *I hope*, she added to herself.

The two revealed the secret to Jacob three days later; Lorcis had refused to see him by herself. She had felt no shame about her pregnancy until Xanthippe suggested that she tell Jacob and ask him to go with her to Regulus. With that, Lorcis suddenly realized how disappointed Jacob would be in her, and she began to feel worse about the situation herself. She sensed that Jacob regarded her as the daughter he had lost, and she did not want to be alone with him when he learned of her condition. Xanthippe had urged Lorcis to talk with Jacob by herself, but when Lorcis flatly refused to go without her, Xanthippe acquiesced.

Jacob said nothing at first. When he finally spoke, he measured his words carefully. "I am pleased, Lorcis, that you and the man you love are going to experience the joy of creating a child. But I am saddened somewhat, too, because according to the teachings of . . . " he checked himself because of Xanthippe's presence, " . . . of my people, children should be born only within wedlock."

Lorcis was stung by his comments. She did not want Jacob's opinion of her lowered; he meant more to her than she yet admitted to herself.

"But," he continued slowly, "I know that in your circumstances such a thing could hardly be. Still, a freeman outside the household fathering a child by one of our slaves—it creates a difficult situation. I agree with Xanthippe, though; Regulus must be told, and I will see to it. But Lorcis, it will be best if you come with me. I'll send word when I'm ready—probably tomorrow afternoon. Now, Xanthippe, I need to speak to Lorcis privately about this."

When Xanthippe closed the door, Jacob smiled—Lorcis had been waiting for that. She smiled back, relieved, and when he held out his arms, she gladly moved into them.

"My child, I am pleased," Jacob said. "It will be an awkward situation because of your status, but I will do everything I can to help you and your child. I wish you had a husband and a home, but in this world we must enjoy what happiness we can."

"I am happy," Lorcis said, "but scared."

"How does Martial feel about it?" Jacob asked. When Lorcis said nothing, he pulled back from her and scowled. "You haven't told him?"

Lorcis shook her head. "I'm just not sure how he'll react. Either he'll leave me because he doesn't want a child or he'll make trouble with Regulus, trying to get the baby. There's no middle ground with Martial."

"I see," Jacob nodded. "I understand your reluctance, but as Xanthippe pointed out in regard to Regulus, a delayed surprise is seldom as welcome as it would have been earlier. I think you should tell Martial as soon as possible."

"I'll think about it," Lorcis hedged.

"He has a right to know," Jacob persisted.

The next afternoon, Jacob sent for Lorcis as promised. When the message arrived she almost felt nauseous again. She put on her prettiest stola, checked her make-up, and went to meet Jacob in the atrium.

He touched her hair, like a father might, and Lorcis instinctively took his hand as together they approached Regulus' study on the other side of the large chamber. The door was open, and when Jacob knocked lightly, Regulus ordered them to come in.

The room was larger and more lavishly furnished than Encolpius' study. There were several chairs, a bookshelf (although she had never seen Regulus read a book), and two large marble-top tables. Frescoes of cupids playing at school decorated the walls, and the floor was a mosaic made up of geometric patterns. Regulus sat at the larger table reading reports from his estates and business interests and making notes. He did not look up until Jacob and Lorcis had stood beside the table for a moment or two.

"Now," he snorted, laying down pen and paper like a man who must deal with some damned nuisance, "what is this important matter with which you insist on taking up my time?"

In spite of his ten years of service under the man, Jacob felt his grip on the situation slipping. Rather than going through his elaborate and rehearsed prologue, he blurted out, "My lord, Lorcis is pregnant."

Regulus' lower lip pouted while he rubbed the bridge of his nose with his thumb and forefinger. Lorcis wondered if she should say anything, but Jacob had given her strict orders not to speak unless she was asked a direct question.

"Who's the father?" Regulus finally demanded.

Lorcis was not sure if he was addressing her or Jacob, but Jacob quickly replied, "That has not been determined, my lord. Given the nature of her . . . duties in the household, I doubt it will be known for certain." That was the story he and Lorcis had agreed to tell, and she hoped Regulus would not press the issue.

"This is an interesting situation," Regulus mused aloud. "Normally I would not be happy to have one of my finest entertainers and one of my loveliest slave girls pregnant. It's not one of the Nubians, is it?" he suddenly interjected. Lorcis shook her head in horror. "I thought not," Regulus said, "but I wanted to be certain."

Regulus stood up and walked around, studying the pattern in

the floor as though he had not seen it before. "Normally I would not allow the pregnancy to continue. Raising a slave child is an expensive proposition with no guarantee that the product will be worth it. I much prefer to buy a mature slave whose character and abilities are already known. Besides, abortions are easy, and the girl can be back to work in a few days with no ill effects."

Lorcis put her hands on her stomach. *You are not going to kill my baby!* an inner voice screamed. The only outward change in her demeanor was a slightly more rapid breathing. She was learning to be a good actress around Regulus and people of his sort.

"But," Regulus droned on, "since Lorcis can perform her particular duties without any interference from, or danger to, the unborn child, I am going to make an exception. If the baby is a girl she'll be raised in this house. If it's a boy, we'll have to make other arrangements."

Lorcis received this news with mixed emotions. At least the initial hurdle had been overcome: she could have her baby. But the fate of her child remained in the hands of a man she knew to be evil, spiteful, and insensitive toward anyone's needs but his own.

He stood directly in front of her and patted her belly gingerly. "So, not everybody's interested in your flute playing, eh?" He laughed in that callous way Lorcis had started to hate the first time she heard it. "If your child is a girl, it will be interesting to see if she inherits your special talent. After all, you aren't always going to be as young and pretty as you are now. It might be worthwhile to start grooming someone to take your place."

His words fell like a death sentence. Her child had not even been born yet, and he was condemning her to the life of a prostitute. She wanted to shout, "You can't have my baby! You're not going to ruin her life. I'll kill her first!" But she had to remain silent. When the passion of the moment had subsided, however, that last thought refused to leave her.

Regulus was ready to dismiss them. "Well, as I said, it's not an ideal situation, but I think we can manage it. I appreciate your frankness in this matter. I'm glad to know that my slaves trust me enough to come to me at once with something like this rather than trying to hide it. Nestor, have Xanthippe look after Lorcis. She knows this sort of business quite well. That will be all."

Jacob and Lorcis bowed and left the room. Once outside,

Lorcis leaned against a pillar to take a breath and steady herself, but Jacob took her arm and led her across the atrium to the stairs going up to the servants' quarters. "Don't stop till you get to your room," he said sternly, "then you can go to pieces if you want. You held up very well. I know you didn't like what you heard, but at least we've bought some time to make plans." He patted her arm then left to attend to his other duties.

"I already have my plan," she thought grimly to herself as she started slowly up the stairs.

CHAPTER XIII

A week later Lorcis lay on her bed. She did not know the time; it was night, early morning, perhaps. With the door closed, the windowless room was absolutely dark. She could not even see her own naked body.

She lay on her back with her hands resting on her abdomen. One hand held a long, slender twig from a tree in Regulus' garden. By indirect questioning over the past week she had learned from Xanthippe that a sharp, thin object inserted into the womb could cause a woman to lose her baby. She had been lying on her bed awake for what seemed hours, talking to herself and her baby about how much better it would be not to be born than to live the kind of life Regulus had planned for her. She had reminded herself that she didn't know if the baby was a girl, but even if it was a boy, Regulus would kill him or sell him. "What choice do I have?" she asked not herself but the baby.

She nerved herself. Xanthippe had said that a careless abortion could kill the mother along with the child. "Would that really be so awful?" she thought.

Slowly, she inserted the stick. It scraped and hurt. Deciding that she would have to do it quickly, she thrust the stick sharply and suddenly into herself. The excruciating pain was so unexpected that she could not stop herself from letting lose with a chilling scream.

Before the sound had faded away, Xanthippe was in Lorcis' room, lamp in hand. She found Lorcis on her side facing the wall with her legs drawn up in pain, the stick poking out.

"Damn!" Xanthippe cried as she began soothing Lorcis. "It's

all right, sweet," she cooed. "Xanthippe's here. Just relax. Now, let go of the stick."

But Lorcis would not relax her grip; even through the pain, her resolve to save her baby from the life of a slave remained firm. As Xanthippe tried to grab below Lorcis' hand to remove the stick, Lorcis continued to push the stick deeper into herself. The older woman, however, proved stronger and more determined to save the baby than her desperate young friend was to kill it.

Nivea, whose room was directly across the hall, stuck her head in the door. "What's going on?" she moaned, still half asleep.

"Never mind!" Xanthippe barked. "Go get Nes— No, forget it! Just go back to bed. Lorcis isn't feeling well." Sending someone to get Nestor, she had realized in time, would awaken the whole slave quarter, and Regulus would be sure to hear about it. Nestor couldn't do anything, anyway. The baby's fate had already been determined.

Lorcis started to cry, and her grip on the stick relaxed. Xanthippe eased it out and dropped it to the floor. There was only a trace of blood on it, and Lorcis didn't seem to be bleeding. "Thank the gods," Xanthippe sighed, "Nestor's included." She would need to watch Lorcis for a few hours to be certain no harm had been done, but if her experience was any guide, the baby was safe.

She laid Lorcis back down, pulled a blanket over her, then went quickly to her own room and got a sleeping potion. By the time Xanthippe returned, Lorcis was almost asleep, but she roused her enough to take the potion anyway. It would relax her muscles and organs, including her womb, and lessen the likelihood of a miscarriage.

Early the next afternoon the slave who arrived to summon Lorcis to Regulus' quarters was told that she was ill. Xanthippe accompanied the slave back to Regulus' room to explain that Lorcis was temporarily indisposed because of her pregnancy. She offered to take Lorcis' place, hoping to distract Regulus and keep him from sending anyone to check on his flute player. After all, he had agreed to let her have the baby on the assumption that it would not interfere with her "work." Xanthippe refused him nothing; he was satisfied.

It took a long bath for Xanthippe to feel clean enough to return to her room later that afternoon. She stopped in Lorcis' room and found Jacob sitting beside the bed. Xanthippe had informed him that morning of what had happened, and he had been in to see about Lorcis several times before Xanthippe left to go to Regulus. He sat watching the sleeping girl intently, his face heavy with worry.

"She's been asleep all day," he said. "Is that normal?"

"Yes," Xanthippe replied, putting a reassuring hand on his shoulder. "She was exhausted to begin with, and I gave her a powerful potion. She'll probably sleep right on through till tomorrow morning. She needs to be as still as she can until we're sure the baby's in no danger." She lifted the blanket to check for bleeding while Jacob quickly and politely turned his head.

When Xanthippe finished her examination and stepped back, Jacob reached down and smoothed Lorcis' hair, letting his hand rest on her shoulder.

"We love her very much, don't we," Xanthippe said. They looked at each other with surprise, as though some other person had spoken.

"Yes," Jacob replied quietly. "The first time I saw her I felt I had always known her. I realize now that God has put me here for her sake—and yours, too."

Xanthippe thought for a moment, without taking her eyes off Lorcis. "I don't know your god, so I don't pretend to know what plan he's working by. But I do know that I love Lorcis and, because of her, I've come to love you too . . . Jacob." She kissed his cheek. "We're going to get her through this. She's going to have a beautiful baby, and then . . ."

"We'll think of something by then," Jacob encouraged. *We've got to,* he added to himself.

It had been easy to put Regulus off, especially since Xanthippe offered her considerable erotic talents instead. Martial, however, was not so easily satisfied. He had few enough opportunities to be with Lorcis, and they had planned an outing late that afternoon. When she didn't show up, he came to the house.

First, Jacob castigated him for even coming to the house, risking revealing his interest in Lorcis. But he was merely trying to avoid the real issue. The shock of learning about Lorcis' pregnancy would be enough, without the news of the attempted abortion.

Martial, however, would not take "She's sleeping" for an answer, and Jacob began to wish Lorcis did not love this obstreperous man so much. True, he was the father of her child, but with that part done, Jacob almost wished the man would just go away and leave their little family alone. Martial just complicated the situation.

The poet was losing his patience. "Nestor, we're friends. If there's something wrong with Lorcis, I have to know. If her feelings for me have changed, she can at least have the decency to see me and tell me herself."

"But she can't see you. She's asleep," Jacob repeated.

"She wouldn't be sleeping at this time of day unless something were wrong with her," Martial insisted. "Now, I am going to walk around you—or over you if I have to—and up those stairs. I am going to see Lorcis."

Jacob shrugged his shoulders and shook his head slowly, then turned and led Martial up the stairs.

When Lorcis awoke she was facing the wall. At first she thought there was someone lying beside her. Then, as her vision cleared, she realized that she was looking at her own shadow on the wall. That meant there was a lamp burning behind her. But why would there be a lamp burning in her room at this hour of the night? What hour was it anyway? Had she dozed off and left the lamp burning?

She was about to turn over when she remembered that the lamp had not been lit when she'd gone to bed. Gradually, the whole awful memory rushed over her, and she recalled Xanthippe talking to her. Xanthippe must be sitting by the bed, but she did not want to turn over and face her.

What had happened? Had she succeeded? With her right hand resting on her abdomen under the blanket, she could not feel any difference. But she couldn't really expect to, she reminded herself, since she hadn't been showing yet. At times, she thought she detected a slight protruding of her tummy, but perhaps she'd only been fooling herself. At any rate, all she felt was clammy, as though she had been sweating and had not had a bath for some time.

A hand touched her shoulder, and Martial's voice broke in on her thoughts. "Lorcis, my love, are you awake?"

Lorcis gasped. "Oh, damn!" she thought. It would have been

difficult enough to face Xanthippe after what she had done—but Martial!

There was no way out of it. Her movements had made it obvious that she was no longer asleep, and Martial pulled gently but insistently at her shoulder. Taking a deep breath, she slowly rolled over.

When Martial reached his hand out toward her, she flinched. He had never struck her but his temper was mercurial, and on occasion she had found herself leaning away from him. He surely had reason to beat her now, but he only touched her hair and gently asked, "How do you feel?"

"Surprisingly well," she answered, "at least physically. I . . ."

"Don't worry about explaining," Martial broke in. "I've had a long talk with Nestor . . . Jacob and Xanthippe, so I know all about it."

Lorcis began to sob. "I killed our baby!" she blurted out, putting her arm up to cover her face.

"Sweetheart, wait," Martial said soothingly. "You don't understand. Everything's all right. Every*body* is all right."

Lorcis looked up from under her arm, wiping her tears. "Everybody?"

Martial nodded. "You haven't killed the baby. You came awfully close, but everything's just fine." Lorcis rolled her head from side to side and began to laugh in giddy relief. "Oh, thank God!" she cried. She took Martial's hand and drew him close to her. "I am so sorry, my love. I must have been crazy."

Martial leaned over and kissed her on the forehead. "In this town everybody goes crazy at one time or another. But everything's fine now. Just rest and be sure you and the baby are strong."

CHAPTER XIV

In June of the second summer after the eruption of Vesuvius, Lorcis gave birth to a daughter. A Roman girl normally bore the feminine form of her father's family name, but Lorcis could not legally call her child Valeria. Under the circumstances, that was impossible as well as indiscreet. She and Xanthippe had been calling the unborn child their "little love," so the Greek name Erotion seemed natural for her.

"The delivery was uncomplicated, and mother and daughter are resting comfortably," Xanthippe explained to Martial that evening when she went to his apartment to give him the news.

"When can I see them?" he asked immediately.

"Well, that is a problem," Xanthippe reflected. "If you show too keen an interest in one of his slave children, Regulus will get suspicious."

Martial pondered silently for a moment. "Ask Jacob if he can add my name to the guest list for Regulus' next dinner—and I hope it's soon."

"There's not another one scheduled for a week," Xanthippe replied, "but that's just as well. Lorcis can use the rest."

"Assuming I can get in, can you arrange for me to get at least a quick glance at them?"

"Yes, I think so. About the middle of the evening—let's say just before the fish course—go out to relieve yourself. Lorcis will be in the atrium with Erotion. Just be sure you're casual."

"I'll be utterly indifferent," Martial assured her with a wave of his hand. "I'll just say, 'Oh, a baby. How nice,' and I'll go on about my business."

Xanthippe chuckled. "I can more easily imagine you picking up Lorcis and the baby in your arms, running into the triclinium, and reciting a poem to everybody about *your* baby."

"You don't think that would be casual?" Martial asked teasingly.

Xanthippe laughed in spite of herself. "It would be catastrophic if Regulus were even to suspect you are Erotion's father. After all, there are laws about sowing your seed in another man's field."

"But Xanthippe, I love her so much. The way Regulus can control her and abuse her . . ." He raised his hands as though he were trying to grab someone by the throat. "And it's more than just Regulus; it's our whole way of life. What kind of society is this? What kind of people are we, to allow women and children to be enslaved? Can the woman I love really be Regulus' *property*?" He shook his head and sat down. "Sorry. I didn't mean to turn into a philosopher."

"Lorcis has had a similar effect on me," Xanthippe said. "Slavery is the only life I can remember, so I never thought much about it. But all of Lorcis' talk about freedom has affected—or perhaps infected—me. Even if I can't be free, I want her and Erotion to be. I think I would even lay down my life to free them."

"Well, until they are free," Martial said ruefully, "we're stuck with the present situation—which means you'd better get back to the house. Take good care of them for me, Xanthippe."

She smiled and kissed him on the cheek. "Don't you worry, daddy. They're in good hands. I'm the best midwife and nurse on the Caelian Hill, and Jacob is turning out to be the best grandfather in all of Rome."

At the dinner seven nights later, Regulus did not notice Martial, and Martial made every effort to remain inconspicuous. Jacob had placed him near the door on a reclining couch that turned him away from Regulus' table. Not that Regulus would have objected to his presence; he usually gave Jacob the names of people who must be invited and trusted his steward's judgment about inviting other fashionable or useful people to fill up the triclinium. But Martial was nervous nonetheless and thankful that no one paid any particular attention to him.

The dinner had Regulus' usual flair for the dramatic. After

all the guests had taken their places, Regulus entered dressed as the Greek hero, Theseus, who had killed the Minotaur and had later married Hippolyte, queen of the Amazons. A few guests were bold enough to smirk behind their napkins at the sight of the portly middle-aged man posing as a youthful hero, but no one dared even whisper a caustic comment to his neighbor.

Sempronia and several of her friends followed Regulus, costumed as Amazons, with their right breasts exposed and their tunics barely reaching their knees. They wore hunting sandals with straps that wrapped around their legs almost up to the knee. Most of them carried bows and wore quivers of arrows.

As they paraded in, one of the guests muttered something about the Amazons cutting off their right breasts to improve their archery. But his whisper was a bit too loud, and Sempronia turned on him. "That is a wholly erroneous myth," she snapped. "A man might just as well castrate himself to improve his chariot driving," she added with a sneer.

To prove her point she had several of her younger friends, including Gallia, put on an archery exhibition in the triclinium. The girls were not exceptional shots, but the guests, grateful that no one had been hit by a stray arrow, applauded them warmly.

During the first course, the conversation turned to the Amazons as warriors and the usefulness of the bow as a weapon. Upper-class Romans had long since ceased to take an active part in the army, which now relied on mercenary troops. As is often the case with noncombatants, however, the less practical experience they had, the more expert they fancied themselves. Not one of them doubted he or she could have ended the Jewish revolt, Rome's most recent war, in less than six months. But no one could voice such opinions without offending the emperor Titus and the memory of his father Vespasian, so the guests talked instead of legendary wars such as those between the Athenians and the Amazons.

A young nobleman named Quadratus, whom Regulus had been grooming as a protégé, irritated Sempronia by asserting the old Roman belief that the bow was not a manly weapon, since it allowed its user to strike from a safe distance with no risk. "A real man—or even someone who pretends to be a man," Quadratus taunted, setting the guests abuzz, "would use sword or knife and not be afraid of hand-to-hand combat."

Gallia sat up on the couch she was sharing with Sempronia.

"Are you calling me a coward?" she snapped at Quadratus.

"I merely said that yours is not a manly weapon," Quadratus replied. "I said nothing about your own standards of personal bravery."

"Typical lawyer's double talk!" Gallia snorted. "It's no wonder you're famous all over town for your flexible tongue."

With that rebuff all other conversation died down. Sempronia started to touch Gallia's arm to rein her in, but Regulus, who was angry at Quadratus because he had recently assisted Pliny in a court case, suddenly interrupted.

"It seems, my friends," he said in his oiliest manner, "that we have here a question of manliness—and a rather perplexing one it is. Who is the more truly masculine: Quadratus, who is by definition a male, or Gallia, who would prefer to be a man?"

By now the other guests realized that Regulus intended to humiliate both Quadratus and Gallia and expected all present to appreciate the humor. The laughter was nervous at first but soon was widespread. Only Sempronia and her Amazons did not join in.

"The only way to settle this, it seems to me," Regulus went on grandiosely, "is to let them fight it out. Since Quadratus, like a true ancient Roman, disdains the bow, perhaps he will stand up for his convictions and engage in hand-to-hand combat." He glanced at Quadratus, daring him to refuse.

Quadratus knew he could not back down and expect to retain any standing in this social circle; these were the most important people in Rome. His success as a lawyer depended on them and their friends. He closed his eyes and nodded.

Regulus then turned to Gallia and merely raised his eyebrows in a question. She quickly nodded her assent.

"Good, good!" Regulus said, rising from his couch and standing in front of it. "It is customary in the arena," he chortled, "for the gladiators to parade in front of the spectators before they make their bets. I think that would be appropriate here." He knew that his gambling-crazed friends would not pass up the opportunity for a bet which had fallen into their laps so unexpectedly.

The musicians struck up a parody of a gladiators' march as Gallia and Quadratus began their tour of the dining room. But Regulus quickly approached them before they'd gone far.

"Just a minute now," he insisted, clasping them each on a

shoulder. The music stopped. "No one can see much about your physical condition under all these clothes." He tugged at their garments. "Get them off!"

The two removed their clothes, Quadratus slowly and reluctantly, Gallia with undisguised pride. Once they were naked, the reasons for their attitudes were obvious: Quadratus, although only in his early twenties, was already running to flab. His admiration for ancient Roman manliness was largely theoretical. Gallia's slender body, on the other hand, showed the results of her regular visits to the gymnasia and baths. As she slipped her short tunic off over her head, murmurs of approval went around the room.

The tour resumed. As they walked, Quadratus hung his head. He knew he could do nothing but endure what was about to happen. An ancient Roman, he reflected, would have killed himself rather than suffer this sort of humiliation. But, he reminded himself disconsolately, no matter how bad it might be, it would be over within a few minutes and forgotten in a couple of days. Roman aristocrats were always seeking some new thrill and remained satisfied with a sensation only as long as the sensation itself lasted.

Quadratus glanced at Gallia walking—prancing—beside him. She was erect, proud, with a slight spring in her step. Although these people all looked down on her, she had a position from which she could even hope for a measure of revenge: Sempronia was her "friend." She sneered at Quadratus—at all of them.

When they completed their circuit, Regulus was waiting with a napkin in his hands, which he would drop to signal the beginning of the fight. "The rules are really quite simple," he intoned. "Anything goes. No holds barred." Signaling to the musicians for a fanfare, he raised the napkin and released it.

As it floated to the floor, Gallia and Quadratus took a few steps back from each other and began to circle warily. Quadratus knew he was no match for Gallia's wiry strength and decided to risk everything on an all-out attack. He lunged at his opponent, flailing his fists and hoping just to make contact. But Gallia stepped nimbly aside and kicked Quadratus as he stumbled past, sending him crashing into a couch. The guests pushed him back toward the middle of the floor, a few even urging him on.

Gallia skipped around the floor spitting insults at Quadratus as he righted himself. After briefly stalking her, he finally cried out, "Your tactics are proving my point! You dance around and taunt me but are afraid to actually fight me." A few murmurs of agreement came from around the room.

Gallia stopped, planted her feet apart, and placed her hands on her slim hips. "So the great dumb beast doesn't want to be toyed with. He prefers for the lion to finish him off. Very well!" She rushed at him, punching him in the face and stomach several times before he could even get his hands up to protect himself.

Quadratus, frantic, realized that he was not going to be able to knock her down with a punch. His best hope would be to grab hold of her and throw her down. When she moved in to hurl another barrage of punches at him, he managed to get a good grip on her hair. But as he gathered his strength to throw her down, Gallia smiled at him in an odd way and very gracefully stepped backwards—leaving Quadratus with only her wig in his hand. As he stared at it in disbelief, he heard a disembodied cackle coming from somewhere behind him: It came from Sempronia.

Before he could recover, Gallia kicked him low and hard. The few spectators who had bet on him cried foul, but Regulus raised a hand to still the protests and shouted, "Anything goes! That was the rule!"

As Quadratus crumpled to his knees, banging his forehead on the floor, Gallia circled him, pummeling him with kicks and curses.

Martial glanced around the room at the avid, leering faces of the guests while an uncomfortable thought elbowed its way to the front of his mind: "What sort of people are we, who humiliate others for our amusement over dinner? Damn," he muttered as he got up off the couch and slipped on his sandals, "I'm beginning to sound like Jacob."

The next part of the evening had been carefully choreographed by Xanthippe and Jacob. Everyone, even Erotion, had lines in the scene so the meeting would appear fortuitous. But as he approached the door of the dining room, he felt a knot in his stomach, a nervousness he had not experienced since his first appearance as a lawyer. "I was nervous then," he thought, "because I knew I was going to be a rotten lawyer. Am I going to be a lousy actor, too?"

He passed into the atrium, trying not to look around as though he were expecting anything or anyone. But he could not keep his head from jerking slightly when he saw Lorcis sitting on a bench ahead of him and to his right, just as Xanthippe had promised. He played his part by merely nodding and strolling on by. As he passed, Lorcis intentionally pinched the baby's little leg to make her cry. "Sorry, love," Lorcis cooed apologetically.

Martial stopped and turned slowly. "I didn't realize you had a baby, Lorcis. It is Lorcis, isn't it?" Fortunately no one was close enough to notice how badly he was playing his part. His only excuse was that Xanthippe had written his lines.

"Yes, my lord," Lorcis replied. "She's only a week old." She rocked the baby gently as the crying subsided.

Martial nonchalantly bent over her shoulder. "And how are you feeling?" he asked, the first spontaneous thing he had said.

"Quite well," she answered. "And very happy," she added softly, the evidence of her feelings clear in her eyes.

"I do like children," he said a bit stiffly. "May I hold her?"

Lorcis laid Erotion in her lap; Martial bent down and picked her up. This was the ritual by which a Roman man legally acknowledged a baby as his. Lorcis then moved over so he could sit down beside her. Holding the small bundle in his arms gingerly, he pushed the blanket back to see her face.

"By the gods, she's ugly," he muttered with a grin. "Couldn't we do any better than that?"

"I know you're joking," Lorcis smiled. "Xanthippe says they're all a bit ugly at this age anyway. But she also says that Erotion is one of the most beautiful babies she's ever seen—and she's seen lots."

"She's not just beautiful," Martial beamed. "She's the most extraordinary child I've ever seen." Lorcis looked around to see that no one was watching, then kissed him on the cheek.

Just as Martial was formulating a plan—actually, a wild urge—to take Lorcis by the hand and bolt out the front door, Xanthippe appeared at the head of the stairs leading to the servants' quarters.

"That's my signal to go," Lorcis said, reaching for Erotion.

"What if I won't give her back?" Martial asked. The lack of playfulness in his voice frightened Lorcis.

"Please, Martial, don't make a scene," she begged.

"Don't make a scene! I'm to just walk out calmly and leave my child and the woman I love in the clutches of a despicable man like Regulus? Is that what I'm supposed to do?" Martial whispered bitterly. "But then she's only my daughter, and property rights outweigh paternal rights in this damnable, cockeyed society of ours."

"Please give her back to me," Lorcis urged. "We'll work something out, but we'll lose all hope if we do anything foolish now."

Martial slowly handed Erotion back to her. "Thank you, my lord," Lorcis said formally as another guest came out of the triclinium and staggered toward the bathroom.

"She is a lovely child," Martial replied in his stage voice. "I hope she grows up strong and beautiful," and he added under his breath, ". . . and free."

Lorcis bowed her head as a servant should to acknowledge a comment from a superior and took Erotion back upstairs. Martial watched every step, not caring if anyone saw him or wondered about his interest in this slave and her child. When they had disappeared from sight, he sat for a moment longer, composing himself. Returning to the dinner did not interest him, but he knew leaving would be discourteous, if not suspicious. He had to cultivate Regulus all the more assiduously now, to gain access to his house at every possible opportunity.

BOOK III

AUGUST, A.D. 81

CHAPTER XV

Regulus decided to stay in the city for the summer because a legal case had come up which presented him with an opportunity to embarrass Pliny. One of the young lawyer's friends was charged with accepting bribes while on the staff of the governor of the province of Mauretania. Pliny was defending the man and Regulus, who was not even sure where Mauretania was, had agreed to act as prosecutor on behalf of the inhabitants of the province who were bringing the suit. So eager was he to win the suit that he was willing to forego summer in the country to prepare for it. He had been waiting for a chance to get back at the "young upstart" after being so soundly defeated by him almost a year earlier.

With everyone who could afford it away at their country villas, Rome was always quiet in August. Those who had nowhere to go simply sat on their steps and sweltered. This year it was especially quiet because people were dying by the hundreds from a plague which was sweeping the city.

The disease had broken out in late July in the Subura, Rome's social and moral sewer. It produced high fevers, sweating, nausea, and in the majority of cases, death within a week to ten days. It was another in a series of disasters which had beset Rome during Titus' two-year reign. The beloved emperor had come to the throne only a month before the eruption of Vesuvius. Less than a year later, a major fire ravaged the capitol, and now the epidemic.

The fever, which was all anyone knew to call it, had swept through the crowded tenement houses in the Subura, but no one in Regulus' circle had been concerned when they first learned of it. Those were poor people, after all, and the deaths of a few thousand would simply relieve the overcrowding in the city. "Even the loveliest forest needs an occasional fire to clear things out," someone observed, and that witticism passed for wisdom in Regulus' circle.

The wealthy only became concerned when the disease cropped up in their own houses. The first victims were the slaves and freedmen who had more occasions to be in contact with the common people outside because they bought the household's supplies and conducted other day-to-day business. But once inside a house the disease showed no particular respect for social standing. By mid-August large numbers of the wealthy were ill, and their doctors could offer little help. By September even the emperor would be taken ill and die.

Regulus had considered fleeing to one of his country villas, but reports from those already out of the city indicated that the disease had been carried into the outlying areas. There seemed little advantage in leaving. He decided to stay put and keep everyone at home as much as possible.

Nivea was the first of Regulus' slaves to fall ill. When she failed to get up one morning, Xanthippe went in and found her weak and shivering. She treated her with what potions she thought might be effective, though she had never before encountered any disease quite like this one.

When Regulus learned that the disease had penetrated his defenses, he adopted an extreme tactic. All healthy slave women were moved from their rooms and sent to temporary quarters in other parts of the house. "We may have to sacrifice Nivea," he told Jacob in giving the order, "but this may help us isolate the problem and prevent it from spreading." But within two days another female slave and three male slaves became ill.

On the day Nivea died, Lorcis woke up feeling nauseous and feverish. Xanthippe had been keeping a particularly close eye on Lorcis and Erotion, checking on them at least twice a day. She herself was tired from the effort of assisting the doctor whom Regulus had called to tend the sick slaves. Unfortunately, the doctor had immediately forbidden Xanthippe to give any potions to the victims, but she had continued taking them herself. She wasn't sure why the particular potion she was using was effective—or even if it actually was—but even before the other slaves became sick and Regulus summoned the doctor, Nivea had seemed to be recovering. The doctor's prescription of cold baths and poultices seemed ridiculous to Xanthippe. Nivea had worsened as soon as she was taken off the potion, and none of the other sick slaves were responding either.

Lorcis became sick. Xanthippe had given her some of the potion, but Lorcis disliked the strong taste and refused to take any more. She was extremely fatalistic and at times even seemed to welcome the idea of death.

At first, Xanthippe tried to keep the news of Lorcis' sickness to herself and to treat her without the doctor knowing it. But Erotion was a problem. Lorcis was too sick to nurse her baby and Xanthippe doubted that it was wise anyway. She fed the baby as best she could by dipping a rag in milk and allowing her to suck, but it was hard to get the milk without arousing suspicion. Besides, she had no idea if the baby was getting enough to keep her alive and well.

When Lorcis' illness became known, the doctor took over and she was moved back to her own room on the hall where all the sick slaves were housed; Xanthippe took Erotion to her own room. After debating with herself for most of an afternoon, she began giving Erotion minute doses of the potion. "You may not have much chance this way, sweetheart," she cooed, "but you've got no chance at all any other way."

Within a couple of days Lorcis was so ill that the doctor gave up trying to save her. Xanthippe stood by and listened as he discussed the household's dilemma with Regulus in the atrium one afternoon. "There's nothing further I can do for any of them," he concluded. "They are going to die within two days at the most."

Xanthippe could not restrain herself. "My lord," she said a bit too eagerly as she stepped forward.

The two men looked up with obvious displeasure at this intrusion into their weighty council. Regulus clearly intended to silence her, if only to show the doctor that he did not tolerate such insolence, but Xanthippe did not give him the chance.

"My lord, since the doctor has given up hope, may I be permitted to try my 'wretched little potions,' as he calls them? They may help."

Before Regulus could answer, the doctor spoke up. "If I may offer a more professional opinion, the potions will not benefit those slaves any more than they did Nivea." Regulus nodded his head and pursed his lips.

"You wouldn't give my potions a chance," Xanthippe objected. "Nivea was . . . "

The doctor interrupted. "It is much more important," he intoned, "to rid the house of the disease. I would recommend that you have the sick slaves carried to the temple of Asclepius and abandoned there. The priests will tend to them and ease their deaths as much as possible. It's an act of charity. You'll also be rid of the necessity of disposing of the bodies. This is what most of the wealthy people in the city are doing."

This last argument convinced Regulus.

"We must then," the doctor went on as he sensed Regulus' approval, "take all bed coverings and draperies from the rooms of the sick and any of their clothing and have them burned. We're not quite sure how the illness spreads, so we must remove everything that a diseased person has come into contact with."

"That sounds like good advice," Regulus replied, "but what about the slaves who carry the sick to the temple? Won't they bring the disease back into the house when they return?"

"That is a possibility," the doctor acknowledged. "Can you give them orders to proceed to one of your estates outside Rome, to remain there until sent for?"

"Yes, I can send them to my place at Arpinum. It's the closest and is understaffed at the moment—they won't endanger so many people. That should take care of the problem." The doctor nodded. "Now," Regulus said, clapping his hands and rubbing them together, "we must get them out of here quickly."

The doctor bowed and left, but Xanthippe did not move. Regulus looked at her grimly. "Xanthippe, go help the doctor," he ordered.

"My lord," she said nervously, "may I be allowed to accompany them to the temple?" She really meant just Lorcis, but she did manage to state the question more generally. She was not certain whether Lorcis or Erotion needed her more, but Lorcis was the sick one at the moment, and her instinct was to stay as close to her as possible.

"No," Regulus replied quickly. "I can only spare a few slaves, and they must be strong ones who can carry the sick. You're needed here to assist the doctor and tend to the child. She is still well, isn't she?"

"Yes, my lord. Feeding her has proved awkward, but I am managing and she's fine."

"Good. Now carry out your orders." His voice was not kind, but it was more human than Xanthippe had ever heard it. His worry over the plague seemed to have softened him, at least momentarily. She did not expect the effect to last.

Panic seized Xanthippe as she trotted up the stairs. Once Lorcis was out of the house there would be nothing more she could do for her. She had to act fast in the few minutes left to her. Stopping at her own room, she got a small vial of her potion and hurried down the hall. Two slaves were already at Lorcis' door when she got there, ready to drag her out.

"Wait!" Xanthippe said, a plea in her voice. "I'd like a moment to say good-bye to my friend. Can't you get the others first?"

One slave shrugged his shoulders and stepped back. The other hesitated but followed his example. "You owe us," he leered.

With the door closed behind her, Xanthippe took out the small vial, unstopped it, and put it to Lorcis' pale, parched lips. "Come on now," she urged, almost praying, "take as much of it as you can." Lorcis swallowed several times, coughed, and groggily turned her head away.

"Well, that will have to do," Xanthippe said.

Opening the small trunk that contained all of Lorcis' personal belongings, she found the wooden medallion wrapped in a silk cloth. Lorcis had not told her the entire story of the picture, but Xanthippe knew it was the one symbol of her freedom and her past that Lorcis cherished. It should stay with her.

There was a knock at the door. "Just a minute," she called.

She pulled back Lorcis' blanket and raised the stola. Placing the medallion on Lorcis' stomach, Xanthippe tore a strip off the blanket, wrapped it around the dying woman's body, and tied the medallion in place as securely as possible. She had just pulled the stola back down when the slaves opened the door.

"Come on!" one of them snapped impatiently. "We've got orders to get her out of here."

Xanthippe stood up and stepped back from the bed. The men entered and picked Lorcis up roughly, one grabbing her feet, the other her arms. She groaned. "Take it easy!" Xanthippe cried. "She's not dead yet."

Xanthippe trailed behind them as they lugged Lorcis down

the steps and across the atrium. A cart had been found, and Lorcis and three males would be loaded onto it and carried to the temple of Asclepius, the god of healing. The two men who had brought Lorcis down were chosen to push the cart. Jacob, supervising the operation, opened the door quickly as they carried each slave out.

Watching from the other side of the atrium, Xanthippe held one hand to her mouth and clutched the other to her stomach as they carried Lorcis out last. "Oh, dear God . . . dear Jesus . . . " she found herself muttering. She did not know how to pray to this strange god that Jacob had told her about, but it seemed useless to call on any of Rome's old gods. If they had survived this long—which she doubted—they must have been done in by the plague. She only hoped that her unarticulated prayer had been heard.

Jacob had simply opened and shut the door as the male slaves were removed, but he kept it open after Lorcis passed through, standing there and continuing to watch until the cart rumbled out of sight down the hill. Xanthippe knew from the way his hands were clasped and held to his lips that he was praying the whole time. "This must be a powerful god, who can hear silent prayers," she muttered to herself.

When Jacob closed the door, it seemed to Xanthippe that he had sealed Lorcis' tomb. Across the atrium their eyes met as he turned and leaned against the door. Would they ever see her again?

Now there was only Erotion. Erotion! The name gave Xanthippe a new focus for her thoughts, a new reason to climb the stairs and return to her room. The baby—her baby now—was awake and fretful. She picked up the child, put her on her shoulder, and together they cried.

CHAPTER XVI

The temple of Asclepius, located on a large island in the Tiber, was awash with suffering humanity. The families of the sick brought their loved ones there in hope of a healing that eluded human power. The Senate had ordered that sacrifices and prayers be offered there according to the rituals prescribed in the ancient Sybilline books, and many wealthy families sent their sick slaves there to be tended to—usually to die.

It had long been the custom to abandon sick or elderly slaves in this fashion to escape the expense of tending to them when they were no longer able to earn their keep. The practice had become so popular and widespread that Emperor Claudius, thirty years earlier, had decreed that any slave who recovered after being abandoned in this manner would become free. This had slowed the tide; only the most seriously ill slaves were now brought to the temple and almost all of them died.

The kindly priests of Asclepius, however, were better able to deal with minor illnesses or psychosomatic conditions than with serious diseases. They were hardly able to do more with plague victims than record the names of those who were brought in and cover them with blankets. This list was kept by the door of the temple courtyard nearest to Rome. On the other side of the island, away from the city, was the door through which the dead were carried out to a funeral pyre on a field at the foot of the Janiculan Hill. Soldiers were stationed there to keep the flames stoked.

The road leading to the temple of Asclepius was always

crowded since it was a main thoroughfare leading out of Rome to the west. As Martial forced his way through, the crowd hardly moved at all. It was simply a long line of people waiting to cross the bridge to the temple.

He had been trying for days to get news of Lorcis and Erotion, but on Regulus' orders, the door of his house was not to be opened except in dire emergency. Martial had no way of explaining to anyone in the household except Xanthippe and Jacob what he wanted, so he had been turned away every time he had gone to "pay his respects" to Regulus. But that morning the door had opened wide enough for someone—he was sure it was Jacob—to slip him a note which read: *Why do you keep worrying us? Go to the temple of Asclepius and pray. You should have been there three days ago. We are only tending to small matters here. Bigger things are being done at the temple.*

It was the sort of note one had to write in Rome. It told the intended reader everything without revealing anything if it fell into the wrong hands.

Martial had run most of the way until the crowd became too heavy. Then, for half an hour he had squeezed and elbowed between and around people. Such behavior would normally have incensed a crowd of Romans, but they were too exhausted and sick at heart to care.

Getting across the bridge was the most difficult part since there was so little room for people to give way. Martial briefly considered swimming the Tiber, but the garbage and raw sewage floating in it quickly dissuaded him.

Finally, around midday, he reached the huge bronze gates of the temple. A squad of soldiers blocked the gate, registering all slaves who were carried in and controlling to some extent the size of the crowd inside the temple courtyard. The tribune in charge asked Martial if he were ill or if he wished to offer sacrifices.

"Neither," he replied. "I'm looking for someone—a slave who was brought here three days ago."

"That list would be in the possession of the priest Severianus," the tribune said. "A tall, thin man with light brown hair." But he gave no order for the guards to open the gate.

"Can I get in to look for her?"

"Other people have more urgent business than yours," the tribune snapped, "and the temple is packed already."

Martial dug into his money pouch, pulled out several coins, and slipped them into the tribune's hand. *Never let it be said that Romans don't recognize a business opportunity,* he said to himself. On the officer's signal the soldiers blocking the gate opened it and stood aside to allow Martial to enter.

The normally quiet, cool grounds were covered with bodies, some writhing and moaning, others completely still—too still. The air was fetid, oppressive. Incense could not sweeten the stench of disease and death. The priests had tried to lay the bodies out head to head, leaving rows at their feet so they could pass among them and tend to them. Even so, the courtyard was crammed. The priests' attention to the ill was devoted mostly to determining which ones had died. Temple servants then removed the bodies so more of the sick could be brought in.

The man Martial was looking for was only a few yards from the gateway, checking a list as the other priests reported to him the names of the slaves who had died. A moment of panic seized Martial: Lorcis' name was on one of those lists! Had it already been crossed out? He studied the faces of those lying ill around him as he walked over to Severianus. There were groans and heavy breathing from people trying to call to him as he passed. He felt like he was walking through a bog on a dark, eerie night.

"Good day, servant of the god," he saluted Severianus formally.

Severianus looked up, apparently surprised to hear anything but names of dead slaves.

"Good day, my friend," he said wearily. "May I help you?"

"I'm looking for a woman who was brought here three days ago."

"We record only the names of slaves so that the question of their freedom may be settled easily should they recover. The others we tend to as best we can, but their names are of little concern to us at a time like this."

"The woman I'm looking for is a slave," Martial replied.

"Then I should be able to help you." The priest began to leaf through the pieces of papyrus in his hand. "Three days ago, you say? I'm afraid I can't hold out much hope that she is still alive; few last that long." He pulled out a piece of papyrus. "Here's the list for that day. What is her name?"

"Lorcis, slave of Marcus Aquilius Regulus."

"Yes," Severianus nodded. "She and three other slaves of

Regulus were brought in on that day. I have no record of her death, though everyone else on the list is marked out. Perhaps there's an error here."

Martial would not yet allow himself to hope. "Where would I find her?"

Severianus waved the sheaf of papyrus pages over the courtyard. "I'm afraid you must simply search. We cannot keep track of where each person is. We just mark names on their feet and place them in the first vacant spot we can find."

Quickly Martial walked down the rows, searching the sea of faces for that dear pointed chin and those blue eyes—open, he hoped, with life, not frozen in death. When he had to kneel down to turn someone over, he found most of the bodies hot with fever; a few were startlingly cold.

He had covered more than half the compound when he knelt to turn over the body of a woman about Lorcis' size. Before he touched her, however, he noticed the face of the woman lying head to head with her—it was Lorcis! With tears welling in his eyes he stepped over to her side.

At first he could only study her face. It was unmarked by any sign of pain or illness. Her eyes were closed and he began to despair—she must be dead! Trembling, he looked carefully to see if she was breathing. He touched her shoulder. She was warm, the warmth he had experienced when she lay next to him asleep. He felt her forehead; perfectly normal. In fact, she did not seem sick at all. Finally, he grew confident enough to call her name.

"Lorcis?"

When she opened her eyes they were tired but clear, and focused immediately on him. Licking her parched lips to moisten them, she tried to speak.

"It's all right," Martial said, leaning down and kissing her cheek. In a gesture of wonder, she raised her hand to touch his face. She did not understand where she was or why they both were there, but she was clearheaded enough to trust him to look after her.

"I'll get you something to drink," he assured her. "Don't go away." She managed to smile wanly at him.

Nearby he found a priest checking for the dead. "Could my friend have a drink?" he asked joyously. "I think she's getting well."

"There's a fountain in the north corner of the courtyard," the priest said. "You get some water while I take a look at your friend." Martial showed him where Lorcis was, then headed for the fountain. When he returned, the priest was sitting beside Lorcis, a look of disbelief on his tired face.

Martial filled the ladle from the small bucket he had found and started to give Lorcis a drink, but the priest blocked his hand and took the ladle. "Just a little bit at a time at first," he explained. "It's natural to want to give her a lot, but her stomach can't handle it yet."

Both men watched anxiously as Lorcis sipped the water. Raising her head on her own was an effort at first, so Martial sat with her head and shoulders cradled in his lap. She held his arm as tightly as she could in her weakened condition.

"I am mystified," the priest admitted. "I remember this girl because of her beauty and because she kept ranting about a baby. She and the others who were brought with her were all on the verge of death. I've seen a few people recover from this illness, but never one who was as sick as she was. Yet she is recovering, I'm sure of it."

He felt Lorcis' forehead again. "I know you're tired, my child, but do you feel well?"

Lorcis nodded her head. "Where am I?" she managed to rasp.

"In the temple of Asclepius," Martial replied, going on to explain how she had gotten there and how he had found her.

"We have some rooms in the building adjoining the temple where she can rest more comfortably," the priest suggested kindly. "Can you carry her?"

"To the ends of the earth, if necessary," Martial replied. He stood and lifted Lorcis easily, pushed aside the blanket which fell off her, and followed the priest.

They crossed the courtyard to a single-story rectangular building usually reserved for visiting priests from other temples of the god. It was occupied now by those who had survived the plague and were recovering their strength, preparing to leave. The priest showed them a room, bare except for a bed and a stool. "Put her there. I'll make arrangements for some food."

During the afternoon and early evening Lorcis drank some broth and ate a few bites of bread, but she slept most of the time. Martial didn't leave her side. At one point he was afraid she was becoming ill again, but the priest reassured him.

"Her body is exhausted from fighting the disease," he explained. "She must sleep a great deal to regain her strength. By tomorrow evening you'll see a considerable improvement."

True to the prediction, the next evening Lorcis was feeling well enough to talk. Her first question was only a word. "Erotion?"

"She's fine," Martial answered with a smile. "Jacob passed me a note yesterday."

Lorcis savored that bit of information and almost managed to smile. "What about the others?" she asked weakly.

"I think they're well," Martial assured her. "Jacob certainly is, and his note didn't say that anything was wrong in the house." As he thought about it, he realized that he was merely inferring things from the guarded wording of the note, but he didn't worry Lorcis with that detail.

"Why me?" Lorcis asked suddenly, a question Martial was totally unprepared for.

"Why were you taken ill?"

"No, why did I get well?"

"I can't answer that," Martial said. "I'm not sure I even want to ask it. The gods might think us ungrateful."

Lorcis laughed. "What kind of an answer is that? You don't believe in any gods."

"No, not really," Martial admitted, "but there's no sense taking chances. You're alive, you're well; that's all that matters."

"I'm also filthy," Lorcis said. "I haven't had a bath in a week, you know, and I've been sweating like a horse and lying in my own . . ."

"Why don't I wash you off a bit?" Martial volunteered quickly and compassionately.

"Oh, I would love that," Lorcis said.

Martial went to the kitchen and returned a few minutes later with a bowl of warm water and a couple of towels. He lovingly sponged off her face and arms.

"This stola is the problem," Lorcis said. "It's never going to be worth wearing again. Help me get it off."

"But you don't have anything else . . ."

"I'd rather just wrap up in a blanket than spend another minute in this rag," Lorcis said, struggling with the dirty, sticky cloth around her body.

"You are getting well, aren't you!" Martial chided her.

Lorcis laughed at herself. "Yes! Yes, I am!"

As Martial helped her slip the stola up over her head, they both stared in amazement at the strip of cloth tied around her waist. He looked at her, obviously waiting for an explanation, but she just shrugged. She ran her hand over the knotted strip and felt something wrapped inside, but it did not occur to her what it might be.

"Help me untie it," she urged.

Martial fumbled with the cloth, but Xanthippe had tied it securely. Lorcis' sweating and tossing and turning had tightened it even further. "I'll have to get a knife," Martial finally conceded.

Lorcis lay back to rest until he returned. She had been so delirious with fever before she was carried out of Regulus' house that she had no memory of anything that had happened. Had Xanthippe wrapped this thing around her? That seemed the only reasonable assumption. *Dear Xanthippe,* she thought, *taking care of me right up to the last moment!*

Closing her eyes, she reflected briefly on the course of her life since leaving Encolpius. She had thought of his house as her haven and remembered the dread with which she had left it. The intervening fifteen months seemed a lifetime, filled with enough unpleasantness and degradation to break even the strongest spirit.

But she was happy! She had two true friends, a man who loved her, and a baby. Everything was not perfect, but she was beginning to feel that things would—or at least could—work out well. For the first time in her life, she trusted someone or something besides herself. Was this all just luck, or was some god's plan unfolding?

Martial came back with a small knife and carefully cut the strip of cloth from around Lorcis' midsection. She unfolded it and gasped as she recognized the piece of silk in which she kept the medallion wrapped.

"Oh, dear Jesus," she said softly. "It's true."

Martial was afraid she was getting delirious again. "Who's Jesus?" he asked with more concern than curiosity. "What's true?" He touched her arm. "Are you all right?"

Lorcis patted his hand. "Yes, Martial, I'm fine. Don't worry." She held up the medallion proudly. "And this is the reason I am. This is Jesus."

Though he said nothing, Martial's face showed his lack of comprehension.

"My mother gave this to me not long before my stepfather sold me," Lorcis continued. " 'Always guard it well,' she said, 'and he will protect you.' "

"I thought you didn't believe in gods," Martial reminded her sardonically.

"I'm beginning to believe in this one. He healed Jacob, raised my father from the dead, and now . . ."

"Wait a minute!" Martial interjected. "Healing sick people I might grant you, but raising people from the dead? Are you sure you're all right?"

"Yes, I'm sure. And I'll explain all this to you some other time, in private." She suddenly recalled Jacob's reluctance to discuss his faith when he could not be sure he was safe from hostile ears. She wasn't ready to call herself a Christian yet, but it seemed prudent not to say any more about the matter until later.

"That's fine," Martial said, intending never to bring the subject up again. "For whatever reason, by whatever power, you are well. Have you realized yet what that means?"

"No," Lorcis said hesitantly, afraid that some unknown factor was about to upset her life again. "What are you talking about?"

He took the hand that was not holding the medallion. "It means you're free." He spoke the words softly, not wanting to shock her too much, just as the priest had advised against giving her too much water too soon.

"Free?" The thought did not surprise her; it had no reality because it seemed so impossible. "How? Why?" she asked weakly, almost as an afterthought.

Martial explained the law to her. "You were abandoned here," he concluded, "but you have survived. Therefore, you are no longer Regulus' slave—or anybody's. You're free! It's as simple as that."

Knowing how much she had longed for this, Martial expected her to show a great deal of emotion, to yell or cry or some such thing. But she merely smiled and shook her head in disbelief. Then suddenly her expression changed.

"What about Erotion?" she asked anxiously.

"She's fine, as far as I know," Martial replied. "I told you that." He tried to remain patient with these sudden shifts of topic, which he attributed to the high fever she had endured.

"No, no. I mean, is she still a slave?"

"Of course. She didn't get sick. She still belongs to Regulus."

"But she's our baby, Martial!" Lorcis cried with the deepest intensity he had ever seen her display. Struggling to sit up, gripping her blanket tightly, she insisted, "We can't just leave her there."

"No, of course not," Martial assured her as though she were a frightened child. "We'll do everything we can to get her out. But she is Regulus' property. However much we love her and know that we have a right to her, if we take her out of that house, we are stealing his property in the eyes of the law."

"Is property so much more important than love in the eyes of the law?" Lorcis protested.

"No one has yet proved to the satisfaction of the law that love even exists," Martial said sadly, "much less measured it or put a value on it."

"But we've got to get her away from that monster!" Lorcis said a bit frantically, clutching both of Martial's arms.

"All right, just settle down," Martial said soothingly. "I want her out as much as you do. But first things first. I'm going to get you some new clothes. Tomorrow morning the priest and I will take you to a praetor who will certify that you are free. Then we'll work on getting Erotion." He had no idea whatsoever how they would accomplish that, but he knew Lorcis needed to hear reassurance.

Once she was calm again he finished washing her off, then left to get her something to wear. Lorcis picked aimlessly at the old strip of blanket in which her medallion had been wrapped. Suddenly her fingers detected something else in another part of it. Unfolding it, she discovered six gold coins, enough money to live on for a couple of months, but not enough to make too large a lump or attract the attention of anyone who might have carried her. Shaking her head at this new evidence of Xanthippe's love for her, she promised herself that she would repay the debt, whether Xanthippe wanted her to or not.

The longer she looked at the coins and turned them over in her hands, the more they reminded her of what she had done to get them. She was free from that life now, but she still needed the money. Although the urge to throw it away was strong, her practicality prevailed. She was on her own now. Her long-desired freedom was hers. What that meant, she now realized, was that for the first time in her life, her next meal was her own responsibility.

CHAPTER XVII

Martial did not actually go into the praetor's house but accompanied Lorcis and the priest to the door and waited there. His attendance was not necessary, he said, and he did not want to attract attention to himself and Lorcis until she was legally free. He was also concerned that the praetor would recognize him, or know his name, and report it to Regulus, who might make some associations in his own mind.

The emancipation ceremony was simple, even businesslike. The praetor, Gaius Cornelius Scaevola, asked the priest a few questions about Lorcis' illness and recovery, wrote out a certificate testifying to her freedom, then called to a servant to knock off Lorcis' fetter with a hammer and chisel.

She was surprised when the servant snatched it up before she could and handed it to Scaevola. She had planned to keep it to remind herself of her hatred for Regulus. But when she asked Scaevola if she could have it, he informed her that it was still Regulus' property, even if she was not.

"Will it be returned to him?" she asked, preferring that he think her dead, giving her time to formulate a plan to get Erotion.

"Of course, it must be," Scaevola responded. "But don't worry. There is absolutely nothing he can do to you, legally speaking. He has given up any claim he had on you." He could see that Lorcis was still uneasy and sensed a chance to capitalize on her insecurity. "Of course, there need not be any hurry about returning it. Things sometimes do get misplaced for a while."

Lorcis looked at Scaevola in disgust. She had lived in Rome

long enough to lose all her provincial naiveté. To think that he would try to extort a few coins from someone as vulnerable as she was! A grave robber seemed honorable by comparison.

She started to protest, but the priest touched her arm. "He has his duty to perform, my child, and he receives no salary. He fulfills this function from a sense of civic obligation. Besides, you're in no position to bargain."

Lorcis glanced at the floor, pursed her lips, and said, "Give me a moment, please."

She found Martial waiting across the street, trying to blend in as a potential customer at the taberna there. Having no money pouch of her own, she had entrusted her money and the medallion to him. "Give me one of the gold pieces, Martial," she snapped. Martial sensed that he had better not refuse or even ask any questions. He meekly opened his money pouch and extracted a coin.

Lorcis gripped it tightly and marched back to the praetor. Holding her arm out straight she declared, "Here, it's all I have." Scaevola opened his hand and she dropped the coin into it, refusing even to touch his flesh.

Scaevola and the priest were both stunned. They had expected her to have only a pittance. Scaevola had even wondered if it would be worth his trouble to try to extort anything from her, but his gambling debts had eaten up so much of his fortune that he was happy to take in even a few sesterces. Over the years he had found that most slaves in this position managed to come up with enough to interest him, especially pretty female ones. Lorcis was not the only slave woman with a free lover, and those men usually took good care of their paramours.

Even an ordinary slave could provide good pickings. Kindly masters often slipped a few small coins into a bag and tied it to a slave who was being abandoned, knowing that if the slave recovered he or she would need something to live on. If the slave died, the priests of Asclepius could keep the money as a donation to the god. The ones who did recover were usually so elated over their freedom and so afraid of losing it that they took the praetor seriously when he suggested that he could nullify their emancipation and would do so if he were not rewarded. He never said it in so many words, of course, because he legally could do nothing. The priests kept quiet about his knavery since they got a portion of whatever came into his greedy fists. But never had a slave barely off her deathbed dropped so much money into his palm! Where did she get it?

"I have a friend," Lorcis said, reading their thoughts. "Several friends, in fact," she added proudly.

"Well," Scaevola finally managed to sputter, "as I said, I will have to return the bracelet and inform Regulus eventually, as the law requires. But the law does not specify how soon this must be done."

"Thank you, your honor," Lorcis said with enough sarcasm to offset the polite bow she made. Then she and the priest turned and left.

On the street, after the priest bid Lorcis and Martial farewell, there was an awkward moment when Lorcis realized she had no place to go. Her assumption, of course, had been that she would go with Martial, but he had said nothing to that effect. Their entire relationship had been colored by the fact that she always had to get back to Regulus' house. But now?

Martial took her hand. "Let's go home."

The walk to Martial's room—their room—was a long one, and Lorcis was not up to it. They stopped twice to rest and to get her a drink. "At least I don't have any luggage," she joked, then instantly became more solemn as she thought of one small bundle she longed to be carrying. She said nothing more, concentrating all her energy on getting home.

At last the apartment house came into view. Reinforced by the stench of death, the familiar aroma of the place rose even stronger. Because no attempt whatever was being made to clean the streets or sidewalks, they had to pick their way carefully through food scraps and the contents of chamber pots emptied from upper windows. Lorcis had to keep reminding herself that this was home now. Somehow, it had seemed more romantic when she and Martial would sneak there for an afternoon of lovemaking. She had tolerated the filth then because she knew she could go home and wash it off.

All her arguments with the other slaves about the desirability of freedom versus slavery began to run through her mind. She had her freedom now, and the life-style that went with it—and it was going to be better than slavery, she was determined. She inhaled deeply, trying to shock her nose and lungs into accepting the new atmosphere as quickly as possible.

As they climbed the narrow wooden stairs, their way was blocked by a man slumped on the steps. "Well, I see the door-man is on duty," Martial muttered. When he poked the man in the ribs, he grunted but barely moved. Whether he was drunk or sick, Lorcis could not tell. As Martial tried to move the man, he lost his grip and the limp body rolled to the bottom of the stairs.

"Shouldn't we see about him?" Lorcis asked.

"If the situation were reversed, he wouldn't even look back at us," Martial replied with a shrug.

"But he might be hurt!" Lorcis protested.

"And what could you do for him? If he has the fever you only risk getting sick again. Besides, if he has a family, they'll soon find him and tend to him. Let's go."

The cross ventilation from the two windows in their room was its only luxury. For the first time Lorcis focused her attention on aspects of the room other than the bed, though there was not much to see. It was merely the rented room of a bachelor who did little more than sleep there. The only personal touch was the table with the pile of scrolls and writing paraphernalia. It stood in a corner away from the windows, which lacked any covering except shutters that kept out light and air along with bad weather when they were closed. The only thing Lorcis could say about the room was that it was light and airy.

"Welcome to your new home, my lady," Martial said. Then he looked around and shrugged as though he were seeing it through her eyes and realizing for the first time how unappealing it really was.

Even as Lorcis was appraising her new home, the praetor Gaius Cornelius Scaevola was knocking on the door of her old one. The plague had abated somewhat, but Regulus was still reluctant to allow visitors to enter the house unless their business was urgent. Because Scaevola was unknown to Regulus, he was not granted entry to the house until he stated his business. With impatience, he handed Lorcis' bracelet to the slave at the door. The slave closed the door, returned a moment later, and hurriedly opened it to escort Scaevola into the house.

Regulus met him coming across the atrium. Scaevola was a person of no consequence to him, and his facial expression and whole physical manner suggested the disdain with which he received him. This was not a man he needed to flatter or court.

"Good day, my lord," Scaevola greeted him. "May I say how pleased I am to be admitted to this . . ."

"No, you may not," Regulus snapped, holding up the bracelet. "Where did you get this?"

"Off the wrist of the young woman whose name appears on it," Scaevola replied, somewhat cowed.

"Are praetors in the habit of robbing corpses now?" Regulus sneered.

"She was pale and somewhat weak, but she hardly looked like a corpse when she walked into my house this morning, my lord."

"Walked into your house!" Regulus sputtered. "But she was carried out that door five days ago all but dead!"

"So the priest of Asclepius informed me, my lord. The other slaves brought in with her did die in a very short time, but Lorcis inexplicably recovered." He paused, waiting for Regulus to say something, then went on to cover the awkward silence. "Under the Claudian law on the abandonment of sick slaves, I had no choice, of course, but to declare her free."

"Of course," Regulus muttered, already beginning to scheme. His ability to comprehend and to react instantly to a new situation had kept him a powerful man through the reigns of six emperors—some of alarmingly brief duration. "Do you know where she went after she left your house?"

"No, my lord. She had a man with her, and they started out in this general direction. He must have been a wealthy man. They gave me a handsome present in gratitude for my services." He stressed the word "gratitude."

Regulus looked distracted and did not respond.

"I was certain you would want to know," Scaevola plugged on. "I felt you would be grateful to learn of this development as soon as possible."

"Hmm? Oh, yes," Regulus said. "Yes, thank you." He turned his back on Scaevola and called, "Nestor!" He said nothing else to the praetor and did not even turn around to face him again until Jacob appeared from the study where the two of them had been going over accounts.

"Nestor, escort the distinguished praetor to the door and express to him my gratitude for the trouble he has gone to in order to bring me some important news."

Jacob returned to the study and filled up a small coin pouch.

He then joined Scaevola and walked to the door with him.

"Come back to the study when you're finished," Regulus called after him, and without acknowledging Scaevola's farewell, he returned to his study.

Jacob pressed the pouch of coins into the praetor's eager hand and politely pushed him through the open door. Out on the street, Scaevola straightened his toga and said aloud, "Well, I guess I showed them that I'm not one to be trifled with." He then set off to the Circus Maximus, where the races would soon begin.

Jacob hurried back to the study, his heart pounding. He had recognized the bracelet when the slave brought it to Regulus. Standing behind a pillar in the atrium, he had listened to the conversation between Regulus and Scaevola without being seen, but had almost shouted for joy on hearing that Lorcis was alive and well—and free!

When Jacob entered the study Regulus was sitting in his customary place but had not resumed work on the accounts. He was fingering the bracelet, which lay atop a pile of papers. Jacob stood by the door, awaiting an order.

"Well, I've lost this little bitch," his master muttered, "and there's nothing I can do to change that. But I doubt if she's finished with me, not as long as her baby is here. She'll be trying to get that child." He tapped his fingers on the bracelet. "But she's mine . . . in more ways than one, perhaps."

Erotion had come to exercise a fascination on the childless Regulus. His threat to raise her as a prostitute had not been made idly, but another idea had cropped up, like a weed unnoticed in the corner of a garden: What if she was his daughter?

It was within the realm of possibility. He had not fathered any children by Sempronia, but he hadn't tried very often. Moreover, she could have aborted any children she might have conceived, and he would never have been any the wiser. He had always had easy access to Lorcis and had availed himself of her frequently. He could not recall if he had actually been with her "in the appropriate manner," but it was entirely possible he had. He knew the sexual proclivities of the three men with whom he'd shared her during that time. Nothing they would have done with her would result in a pregnancy. This vagueness about the child's paternity made him more determined not to take a chance on losing her.

Finally he looked up, ready to embark on a course of action. "I want Erotion moved to a room in my quarter of the house, and a guard is to be placed in front of the door: four-hour watches, day and night. No one is to go in there except the wet nurse and Xanthippe. Is that clear?"

"Yes, my lord."

"Then do it!"

Jacob scurried from the room and rushed to the steps leading up to the servants' quarters. He started taking them two at a time, but his tired old body rebelled about half way up. When he reached Xanthippe's room, where she was caring for Erotion, he looked like a wild man. Between his excitement and his exertion he could hardly make himself understood. All he could gasp was "She's . . . alive!"

CHAPTER XVIII

It wasn't being free that was making her miserable, and Lorcis had to keep reminding herself of that fact. She just was not fully recovered from her illness and was consequently weak and irritable. There was no one to talk to when Martial went out, and he was out a great deal. He had to meet people and keep his name and poetry in the limelight. She had to stay indoors as much as possible to avoid meeting anyone who might report her recovery to Regulus, something she thought was still hidden from him. Left alone for hours at a time, she had nothing to do but long for Erotion.

If she could just get a good night's sleep, she assured herself, she would feel much better. But the noise all around her prevented that. Because of the overcrowding in the streets, it had long been the law that no vehicles could enter Rome during the day. This meant that wagons and carts carrying supplies for bakers, potters, shoemakers, and all tradesmen had to make deliveries during the night. The noise had never bothered her before because there were few shops in the district around Regulus' house and because the walls of the house were thick and windowless. Now, however, she was practically sleeping on the sidewalk, and the creaking of the axles, the cracking of whips, and the curses of the drivers all combined to keep her sitting up with her eyes open all night.

During daylight hours, drunken neighbors fought or sang, while their dirty, half-savage children played at full tilt in the halls or on the sidewalks. The building never emptied because the generous government welfare system and gifts from wealthy patrons made it unnecessary for people in Rome to have to work except to relieve their boredom. Thus, a large class of idle poor relied on wine, the games, and the baths to fill their days. But even the best Falernian vintage and an arena full of blood could not mask forever the futility of their existence. Lorcis recalled the conversations in which the other slaves in Regulus' house had described the realities of freedom, but she was going to hold out against despair as long as she could. If only she could sleep.

On the morning of the third day of her freedom she was lying on the bed, trying to get a bit of relief from the exhaustion which threatened to overwhelm her. But even the scratching of Martial's pen over the papyrus was like a lion's roar in her ears. Then someone pounded on the door. It was actually only a light tap that Martial did not even hear the first time, so absorbed was he in his writing. To Lorcis' battered senses, however, the knock sounded like a drumbeat.

Lorcis was too tired to answer the repeated knocking; it was probably just some neighbor child aggravating them, anyway. But then a voice murmured, "Lorcis? Martial? This is Xanthippe."

Was this a dream? What would Xanthippe be doing at Martial's apartment? Who knew she was there besides Martial? The tapping came again. This time Martial looked up, so Lorcis knew it was real. She rose from the bed, stepped to the door, and threw it open.

When the two women had hugged and cried enough Xanthippe said, "I can't stay long. Regulus is still leery about letting anybody in or out of the house, but I told him I needed some things for Erotion."

Lorcis wrung her hands. "She's all right, isn't she?"

Xanthippe laughed. "Yes, she's fine. That was just the one excuse I could think of that was sure to get me out of the house for even a little while."

"I want to get *her* out of that house—permanently," Lorcis said with her teeth clenched.

"It's not going to be easy," Xanthippe replied, going on to explain how Scaevola had brought the news of Lorcis' liberation on the very morning that it had happened.

"Damn him!" Lorcis shouted. "I knew he was a scoundrel, but I thought he would at least feel bound by a bribe."

"He certainly put Regulus on his guard," Xanthippe continued. "Jacob and I have tried to come up with a plan, but there's the problem of the guard, not to mention the nurse. And even if we could manage to get Erotion out of the house, she'd be missed immediately. Regulus has taken to sticking his head in the door without warning, just to be sure she's there. That's what has us stymied. There has to be a baby in that house—in that room—at all times."

"But does that baby have to be Erotion?" Martial asked from his corner, where he had almost been forgotten by the two women.

"What do you mean?" Lorcis asked.

"It's simple logic," Martial said. "We want Erotion out of Regulus' house, but there has to be a baby in the house at all times. Ergo, the baby in the house must be someone other than Erotion."

"You mean, switch children?" Xanthippe asked.

"It's the only way," Martial repeated.

"But how?" Lorcis wondered. "We don't have another baby to begin with. Assuming we could get one, how would we get her into the house? And assuming we accomplished that simple task, how would we get her past the guard? And then, what do we do, bribe the nurse to turn her back while we switch babies? And then how do we get Erotion out of the house?" She threw up her hands. "It's hopeless!"

"Not if we take it one step at a time," Martial assured her with a playful gleam in his eye. A plan was taking shape. It was like writing a poem. He had his theme; he just had to work out the meter and arrange the words.

"Where are we going to get another baby?" Lorcis protested.

"That's the easy part," Martial replied. "And it's not really where we need to start. We have to start at the crucial point, the place where the switch will be made. We need a wet nurse there who is absolutely dependable, who under no circumstances will ever reveal what happens."

"There's no such person in Rome or in the whole empire," Lorcis fretted. Scaevola had shattered her faith in the bribe.

"There's one woman I know we could trust," Martial said smugly.

"Who?" Lorcis challenged him.

"You," Martial smiled.

Lorcis was too shocked to say anything, but a snort exploded from Xanthippe. "You expect her to walk right up to Regulus and say, 'I'd like to be my daughter's wet nurse until I can get her out of here'? I thought you had a serious plan." She waved her hand in disgust.

"Just hear me out," Martial said patiently as he began to unfold his plan.

The main streets of Rome were narrow and dirty, but the side streets and alleyways were little more than open sewers in which people dumped anything and everything, including unwanted babies.

Exposure of surplus infants had been legal from the very beginning of the republic, just as it was a common practice among most other peoples of the Mediterranean at that time. The early Roman law had even required that deformed children be left to die since they would never be able to contribute to the state and would in fact be a drain upon it.

Female children were exposed more often than males. If a father raised a daughter he had to provide a dowry for her marriage. If he could not provide the dowry he faced the prospect of supporting his old maid daughter all her life. Thus, some fathers exposed all female children after the first or second.

But such children did not always die. Among upperclass women of the empire it was not fashionable to give birth to children. It was so time-consuming and so harmful to the figure. But upperclass men continued to want children, if only because the law provided that only fathers were entitled to inherit property or to hold certain political offices—unless the emperor granted exemptions, as he had done for Regulus. The slaves of upperclass families frequently combed the alleyways of Rome at night in search of abandoned infants to fill their masters' needs.

Lorcis and Martial saw several such groups as they spent the next few nights prowling the streets in search of a child to switch for Erotion. Each time they found a newborn already dead from exposure, Lorcis was unable to stifle a cry of anguish. She was especially distressed when she came upon the first little girl. The baby was lying in the open where she must have been seen by others, but the deformity of her spine had caused her to be rejected, even by the scavengers who picked up female infants and sold them to be raised as prostitutes.

"I can't go through that again," Lorcis said one morning, before she had even gotten out of bed. "It's unbearable to think of those children just being thrown away like so much garbage."

"Well, I don't think we'll have to," Martial said. He had already been out, visiting the home of a patron for the "morning greeting" which Roman aristocrats customarily received from their dependents. "I stopped to buy some bread on my way home. The man next to me was complaining about all the children he had to feed, and now he has a new baby girl in the house. 'She's only three months old,' he said, 'and already I can see the expenses ahead.' I sympathized with him as we walked together for a few blocks. He already has three other daughters and had hoped this baby would be a son. If he weren't such a kindhearted man, he assured me, he would have exposed her at birth."

He sat on the edge of the bed and handed Lorcis some fresh bread, some raisins, and a cup of water. "So he's been looking for just the right opportunity to sell her, hasn't he?" she asked. Apparently her stepfather wasn't the only heartless man in the world.

"That's exactly it," Martial replied. "I explained to him that my wife and I had recently lost a daughter that age. You were so distraught, I told him, that you were scouring the streets to find an abandoned baby to take her place. I said we would give a baby girl a good home"—he paused to look around—"well, at least a lot of affection, and would be quite grateful to him and his wife if they would let us have their child."

"How grateful did he expect you to be?" Lorcis asked.

"Three gold pieces."

Lorcis whistled. "That's a lot of gratitude!"

"But we're not just buying some stranger's cast-off child. We're ransoming Erotion."

"I know. It's just that we don't have much money now, and who knows how long we'll have to hold out before we have Erotion?"

"You know the plan. It'll only take a few days once we get a baby to replace her. And here's our chance to get one that's exactly the right age and in excellent health."

He stood up and walked over to the window to throw out the scraps of his breakfast.

"Besides," he went on, "things are looking up." Then he drew a money pouch from the belt around his tunic. It was fat with sesterces, copper coins that were the everyday currency of Rome. Opening it, he poured them out on the bed for Lorcis to count. There were more than enough to equal the three gold pieces they were about to spend.

"Where did you get this much money?" Lorcis asked in delight.

"I went to your friend Pliny this morning and managed to get a word with him privately. I told him that you were free and that we were trying to protect you from Regulus. That was the magic word. He even invited us to come and live in his house. I think he would've given it to us if I'd asked. But I told him that would cause too much talk, and we wanted most of all to keep you out of sight for a while. This was all the money he had handy at the moment, but we're to feel free to come back at any time and ask for whatever we need. And," he paused dramatically, "he's given us a small farm a few miles outside of town."

He leaned over her, putting his hands on the bed on each side of her. "He's really quite fond of you. Anything I should know about that?"

"He's a very dear friend," Lorcis replied, "and you are a very jealous lover." She tweaked his nose lightly.

"Well, lover, you need to get up," Martial said, "so we can get ready to go."

"Where?"

"We have to see a man about a baby. We're meeting him in an hour at a taberna near the Circus Maximus."

As they approached the restaurant they saw a man accompanied by a woman carrying a baby walking slowly from the opposite direction. The plan which Martial had devised would protect everyone's anonymity. The two couples would enter the taberna together and sit at the same table, with the women side by side, pretending to know one another. While they had something to drink the baby and the money would be exchanged as casually and inconspicuously as possible. Then the couple selling their baby would leave. After a suitable interval, Martial and Lorcis would do the same.

At first Lorcis was dismayed by the crowd, people having a few drinks to get them in the mood for the upcoming chariot races. But she soon realized how that would work to their advantage. People weren't paying them any attention. The two couples talked desultorily about their favorite driver or team. Having never been to a chariot race, Lorcis just listened and nodded her head.

By a gesture and a smile she asked if she could hold the baby. The woman handed her over with no noticeable reluctance while the conversation and the drinking continued. Then the man patted his newly enriched money pouch and told his wife it was time to leave. They never looked back, which caused Lorcis to hold the baby a bit more tightly.

The innkeeper glanced at the departing couple, then at Martial and Lorcis. Martial noticed his quizzical observation and suggested to Lorcis that she nurse the baby.

Pulling her stola down over her left shoulder, Lorcis held the infant to her breast. The eager sucking gave her an intense satisfaction, though she was not providing much milk. Part of her unhappiness the past few days had arisen from the lack of this relationship with her baby.

When the child had nursed for a few minutes, Martial said, "I think we've made our point." He called the owner over to the table, paid for the drinks, and he and Lorcis left.

As they walked back home, Lorcis' attention was entirely on the baby. Her arms felt so good, so natural, with this burden in them, even if it was not her own baby. Martial, however, nervously watched the street around and behind them. He could think of no reason for the couple to follow them, but he was uneasy. Things had to go exactly right, and yet he was uncomfortable because they were.

Xanthippe came to their room again two days later. She had received Martial's note indicating he was "ready to write the next verse" of his latest composition for her. That was her signal to put the second step of their plan into operation.

"Erotion's wet nurse," she told them, "was taken ill yesterday."

"How convenient!" Lorcis said sarcastically.

"A miracle of modern medicine," Xanthippe replied. "She'll be fine in a couple of days, as soon as my potion is out of her system. In the meantime, Regulus is sure she's got the plague and has already ordered her out of the house and told Jacob to find someone else. And, of course, we have an excellent candidate for the job."

"Are you sure this is going to work?" Lorcis asked dubiously as she removed her stola and sat on a stool in the middle of the floor. "I shudder at the thought of going back into that place."

"By the time we get through with you, no one will recognize you," Xanthippe assured her. "Regulus probably won't even take a good look at you—and Jacob certainly will not suggest that he do so." With that, she took a pair of scissors from her bag and began whacking off Lorcis' hair.

Watching the pile of hair grow around her on the floor, Lorcis mused. "One thing is starting to bother me about this, though. What's going to happen to this baby here once we've made the switch?"

"She'll grow up to be Regulus' slave, Erotion," Xanthippe replied matter-of-factly.

"That's what troubles me. Do I have the right to consign this child to a life of slavery to that obscene monster? Is my child any more valuable than this one?"

Xanthippe stopped cutting. "By the gods! The questions you raise! One of your ancestors must have been a philosopher."

"Worse than that," Martial broke in. "He was a Jew."

"All we're concerned with now is getting Erotion out," Xanthippe lectured her. "I shouldn't even have to remind you of that. The world is already so hopelessly unjust and corrupt that the fate of one child is not a major concern. Besides, she will lead a more pleasant life in Regulus' house than in some sweltering tenement like—like this one, if I may say so—where she would be neglected or abused by her parents. You've seen both sides of it now, Lorcis. Aside from being with Martial, is this life all you had hoped it would be?"

Lorcis did not respond, but she had to turn her head and look away from the baby sleeping in a basket at the foot of the bed.

Once she had clipped as much of the hair as she could, Xanthippe shaved around the edge of Lorcis' head. Then from her bag she produced a blond wig, crafted from the hair of German captives. She placed it on Lorcis' head, making sure no telltale black hairs peeked out from under it.

"Now," she said with one final pat, "all you have to remember is 'Ich bin Helga,' 'Ja,' and 'Nein.' And if you don't pronounce it right, don't worry. Nobody in Regulus' house knows German anyway."

She walked around Lorcis, admiring her handiwork, then stood back and cocked her head. "What do you think, Martial?"

"It's remarkable," he replied. "The different color and style make her a totally different person. I don't think I even love her anymore. Maybe I'll look around for someone else." He grabbed Xanthippe and smooched her.

"Watch it, you two!" Lorcis squealed.

"You watch it," Martial countered. "Remember, only German. 'Ja' and 'Nein,' and be sure you don't let your eyes betray you. Don't look at people as they speak. And don't look from one person to another in a conversation, as though you can anticipate when they're going to respond to one another."

Lorcis sighed and nodded. "Ja, ja. Ich bin Helga."

Later that afternoon Jacob reported to his master that he had secured a new wet nurse for Erotion, a German girl, the young wife of a retired soldier, who had recently lost her own child. "She speaks no Latin or Greek but seems to understand the arrangement. Would you care to meet her?"

Lorcis stood outside the door with her heart in her throat. She had not known Jacob was going to say that!

But Regulus, in the midst of his bath with Thais, merely shook his head and waved Jacob away.

Jacob escorted Lorcis back through the house to Regulus' quarters. They could hear Erotion crying as they turned the last corner. Beside the door sat the guard, studying a list of gladiators scheduled to fight in the next day's games. Lorcis recognized him, but he was not someone she had known well when she was in the house. Jacob told the guard her new name and explained the situation they had invented for her.

"Glad to see her," the slave muttered. "That brat's been howling all day. Be a relief for everybody to get one of those tits stuck in her mouth."

Jacob smiled weakly and led Lorcis into the small room. Xanthippe was trying to satisfy Erotion with a cloth dipped in milk, but it was having little effect. If her baby had been sleeping or awake and happy, Lorcis might have had time to react to seeing her for the first time in two weeks. As it was, she quickly picked her up and placed her to her breast.

She sat on the bed and held her child in her arms the entire night.

CHAPTER XIX

The next morning Xanthippe, with Jacob's permission, went shopping for baby items. She returned around midday with a supply of new linens protruding from the top of her full bag. Snuggled safely in the bottom was Erotion's alter ego. The infant was gagged to keep her quiet and wrapped tightly to prevent her from moving. Xanthippe and Martial apologized profusely to her as they trussed her up and, as if she could understand them, assured her it would only be for a few minutes.

Xanthippe went directly to Erotion's room. She approached the door nonchalantly, since she expected to go straight in as usual, but the guard blocked the door.

"What do you think you're doing?" Xanthippe demanded.

"Regulus says all packages carried into and out of this room are to be searched," the guard replied.

Xanthippe squelched her panic. "When did he give that order?"

"This morning. He caught the fellow on the shift before mine sleeping at his post and decided we didn't have enough to do."

"Well, all I have are some fresh linens for the baby." She held up the bag.

"I've got to see what's in there," the guard persisted.

How could she distract him so quickly and deftly that he would not realize he was being deceived? She was standing close enough to him to reach out and rub her hand across his crotch. "Let me see what you've got in your linen," she purred.

The slave grinned stupidly. He was ready to take her on the spot.

"Let me get rid of this stuff," Xanthippe stalled, with an eyebrow raised suggestively. "It'll just take a minute." She kissed his cheek as he stepped aside and opened the door for her, patting her bottom as she passed by.

Once inside the room, she signaled Lorcis to be quiet in case the guard's new orders included listening at the door. She unloaded the few pieces of cloth on top of the bag and the baby underneath. She and Lorcis quickly bundled up Erotion in similar fashion and placed her in the bottom of the bag. Before Xanthippe could put anything on top of her, Lorcis pulled up her stola and removed the Jesus medallion, which she had been wearing wrapped around her waist in the same way Xanthippe had fashioned it. She placed it in the cloth that bound her daughter.

Xanthippe then placed a few clean pieces of cloth loosely over Erotion, turning her so that her face was to the side in a small pocket of air. On top of this she laid the wet diapers that needed to be taken out. "Sorry, dear," she whispered to the baby.

Lorcis picked up the substitute baby and began nursing her. "In less than an hour," Xanthippe said softly with a smile, "Erotion will be with her daddy. Then we'll just have to slip you out."

Lorcis smiled in reply, but she still was not sure this scheme would work. It was so bold, so apparently foolish. But Martial had assured her that this was precisely why the plan would work—it was something Regulus would never anticipate.

Xanthippe gently hefted the laundry bag. Then, taking a deep breath, she squared her shoulders, practiced a seductive smile, and opened the door. The guard reached for her as soon as he saw her, but she held the bag up in his face. "Don't you want to inspect this?"

He jerked away, gagging.

"Then just let me get rid of this mess," she said apologetically, "and we can concentrate on more pleasant things."

The guard nodded, holding his hand over his nose and mouth as Xanthippe passed. About halfway down the hall she stopped and turned. "What happened to the man who was caught sleeping on duty?"

"He was whipped," the guard replied thoughtfully.

"Am I worth that?" Xanthippe teased.

The guard shrugged. "Are you?"

"Maybe we'd better get together later, when you're off duty." She waved as she turned the corner.

After Xanthippe was out of sight, the guard began to reflect on the events of the past few minutes. Admittedly, he had not looked in the bag—a direct violation of Regulus' order. What if Xanthippe were to report him? What if . . .?

He took a few hesitant steps after Xanthippe, then glanced back at the door he was about to leave unguarded. How could he challenge her without acknowledging that he had failed in his duty? He bolted back to the door, banged it open, and found Lorcis smiling up at him while she nursed the baby.

"Ja?" she said.

"Oh, ah . . . nothing," the guard stammered. "I mean, I thought I heard. . . . Oh, hell, why am I trying to talk to you anyway?"

"Ja?" Lorcis repeated.

The guard closed the door and leaned against it, blowing out a long sigh of relief.

Xanthippe was exhilarated by her success, a triumph made even more spectacular by the unexpected confrontation with the guard. Wait until she told Martial!

The rest was simple. She would meet Jacob in the laundry room where they would place Erotion in the bottom of a basket, under a toga which was ready to be cleaned. Because of their size and because custom required that they be brilliant white, the togas which the Romans wore on formal occasions had to be cleaned by professionals known as fullers. It would be nothing out of the ordinary for Xanthippe to carry out of the house a basket with a couple of togas in it. She would just have to make one quick stop at Martial's room before she continued on to the fuller's.

She and Jacob arrived at the laundry room almost simultaneously, but there was another slave there sent on some task by Regulus himself. Xanthippe tensed but tried to reassure herself that everything was going according to the plan and this minor difficulty could be overcome.

Jacob glanced at Xanthippe, who said nothing as she went to the place where Erotion's soiled diapers were usually piled. The two dallied at their jobs, hoping the other slave would finish and leave, but by the time Jacob finished going through the few dirty togas, the slave still gave no indication that he would depart soon.

Finally, Jacob ordered him to take some clean linens to Sempronia's room. Already suspicious because the steward himself was working so long in the laundry room, the slave studied both of them, but left sullenly to carry out the order. He arrived at Sempronia's room as she and Gallia were reading and acting out for some friends the myth of Iphis, a young girl raised as a boy and transformed into a man on her wedding day.

Infuriated by the interruption, Sempronia sent the slave packing with his armload of clean bedclothes. His suspicions now fully aroused and desiring to ingratiate himself with Regulus before Sempronia complained about his intrusion, he hurried to report Jacob's peculiar behavior.

Regulus was aware that Xanthippe and Jacob were close friends of Lorcis so his first reaction to the guard's report was to check personally on Erotion. He was satisfied to see the nurse holding the baby on her lap. Fortunately, in the dim light of the room, he was not able to take a close look at the nurse herself. Besides, she was immaterial as long as Erotion was still there.

"They must be trying to steal something," he muttered half aloud as he walked back toward the atrium. "But what—and why? That's not like them." He took a few steps in silence, then jabbed at the air. "Of course! Money for Lorcis."

He grabbed the nearest slave by the arm. "Put a guard at both doors. No one leaves the house without being thoroughly searched. Keep an eye especially on Xanthippe and Nestor, but search everybody. Someone else may be in this with them."

When Jacob and Xanthippe entered the atrium a short time later, they heard the argument going on at the door. One of Sempronia's friends was enraged because she was being searched before she was allowed to leave the house.

"What is the meaning of this?" she screamed. "Get your hands off me!"

"Beg pardon, my lady," the slave replied, "but our master has given strict orders. Everyone and everything going out of this house is to be searched. Apparently there is some thievery going on."

"Do I look like a thief?" the woman screeched.

"I'm only following orders, my lady."

Jacob quickly reacted. "It occurs to me there is another toga we have forgotten." Taking Xanthippe by the arm, he turned her around and the two began casually retracing their steps.

"What are we going to do?" Xanthippe asked in a panic. "They suspect something. What's happened to Lorcis?"

"I doubt if anything has happened to her," Jacob replied with more confidence than he felt. "If they were looking for Erotion specifically, they wouldn't be searching Sempronia's friends. They don't seem to know what they're looking for."

Back in the laundry room Xanthippe almost cried. "What are we going to do, Jacob? It was going so well. Now how are we going to get her out—and what's going to happen to us if we're caught with another baby in the house?"

"Well," Jacob answered slowly, "our friend Martial would tell us to approach the problem logically. We can't get Erotion out through the door, so what are our other possibilities?"

"That's just it," Xanthippe agonized. "There are no other possibilities. We can't throw her over the wall or drop her out a window!"

Jacob hung his head and stared at the floor, pretending to be formulating a plan. In reality, his mind was blank.

Suddenly he realized his eyes were fixed on the drain leading into the sewer. It was a particularly large drain since all the other household drains fed into it. Rome's sewers were constantly flushed by the running water which was piped through them. They were, in fact, nothing more than rivers of sewage.

Then an image popped into his mind: a baby in danger, a basket floating in a river.

"We can get her out," he said, trying to contain his urge to shout.

"How?" Xanthippe asked in a loud whisper that conveyed her anxiety.

"No time to explain," Jacob snapped. Checking to be sure no one was around, he pulled some clean linens and a smaller basket from a storage shelf. He then switched Erotion and placed the clothes on top of her. "Take her to your room and stay with her until I get back."

"Where are you going?"

"To tell Martial that he's going to have to play the part of Pharaoh's daughter pulling Moses out of some rather smelly bulrushes."

"What on earth are you rattling on about, Jacob?"

"It's an old story," Jacob smiled, "a very old story. For now, just take care of that little bundle for an hour or two and find some kind of small box with a lid on it."

Within minutes after Jacob left his apartment, Martial started up the street toward Regulus' house. They had agreed it was best for them not to walk together even though they were following the same route. Martial had been dismayed to hear about Regulus' vigilance and blamed himself because his plan had gone awry, endangering them all. When Jacob optimistically suggested that all they needed was another escape route, Martial's spirits revived—until he heard what the route was and what his role in the revised plan entailed.

Jacob had assured him that he would find an entrance to the sewer about two hundred feet down the hill from Regulus' house, in the back of an alley. Indeed, after probing through a good deal of filth, there it was. The grate covering the hole had long since been removed and broken to serve, perhaps, as weapons or firewood. Finding a long stick about equal to his height, Martial sat down on the edge of the square opening and peered down into the abyss before he lowered himself into it. The stench almost forced him back.

The sewage tunnel was large enough to move around in comfortably, Jacob knew, because the emperor Vespasian had made an inspection trip only five years earlier. Regulus and Jacob, along with a party of noblemen and their servants, had accompanied him. They had used a ladder, held steady by slaves, to descend into this netherworld. Martial, however, would have to rely on protruding bricks in the wall designed as a rudimentary ladder. There would be a ledge, according to Jacob, on each side of the channel. The tunnel was about seven feet high at the point of its arch and about six feet across at the bottom. Normally the water was only a foot or so deep, but the tunnel had been made large enough to handle sudden runoffs and to accommodate workmen.

As his feet found the first slimy brick, Martial recalled Jacob's warning about the inhabitants of this subterranean world. A squad of soldiers had gone with Vespasian's party to fend off the rats and to frighten away the homeless vagrants who often slept in the dry spots in the tunnels, and the criminals who used them to hide from the authorities. Martial would have to find Erotion quickly before she fell prey to any of these vermin.

Descending to the ledge, he heard furtive scurrying noises from each side of him and the squeal of small creatures whose identities he was just as happy not knowing. What surprised him was that he heard voices and saw lights—he had expected that people hiding in the tunnels would be quiet, ghostly types. Downstream he could make out a place where enough bricks had been removed from the wall of the tunnel to make a doorway of sorts. Apparently a cave had been carved out behind it, a light shone from within. At other points up and down the tunnel he could see more torches and burning lamps. "By the gods!" he muttered. "Rome is bigger than I thought."

His plan had been to crouch by the water with his stick placed across the channel to catch Erotion's basket as it floated by. Now he decided instead to move upstream, closer to Regulus' house, so he could intercept the basket before the denizens of the place spotted it. Once his eyes became accustomed to the dimness, there was enough dull light to allow him fair visibility.

Martial calculated that fifty steps would get him within range of Regulus' house without the risk of taking him beyond it. Gripping his stick with both hands, he set out upstream.

Xanthippe slammed the door to her room. "Damn him!" she cried as she started down the hall carrying a medium-sized wicker basket in her arms. Pieces of papyrus covered with writing peeked out from under the lid.

Other doors opened along the hall and slave women looked out of their rooms in curiosity. Xanthippe looked so angry and determined about something that no one dared say anything at first. Procne, however, finally stepped out into the hall as Xanthippe passed her room at the top of the stairs.

"Where are you going with your letter box?"

"To dump it in the sewer!"

"Why?" several of the women squealed.

"Because Gorgias has played me false. I am through with him!"

Procne trotted behind her down the stairs. "But he wrote such exquisite love letters and poems. Couldn't we read them over one by one and then burn them?"

"No," Xanthippe snapped. "Burning's too good for them. It

would purify them. They are fit only for the sewer!"

Procne reached for the box as they got to the bottom of the stairs, but Xanthippe held it away from her. Just then, Jacob approached.

"What is the meaning of all this ruckus?"

"Oh, Nestor, stop her," Procne whined. "She's getting ready to destroy some of the most beautiful love letters ever penned. The way Gorgias writes, I swear it makes my heart pound just thinking about it," she sighed.

"Well, then," Xanthippe relented, "take a couple of those that are sticking out and go read them—amuse yourself for all I care."

Procne snatched a few pieces of papyrus and hurried back upstairs as the other girls surrounded her. Xanthippe continued to march purposefully toward the back of the house with Jacob trotting along beside her. The few other slaves who encountered them heard Jacob advising Xanthippe to consider carefully what she was doing. "You might regret such a rash, irretrievable action once your disagreement is resolved," he counseled. But Xanthippe remained adamant.

When they reached the laundry room, Xanthippe asked Jacob to lift the grate over the drain. Once again he asked her to reconsider, and when she refused, he shrugged his shoulders. "All right, if that's what you want."

The other slaves working in the room made no effort to help the old man as he struggled with the awkward grate. Dramatically, Xanthippe hesitated as she knelt over the opening. Then, with great deliberateness, she deposited the box rather than threw it into the sewer. This side tunnel was only about two feet high so the box scarcely splashed as she carefully released it into the water. The two watched for an instant as the sluggish current caught the little parcel and pulled it away. Since the other slaves could not see her, Xanthippe mouthed, "God go with you, little love."

With a smug, satisfied look on her face, she stood up and dusted her hands off as Jacob lowered the grate back into place. "Now, all I have to do is explain this to dear Gorgias," she thought as she turned to leave.

Creeping along the small ledge beside the sewer, Martial noticed other openings in the wall which did not seem to be in use, at least at that moment. He peered into one and saw that it was an opening to a crude stairway; the actual dwelling place was farther below the ground, in deep darkness. The sewer dwellers, of course, had to avoid the foundations of the buildings above them.

His tour was interrupted by a sharp whistle up ahead, obviously a signal of some sort. At first he feared he'd been spotted, but then a rough, unpleasant voice echoed, "Well, we got a package being delivered. Let's get it before the rats do!"

Before Martial could react, several men clambered out of a hole in the opposite wall of the tunnel, stepped without hesitation into the foul water, and gathered around the wicker basket floating there. Their already ugly, unshaven faces took on veritable demonic aspects in the murky, flickering torchlight which one of them held.

"Damn! Nothing but letters," the torchbearer spat out.

"But it's floating awful low just to be full of paper," another one observed.

"We won't know what all's in it till we open it, will we, knotheads?" sneered a large man with a patch over one eye.

As the man started to bend over the basket Martial's stick landed solidly across his back. Something cracked, and Martial feared at first it was his stick. But when he drew back for another swing he found he still had the full length of the weapon. Flailing wildly, he made contact again and again—often enough to drive the other three back into their hole. In the skirmish, the torchbearer had dropped his light and the tunnel was plunged into complete darkness.

Where was the basket? Had it floated past him in the confusion? Stumbling around, probing with his stick, Martial fell face first over the body of the large man whose back he had broken. The thief had fallen on his side so his body blocked the entire channel of the sewer. Against his midsection, bumping gently as though impatient to get on with its journey, Martial found the precious basket.

He pulled out a few pieces of papyrus to wipe some of the filth off his face and hands, picked up the basket, and set it on the ledge. With pieces of papyrus scattering everywhere, he jerked the lid open and lifted out his daughter. Though slightly damp, she was trying her best to move against the bands of cloth which confined her.

"Sorry we can't stop to get acquainted, my dear," he said, "but we need to get out of here before those scum come back with reinforcements."

Two days later, Regulus summoned Jacob to his quarters and told him to bring Erotion's nurse to him. Before he could leave the room, however, Regulus said, "By the way, have you seen Lorcis since her miraculous recovery?"

"My lord, I've not been out of the house in almost three weeks," Jacob answered, not untruthfully, "except for one trip a couple of days ago, at your request, to deliver that money to Fundanus."

"But you and Lorcis were close friends," Regulus persisted. If he asked enough questions, he had learned, he would eventually trip up even the cleverest liar.

"Yes, my lord. We do come from similar backgrounds. But you could hardly expect her to come back here for a visit."

"I know that without your sarcasm," Regulus muttered. "I'm sure she wouldn't come within sight of this place. But if I ever find out that you or any other member of this household have given her money or anything else out of my house, I'll have you crucified for a thief."

"It would be impossible for anyone to get anything out of the house, my lord," Jacob said with a bow, "even if he intended to," he added hastily.

"Slaves," Regulus huffed, "have ways of doing any damn thing they please. As Homer put it, 'Zeus takes half the good out of a man on the day he becomes a slave.' "

"Perhaps the problem is not in the man but in the system which makes him a slave," Jacob offered, knowing it was a risky comment but feeling good enough about his success in spiriting Erotion away that he had the audacity to say it.

"Don't get philosophical, Nestor," Regulus replied. "You know how tiresome I find philosophers. Just go get that nurse."

Jacob bowed and left, suppressing a smile until he was out of the room. On his return, he was accompanied by a short, dumpy woman in her mid-thirties, a peasant woman old before her time. She was carrying the new Erotion.

Regulus looked perplexed, then disappointed. "Who's this? Where's the German girl?"

"She was not satisfactory, my lord," Jacob replied in his

most businesslike tone. "She was very distraught over the loss of her own child, and I began to worry that she posed a threat to Erotion. You were engrossed in a legal matter, so I took it upon myself to dismiss her and bring in Felicia here, who is well-known for her care and feeding of babies."

Felicia bowed. "Did you require something, my lord?" she said with an almost toothless smile.

"No," Regulus said with a dismissing wave of his hand. "Just take good care of the child."

Watching her leave, Regulus sighed. "I am disappointed. If I hadn't been so busy the past few days, I'd have gotten to that German girl right away. A tired palate always appreciates a fresh dish. A barbarian like that would have been a real novelty. But I guess you've done the right thing."

Jacob bowed to acknowledge the compliment.

"Of course, I know you did it more out of your love for Lorcis and her baby than out of loyalty to me."

Jacob looked straight at him but said nothing.

"Still, the right thing was done, so it all comes out the same, I suppose. Go on about your business."

BOOK IV

March, A.D. 85 - June, A.D. 87

CHAPTER XX

That's pretty, Mommy!" Erotion said, clapping her hands gleefully and running up to look at the fresco depicting children rolling a hoop; Lorcis had just finished painting it on one wall of her daughter's bedroom.

"Thank you, darling," Lorcis said, proud of her work and still surprised at the artistic talent she'd discovered within herself through the years. Glancing at the medallion which now sat on a shelf over her child's bed, she wondered if her talent was a gift inherited from her father.

"Don't touch it, hon," she cautioned Erotion. "It's not dry yet."

One more job done, she thought with a sigh as she wiped off her brush and picked up her materials. *There's always two more to be done on this place, though, especially with spring coming.* Painting wasn't the most essential thing on her agenda, but it had helped pass some long hours during a particularly hard winter, the hardest in the four years since she and Martial had escaped from Rome and taken up residence on the farm at Nomentum which Pliny had given them, six miles north of the city.

The place was built to be a working farm, not a country villa serving as some aristocrat's summer retreat. Unfortunately, the previous tenant had done little more than repair the roof and patch the largest cracks in the walls. He and his wife had devoted themselves to working the land and managing the animals; decorating and cleaning did not produce income, so they had done virtually none of either.

With aristocratic tastes and a plebeian budget, Lorcis had to provide the labor for her projects herself. Although her duties as a slave had never included hard physical labor, she had been surprised by her ability to figure out how to do anything that needed to be done. Her methods weren't always traditional, but they were usually effective. She derived tremendous satisfaction from whatever she did on the farm, in spite of aching muscles and calloused hands. Xanthippe and the other slave women in Regulus' household had been right: the life of a free person involved a good deal of drudgery, but she was determined to show them—and herself—that it was a better life than she had known before.

It would be easier if she had some help, of course, but Martial spent most of his time in the city. At first he had come out to the farm—a two-hour walk—every other day. He now stayed in Rome for as long as two weeks at a time. "As my poetry becomes more popular," he explained, "I have to make myself available to people who want to hear me read. I have to be able to accept dinner invitations."

You poor dear! Lorcis thought. But his efforts seemed to be paying off. He brought generous sums of money and gifts when he did come home—at least Lorcis thought of the farm as his home, whether he did or not—and boasted of the fact that he was no longer relegated to the rear of aristocratic dining rooms. *If only he would eat in his own dining room a little more often,* she brooded.

"Let's get some dinner ready," she suggested to Erotion with more spirit than she felt.

"Will Daddy come home tonight?" Erotion asked hopefully.

"Oh, I'm sure he will. It's his birthday."

Erotion took her mother's hand as they walked across the courtyard and into the cavernous kitchen. It was a trusting gesture that told Lorcis she was not as bad a mother as she sometimes felt she was. By the gods, how much she'd had to learn in the past four years! No one had ever told her how to raise a child. She couldn't even fall back on her own experience for she had been raised as a slave, not as a child. Somehow, however, she was doing it, joyfully if clumsily.

"Can I chop the onions?" Erotion asked. "They always make you cry, and I don't like to see you cry, Mommy."

Lorcis leaned down and hugged her. "That's sweet of you, dear." If only she knew how much crying her mother did at night when she was asleep and her father was . . . somewhere in

Rome. "Will you handle the knife carefully?"

"I'm a big girl, Mommy. I can do it." She stepped up onto the old milking stool she used whenever she helped her mother in the kitchen.

Her daughter provided Lorcis with some very valuable help in the kitchen, as long as the appearance of the dish didn't matter. And since they never had company apart from infrequent visits from Jacob or Xanthippe, the appearance of the dish didn't matter.

Not that her culinary skills were anything to brag about. Flute players did not trouble themselves with how the food they ate at banquets had been prepared. At first, she and Martial had often gone hungry, or had eaten meals that were overdone or undercooked. Her first effort at baking bread had produced a tasty but flat loaf. She had deduced from taste the ingredients that went into bread from the bakery—but yeast has no taste. Out for a visit that day, Jacob had complimented her on her unleavened bread and went on to tell a long story about some ancient Jews who had baked it that way deliberately.

At least she had been able to teach Erotion some things as she had learned them herself. Her daughter, singing to herself and hacking away contentedly at two large red onions, would grow up able to manage a house; she would be adept at something other than pleasing men.

Lorcis smiled. She did this frequently around her daughter, sometimes at things Erotion said or did, sometimes just because she was there. What a marvel! She and Martial had actually produced this happy, delightful child. Could this loving, giving little girl actually have come from two people as self-centered and strong-willed as she and Martial were? These were painful admissions to make, but she'd had more time than she needed to think about them and her relationship with this delightful child's father.

Leaving aside consideration of her personality, could a Syrian Jew and a dark-haired Spaniard give life to a child with golden curls that ought to grace the head of some German chieftain's daughter? Erotion's blonde hair puzzled her more than anything about her daughter. She could see Martial's nose and mouth in the child and suspected that she had also inherited more than a dash of his wit. Her eyes and her love of music seemed to come from her mother. So where did the blonde hair come from? Xanthippe had assured her that the parents' hair or eye color was no guarantee of what their children would have, and Xanthippe was very wise in such matters. She even told stories of Ethiopians who had borne fair-skinned children. Anything was possible, it seemed.

"Sing me the song about the peacock, Mommy," Erotion asked, interrupting her mother's reflections.

By sundown Lorcis knew Martial would not be coming home that night. No Roman in his right mind traveled after dark unless he was hiding from the law or facing some desperate emergency. In spite of the emperors' best efforts, bandits virtually owned some stretches of the roads after sundown.

"Why doesn't Daddy come home more often?" Erotion asked as Lorcis put her to bed. "Doesn't he love us?"

"Of course he does, darling. That's one reason why he stays in Rome. It's important he stay there so he can meet people. If they like his poems, they'll give him money, and that helps us buy the things we need."

"But don't we get enough money from selling the things that grow on our farm? Couldn't Daddy just stay here with us?"

Lorcis had to suppress a laugh at the notion of Martial being a farmhand. He'd written several epigrams about the joys of life in the country, but the only thing he dirtied his hands with when on the farm was ink.

"We wouldn't make enough money for everything we need, I'm afraid," Lorcis replied. *At least, not everything Martial thinks we need,* she added in her own thoughts. "I'm sure he'll be home soon."

"How long will he stay?"

"I don't know, sweetheart. But I'll bet if *you* ask him to stay a few days, he might do it."

For all her resentment of his prolonged absences and his seeming indifference to her loneliness, she had to admit that Martial did adore his daughter. He played with her like an overgrown child himself, bringing her lavish gifts and indulging her every whim when he came to see them. Because Martial was more of a father to Erotion than any man had been to her as a child, Lorcis tried not to be overly critical. Besides, Martial had to live a life that suited him; she could not expect him to tie himself down with a freedwoman, a child, and a herd of pigs.

She could accept his frequent absences, though not happily. What frightened her, though, was her uncertainty that he wanted to come out to them at all. Their torrid love affair had become awkward once they settled down to the routine of daily life together. Lorcis gladly abandoned Rome and the society which had enslaved and debased her, but Martial had grown impatient after a few days and longed to return and immerse himself in it. He was like his poems: brief, flighty, never focusing on one thing for very long.

Late in the afternoon three days later, Lorcis heard a wagon stop on the road which ran about fifteen yards to the west of the house. From the laughter and raucous farewells, she guessed some of Martial's well-placed friends were dropping him off on their way to some country estate. She started to walk out to the gate to greet him but stopped and remained unobserved when she heard their conversation.

"Are you sure this is the place?" a laconic, aristocratic voice asked. "It looks like the sort of hovel where Baucis and Philemon received Jupiter and Mercury in disguise."

"I was thinking more along the lines of the swineherd's hut in the *Odyssey*," another young fop volunteered.

Martial laughed as loud as the rest of them. "It's not much to look at," he admitted, "but the freedwoman who runs it for me has made it my most productive piece of property."

Then, before Lorcis could stop her, Erotion burst through the gate and ran down the path yelling, "Daddy! Daddy!"

"Looks like the place has produced a bumper crop, old man," one of Martial's friends said, hardly able to contain his glee. Though many Roman aristocrats fathered children by their female slaves and freedwomen, they did not like to acknowledge such offspring publicly. The legal status of such children was derived from their mothers, and they had no rights of inheritance.

"We'll leave you to sow your spring crop," the other young man said. Their gales of laughter followed Martial as he took Erotion's hand and walked with her up the path to the gate.

"You missed your birthday, Daddy," Erotion said, sticking out her lip. "We fixed you a nice dinner."

"I'm sorry, love. I needed to see somebody in Rome, and that was the only day I could do it. I hope you enjoyed the dinner anyway."

"Mommy fed most of it to the pigs," Erotion said matter-of-factly.

"Oh. Well, I hope the pigs enjoyed it."

"Daddy," Erotion said in exasperation, "you know they eat anything, especially the one we named Old Regulus."

Martial now noticed Lorcis standing by the gate. She did not move toward him or speak.

"Hello," Martial said with the tentative smile of a man who hopes for a better welcome than he knows he deserves.

Bowing like a servant, Lorcis said, "Good afternoon, my lord, and welcome to this humble but productive estate. We regret that we aren't adequately prepared for your visit, but we weren't expecting you today. Three days ago, we were ready for you. You would've gotten a royal welcome and a dinner fit for a king."

"I'm sorry I wasn't here—truly I am. There was a good reason."

Lorcis snorted in scorn. "I'm not sure that even a poet can come up with a good enough reason to justify disappointing his little girl."

"Could we discuss this later?" Martial said, making little effort to disguise the edge in his voice. "I've had a dusty trip with some tiresome company, and I'd like to see my daughter for a while before we eat."

"By all means, my lord. While you take your ease, your humble freedwoman will prepare a meal that befits a guest."

Martial kept Erotion up long past her usual bedtime, but Lorcis did not object. The child loved her father, and the problems which might exist between the adults in the family were no reason to deprive her of something so precious as this relationship. Besides, the longer Martial played with Erotion, the longer they could forestall the painful conversation they both knew was inevitable.

At last Erotion went to sleep in her father's lap, listening to him extemporize childish poems for her. Martial put her in bed and came to the kitchen where Lorcis was kneading dough. She turned the lump over and threw it onto the table with considerable force.

"Is that supposed to be my head?" he asked, watching her from the doorway.

"It's about the same consistency," she shot back without hesitation.

"I'm not going to be able to soften you with honeyed words from Homer, I see."

Lorcis stopped work, turned around to face him, and leaned against the edge of the table. "You make your living by twisting and manipulating words to amuse people who no longer recognize an honest expression of opinion when they see it. For me, I wish you would just say what you have to say."

"And then leave?"

"I didn't say I wanted you to leave. I'd like for you to stay out here with us."

"I'd be miserable out here. We both know that. Why don't you come to Rome with me?"

"Is that really what you want?"

"Yes, of course."

Lorcis smiled sadly. "You've been living in Rome too long. You believe your own lies and think that other people can't see through them."

He stepped toward her. "Darling, I'm entirely serious. Think what great fun it would be. With your charm and wit and musical ability combined with my growing fame, we'd take Rome by storm."

"Storms never last very long. Besides, I'll never live down being Lorcis the flute player, Regulus' slave."

"Oh, she was forgotten long ago. Regulus probably wouldn't know you if he bumped into you in the street. He's thrilled with the child we left him—treats her as his own. Nobody remembers you in Rome. You'd be starting over."

"That's precisely my point. Rome uses people up, consumes them, then throws the unrecognizable remains out into the street like so much garbage. I've escaped. Why should I go back?"

Martial stood close to her, running his fingers through her hair. "Because you love me?"

Lorcis wished his touch didn't feel so good. "That has nothing to do with it. I could say that if you loved me, you'd stay out here and be a father to our child."

"So we've come full circle in the conversation and resolved nothing," Martial said.

"It looks that way. I don't want to lose you, but I won't lose myself by going back to Rome."

"What if I promise faithfully to come out here more often?" Martial asked, kissing her on the neck.

Lorcis wasn't ready to give in yet. "How can I believe you? You couldn't even get out here for your birthday."

"That was also the day my second book of epigrams appeared in the bookstore, and Regulus gave a dinner in my honor that night. Then Calpurnia had a party for me the next night. I just couldn't get away. I'll do better, though—I promise."

Lorcis' doughy fingers were in his hair, her lips close to his. "You are the most exasperating man!"

CHAPTER XXI

"Damn you, Jesus!" Lorcis screamed. "Damn you!" Yanking the Jesus medallion off the shelf where it had sat over Erotion's bed for almost six years, she hurled it across the room. Then she rushed over to where it had hit the floor and began stomping on it.

"She's dead! Do you hear me? Erotion's dead!" she sobbed. "Why didn't you save her?" She spat on the picture. "You can't save anybody, can you! You're just like all the rest of them," she shrieked. "You're no more a god than Jupiter or Apollo."

She stumbled from the room in tears, not knowing where to go. There was no place in or around the house that did not remind her of Erotion. She could see her blonde curly hair blowing in the wind as she ran across the yard, hear her slight lisp as they chatted while fixing supper together and her hearty laugh as she played in her bath.

And now she was dead! Stricken suddenly by a disease that had left red splotches all over her fair skin and driven her fever up until she had writhed deliriously on her bed while Lorcis stood by, helpless, longing for Xanthippe and her potions, praying to Jesus.

She was dead, a week before her sixth birthday. Just that morning Lorcis had bathed her body, mixing her tears with the water, and dressed her in the new dress she had made as her birthday present. Martial had insisted that the body be burned, as befit the child (albeit not officially acknowledged) of a Roman knight. Lorcis had wanted to bury her, in the Eastern fashion, for she could not bear the thought of committing that beloved body to flames. But Martial, carrying the child in his arms, had just left to see to the cremation. Meanwhile a hired laborer—Lorcis would not allow Martial to own a slave—was preparing a grave behind the house in which the urn containing Erotion's ashes would be interred.

Suddenly, this farm, Pliny's gift which had seemed so perfect, had become the most hateful spot on earth. Sitting on the threshold of the back door, Lorcis did not notice at first the squirrel which had come to sit at her feet, expecting its usual feeding from her and Erotion. The child had regarded it as a pet, even giving it a name. When Lorcis realized the animal was there, she picked up the first rock she could lay her hands on and threw it as hard as she could. Even though her vision was tear-streaked, the rock found its mark.

When Martial returned home late that afternoon he found Lorcis sitting on Erotion's bed, staring vacantly at the opposite wall, with its mural of children at play.

"I've . . . finished," Martial said softly. "She's buried in that spot over the hill where you wanted her. We piled up some rocks to mark it until I can get something more permanent."

Lorcis gave no sign that she was aware of his presence. As he stepped toward her his foot came down on the splintered medallion, still lying where Lorcis had smashed it. He bent down to pick it up, but Lorcis snapped savagely, "Leave it alone! It's no worse than he deserves."

For two days she scarcely moved from that spot. She ate virtually nothing and refused to talk except for occasional short outbursts aimed mostly at Jesus. She wept steadily at first, then intermittently. She would not let Martial sit with her or even touch her, nor would she converse with him for more than a sentence or two at a time. "When I sit here quietly," she explained at one point, "I can still see her and hear her. I painted her into that picture, you know, over there on the left. Now it's all I have of her to hold on to."

For over a month Lorcis returned to that room each day at noon. During the two or three hours set aside in the Roman day for rest she sat and stared at the blonde figure in the corner of the mural. At first she wept, then her grief settled into deep moans with her hands gripping her hair so hard it hurt.

That was where Martial found her one afternoon when he returned from Rome. "We have a visitor, sweetheart," he said hopefully, stepping aside to reveal an elderly man slumped over and walking with difficulty.

Lorcis had not acknowledged Martial or reacted to what he said but gasped when she recognized Jacob. Shuffling across the room, his arms extended, he seemed incredibly older—more like the Homeric Nestor who had lived through several generations—than the last time she had seen him.

Lorcis held out her arms to him and hugged him tightly. Sitting on the edge of the bed beside her, he gently touched her hair and face.

"My dear child," he whispered hoarsely. "It really is you. My eyes are not so keen these days, especially in a gloomy room like this." He turned to Martial. "Please bring us another lamp."

While Martial was gone he said, "I am sorry I haven't been out to see you. Regulus is getting richer than King Midas and keeps me busy, especially now that I don't work quite as fast as I used to. I've thought about you so much, though, and of course I've been fortunate enough to see Martial once in awhile."

"I'm happy to see you," Lorcis said evenly, with little emotion. She knew why Martial had brought him and resented it. She did not want to be consoled no matter how much she might love Jacob.

"How's Xanthippe?" she asked casually, just to keep Jacob from directing the conversation. "She used to come out once in awhile, but she hasn't been here in months."

Jacob's eyebrows arched. "Martial hasn't told you?" It was an accusation as much as a question.

Lorcis shook her head. "Told me what?"

"Oh, dear. This really isn't the time to tell you this, but I suppose it can't be avoided."

"Is she dead?" Lorcis asked, suddenly anxious.

"Nothing so fortunate," Jacob sighed. "Regulus sold her to a man who owns several brothels in Massilia."

"Why?" Lorcis gasped.

"She was too old to suit him anymore," Jacob said with disgust. "No more reason than that. Why keep a thirty-six-year-old slave whose beauty is fading when there are plenty of eighteen-year-old ones available to replace her?"

"He could have freed her," Lorcis said bitterly.

"There's no profit in that."

They fell silent when Martial brought in the lamp. He looked like he wanted to stay but knew it would be better if he left. Jacob and Lorcis didn't quite have the heart, however, to tell him point-blank to leave, especially after he had been concerned enough to bring them together. No one spoke until Martial finally asked, "Do you need anything else?"

"No, that will be all," Jacob replied, and Martial left like a slave dismissed by his master.

Jacob squeezed Lorcis' hands affectionately. "When Martial told me what had happened, I wept. I wept most of the way out here in the litter. But now the time for weeping is past, my child."

Lorcis had looked at the wall as soon as he mentioned weeping. She turned to face him. "I'm not weeping. My eyes are dry. See?"

"But you're still grieving."

"Damn it, I lost my daughter!"

"I know that, and it's a terrible loss. But you cannot dwell on it for the rest of your life." He patted her knee tenderly. "There is a story in the Scriptures about King David. A child born to him by his favorite wife was taken ill. As long as the child was ill, David lay on his bed, refusing to eat or speak to anyone. When the child died his servants were afraid to tell him for fear his reaction would be more extreme. But when he perceived from their whispering that the child was dead, he got up, bathed, dressed, and ordered that food be brought. Everyone was shocked, but David explained that as long as the child was alive there was some hope that he might be saved by prayer and fasting. Once the question was settled, even in the most regrettable way, there was no further need for an outward show of grief. Life must return to normal."

"He was a heartless, insensitive man," Lorcis objected. "Or maybe it's enough just to say that he was a man."

Jacob put his arm around her shoulder. "Do you think men feel nothing when they lose a loved one?" A hint of anger edged into his voice. "Can you say that to me, when I watched my wife starve to death in my arms and saw my daughter raped and butchered in the street by Roman soldiers?"

"Oh, my god!" Lorcis gasped, her hand to her mouth. She knew he had lost his family, but he had never told her the details.

"Yes, I grieved," he went on, "but grief cannot be a permanent state, any more than happiness can. Can you go on sitting here for the rest of your life? Erotion is with God now, and those who are in his keeping are infinitely better off than we are. You have your life to lead. It has its own purpose, God's plan."

Lorcis jerked away from him. She knew he had been leading up to this, and it was precisely what she did not want to hear. "Damn your god!" she cried. Despite Jacob's crushed look, she rushed ahead. "I'm sorry you lost your family, but can't you see that no god who is good could have planned such a thing? If your god's plan for my life involves killing my child, then I want nothing to do with him. Surely you can't expect me to worship some deity who has struck down my only child!"

Seeing the pain that her attack was causing him, Lorcis softened and touched Jacob's arm. "Oh, Jacob, I don't mean to hurt you. How could I? You've been so good to me. But I can no longer tolerate your blather about this god. I once made a vow that I would never trust another man. I broke that promise because of you and Martial. Maybe I shouldn't have condemned all men. A few are good; more are bad. Most are indifferent, with their brains focused on their groins. But when it comes to gods, it is universally true: either they do not exist or, worse yet, they exist only to torment us."

Jacob stood up and reached out to her, but she stepped back to avoid his touch. "You are simply angry at God," he said, "because his plan does not please you. But it is not his business to please you."

"Nor is it my business to please him," Lorcis shot back. "So it looks like he and I have nothing further to do with each other. I intend to work on my own plan for my life," she boasted, though she could not have told him what it was if he had pressed her at that moment.

"My child . . ."

"It has been good to see you again, Jacob, but I think our visit had best end while we're still friends." She took his arm and began guiding him to the door. As he shuffled across the floor one sandal brushed over the medallion which Lorcis had not looked at since the day Erotion died. Jacob glanced down to see what his foot had touched.

"Oh, my dear Jesus!" he cried when he recognized the image. "Lorcis, what have you done?"

"Nothing worse than what he has done."

Awkwardly, Jacob bent down to pick up the three pieces into which the medallion had been broken. Lorcis did not try to stop him, nor did she offer to help.

"May I have this?" he asked pathetically. "It means so much to me."

"It means nothing to me anymore," Lorcis snapped, refusing to look at the object, "so do whatever you like with it."

The litter-bearers Martial had hired to bring the old man out to the farm were still waiting, lounging in the shade of the large oak across the road. Lorcis stopped at the front door and watched while Martial slowly escorted Jacob to the litter. But by the time he had taken his seat and turned to glance at her once more, the doorway was empty.

During the following week Lorcis tried to collect herself, and Martial was satisfied that Jacob's visit had served its purpose. Lorcis, however, would not admit that to herself. The surprise of seeing him had lifted her from the depths of her despair, but his words had brought her no comfort. Though she no longer sat in Erotion's room, she could not escape her memory. Martial advised her to keep busy, to distract herself from her grief. It certainly seemed to work for him: he was gone to Rome most of the time. During his brief stays at the farm, Martial was restrained and sympathetic, but Lorcis only grew angry at his apparent lack of grief.

When she confronted him one night, he replied with thinly controlled impatience, "A man does not show his grief as openly or as long as a woman. I wept as I carried my daughter to the cremation ground, but it does not befit a man to show excessive emotion."

Having experienced his ardent lovemaking and having seen him delight in Erotion to the point of silliness, Lorcis found his statement incredible. Surely he could not believe it himself, but before she could object he went on. "I happen to express my feelings in more suitable ways. I have composed a poem—the finest thing I've ever written, I think—and had it carved on a monument which will be placed on Erotion's grave tomorrow. Having done that, I can do no more. Surely you know how I am. If I could, I would bring her back. You must know that. But no one can. Life is for the living, Lorcis. It's time you accepted that."

Lorcis made no reply, and Martial seemed uninterested in

prolonging the conversation. It was already quite late, and he was planning to be up before dawn to go to a patron's house in Rome. He did not even call after Lorcis when she ran out the back door.

About fifty yards behind their house the ground sloped gently up to a small rise. A few trees stood on the top and on the other side of it, but the side nearest the house had been stripped for firewood years before. On the other side of that rise lay Erotion's grave. Lorcis had insisted that it be out of sight of the house, and she had not yet visited the place. Although she could not have articulated the reason, it was simply because she sensed that seeing her daughter's grave would be to acknowledge her death, to let go of her entirely.

Her steps slowed as she approached the top of the rise. The night was clear and warm, even though it was midnight or later, as nearly as she could figure. The full moon made it easy to see the pile of rocks that marked Erotion's burial place. Lorcis approached it and dropped down beside it, not really looking at it and not even certain that she felt any closer to her daughter. After all, those stones covered only an urn containing a handful of ashes, indistinguishable from any other ashes. This place symbolized her loss of Erotion; it broke, not strengthened, the bond between them. She had to come here once, but she knew already that she could never come here again.

She lay back on the grass and cried herself to sleep, not with the hard sobs that had wracked her over the past six weeks, but with slow, silent tears that eased their way out of her eyes like the last drops of wine from a goblet.

She was awakened the next morning by a stranger's gruff voice calling, "Halloo! Anybody here?" When she peeked over the rise she saw three men standing in the yard around a wagon carrying a large tombstone. Fully awake, she realized it was already an hour or more after dawn. Martial must be half way to Rome at least.

"Up here!" she called, standing on top of the rise.

The men turned and one of them waved to acknowledge her. Another tugged on the oxen's bridle to turn them, while a third goaded them with a sharp stick. As they approached, she noticed them smiling and glancing at one another. She self-consciously looked down, wondering if her gown was especially dirty or in disarray. She took in a quick breath when she realized that the sun, still low in the sky behind her, was revealing the outline of her body through her lightweight summer gown. She did not move at once, however. It had been six years since any man but Martial had admired her. It was flattering, even reassuring, because it gave credence to the plan she had formulated during a brief period of wakefulness in the night.

It required a good bit of cursing and tugging to get the oxen up the rise with their load. The foreman of the crew—a freedman who owned the other two men—greeted Lorcis civilly and consoled her but did not try to strike up a conversation. He preferred not to have to deal with grief-stricken women and was hoping she would go back to the house. She disappointed him.

Lorcis did, however, step back out of the workmen's way as they cleared the pile of rocks from the grave and dug out and leveled a spot for the monument. Although she did not really want to watch the operation, she could not turn her back on it. She found herself facing partly away from the men, glancing at them over her left shoulder.

Having prepared the spot, they moved the wagon into place, then unyoked the oxen and tethered them nearby. After chocking the wheels, they used rough-hewn planks to set up a ramp from the wagon bed to the grave. Guiding the stone down the ramp with a lot of grunting and sweating, they brought it to rest in the shallow hole with a thump. Lorcis flinched, almost feeling the weight of it pressing down on her.

After packing the dirt tightly around the base, the men hitched up the oxen, offered condolences again, and plodded off down the rise. Lorcis watched them until they were past the house and on the road to Rome. She wanted to be sure they stole nothing, but she was also hesitant to turn and confront this all too solid evidence of the finality of Erotion's death. For a moment she toyed with the idea of walking straight down the hill without even looking back. But she had come here for this purpose—to see what Martial had written for the stone. She wanted the words to be proof of his grief since the stone was surely no consolation in itself.

Turning slowly around, Lorcis took a few steps toward the stone until she could read the lettering. It was not a typical epitaph. Martial had written in poetic form a letter to his parents, committing Erotion to their care in the underworld:

Father Fronto, Mother Flacilla,
I entrust to you this girl,
my sweetheart, my delight;
so that little Erotion may not shudder
at the dark shadows and the monstrous mouths
of the underworld's guardian hound.
My little love died
only six days before her sixth birthday.
Between guardians so venerable may she lightly play
and chatter my name with her innocent tongue.
O, earth, do not rest heavy on her!
She was no burden to you.

Lorcis was touched but not deeply moved. It bothered her that Martial could express his emotions so facilely, in such a neat literary fashion, complete with mythological allusions he did not believe in. If that was as deep as his feelings went, then the decision she had made during the night was correct.

CHAPTER XXII

With some reluctance, a servant entered Pliny's study. His master normally devoted this part of the day to polishing and rewriting speeches or poems he had composed the preceding afternoon, and he did not like to be disturbed. But the visitor waiting in the atrium was determined to see him and seemed unlikely to go away until the request was granted.

Somewhat annoyed, Pliny asked, "Did she give her name?"

"Yes, my lord," the servant replied with disdain. "She says she is someone called Lorcis, wife . . ."

But Pliny was already out the door, striding rapidly toward the atrium. Lorcis stood up and smiled weakly when he came into view. He had not changed except that his face looked thinner and harder. It bore the insecurity and insincerity that characterized the faces of most aristocratic Romans. Suddenly, she was not certain of her reception here. People who were not seen in Rome were quickly forgotten, and she had not been in the city in six years. But his smile relieved her fears at once.

"My dear Lorcis," he almost shouted. "By the gods, it has been so long!" He took her hands, then hugged her. "Did you bring Erotion with you? How is she?"

"Erotion died of a fever over a month ago," Lorcis replied matter-of-factly. She had herself under control enough that she could say that much without visible pain, but she said nothing else.

Pliny was left stunned, off balance. "I am so terribly sorry," he finally managed to stammer. It was obvious he did not know what to say next and had no inkling why Lorcis was in his house.

After a moment she took him off the hook. "I've decided to return to Rome. I can no longer bear to live on our farm. I am more grateful for your generosity than I can ever express, but the place now has too much pain associated with it, for me at least." She had no doubt Martial would continue to live there. He had his heart set on becoming rich and would never willingly give up so valuable a piece of property.

"Yes, I can understand your feelings," Pliny murmured. He felt an urge to put a comforting arm around her shoulder, but she seemed to be withdrawing from him, though there was no perceptible movement of her body.

"I came to town this morning," she informed him, "and rented a room in the Insula Feliculae."

Pliny's lip curled involuntarily. This monstrous apartment house had a reputation for attracting less than desirable tenants. Rooms were always available because the rate of death or disappearance among that sort of people was atrocious.

"Couldn't you find some place less dangerous?" he asked anxiously.

"Not for what I can afford to pay," she sighed.

"I'll be happy to help you. You know you have only to ask."

"I don't want to ask for money from my friends," Lorcis replied icily. "All I want is a chance to get back into society as a freewoman. If I can just get started, I'll be able to take care of myself, I think."

"There's something about your tone that disturbs me, Lorcis," Pliny admitted. "You're out to beat Rome at its own game, aren't you?"

"Yes," Lorcis said proudly. "These people—or others just like them—took most of my life away from me. They can't give me those years back, and they can't erase the abuse and degradation I've suffered, so they must pay for it."

"Don't you know the kind of people you're going to encounter? Regulus is admirable in comparison with some of them," Pliny cautioned.

"I think I have been in an even better position than you to observe just how despicable they are, Pliny. You may be the only decent person in the lot."

"Can there really be only one? Could I remain uncorrupted

for so long? Perhaps you've been deceiving yourself."

For an instant Lorcis despaired. "Please don't joke with me like that. I have no faith left in anything or anyone else."

"I appreciate your trust in me," Pliny said with a diffident smile. "I just wish you would trust me a bit more when I warn you against trying to take your own vengeance against these people. They'll crush you without thinking about it."

"I know the risk I'm taking," Lorcis assured him. "That's one reason I hope to enter a circle of people who share at least some of your graciousness and humanity. I thought you might have room for me at your next dinner party—as a guest," she added, to be certain there was no misunderstanding.

"How can I refuse any request from you, my friend? In fact, I'm having a small dinner tonight. You will be more than welcome."

"Thank you," Lorcis said. "Then I'll need to get a bath and a new dress." Picking up the bag containing her flutes, which she had not dared leave in her room, she turned to leave.

"At least let me buy you a dress," Pliny called after her. When she turned around, ready to refuse, he quickly added, "For old times' sake—Vesuvius and all that."

"All right," she nodded. It was fair, she argued with herself. She had ruined a perfectly good stola helping him save his mother's life.

The size of the money pouch Pliny brought back from his study surprised her, but she took it without comment other than her thanks. After all, she told herself, she hadn't asked for any money. Whatever he gave her was given of his own free will. That's the way the game was played in Rome. She didn't like herself very much at that moment, but she felt she could succeed at what she had in mind.

"This might also be helpful to you," Pliny said, offering her a sealed letter with a name written on the outside. "That man, whose house is on the Aventine Hill overlooking the Circus Maximus, has several pieces of property for rent here in the city. He might be able to help you find a more suitable—and safer—place to live."

Suddenly unable to speak, Lorcis just nodded. Fortunately, Pliny distracted her with another question.

"By the way, where's Martial? Does he know what you've done?"

"I left him a note," Lorcis sniffed. "It was one of my best efforts, I thought."

The dinner party that evening went well, at least from Lorcis' point of view. Pliny's friends were quieter, more cultivated, than the people Regulus had associated with. The primary topic of conversation was poetry, especially the merits of older writers like Catullus and Calvus measured against the new school of which, she was surprised to learn, Martial was considered the leading light.

Her easy acceptance in the circle gratified her. One reason for it, she kept reminding herself, was that these people, whether they would admit it or not, were bored with seeing one another over and over, night after night. Any new face was welcome, and someone with her beauty and charm was bound to become instantly popular. By the end of the evening she had received invitations to dinner for the next five days. She had to laugh inwardly at the way these fops fought over her.

At the beginning of the evening she had felt unsure of herself. She was attempting to establish herself as a freed woman, under no man's control, in a society in which men, at least theoretically, dominated. But she had observed during her years as a slave that Roman men seldom asserted themselves against their women. The men around her reminded her of the lotus-eaters in Homer's *Odyssey,* lacking any serious ambition, unconcerned with anything except their own pleasure.

Part of the reason for their lethargy was that they had been stripped of all political and military power by the emperors. The senate still met and discussed issues and magistrates were still elected, but their decisions were entirely subject to the emperor's will. They never even expressed an opinion until they were sure of imperial favor. Being accustomed to this sort of passive behavior for several generations, they seldom expressed themselves, even in the privacy of their own homes. The new emperor, Domitian, unlike his father and brother, gave a ready ear to informers; any offhand comment could be twisted to support a charge of treason. Deprived of political and military power and afraid of their wives, these wealthy aristocrats, who had once been called "an assembly of kings," dabbled in poetry and took out their pent-up hostilities on their slaves—the only persons in Rome more powerless than themselves.

Women had gained a prominent place in this society. Looking around her, Lorcis saw that almost a third of the guests were women, some of them unaccompanied, others with handsome young men by their sides. Many women felt no need to marry. Those who had been widowed or divorced often preferred not to marry again, and their inherited wealth or divorce settlements left them independent.

Even married women lived as they wished. Sempronia and Regulus were not a unique couple. Since the reign of Emperor Claudius, it had been legal for women to own, inherit, and bequeath property in their own names without the legal fiction of a male guardian. Many women like Felicula, the apartment house owner, ran their own businesses and were quite wealthy in their own right. Could Lorcis, the flute player, the former slave, hope to find a place for herself in such society?

Her reception at the dinner eased her mind and raised her hopes. She was introduced as Pliny's friend, but she did not share his couch so she could not be mistaken for his mistress. There were few questions about her background because some of the other guests had come from origins no more illustrious than hers, making their way up in society by hard work or opportune marriages. She learned that the man next to her, Larcius Macedo, was the son of a former slave. No legal stigma was attached to him because of his ancestry, but he himself felt some inadequacy because of it. Lorcis noticed a sharp edge in his comments to the slaves attending him.

Lorcis was able to evade the few polite questions by replying in good Roman fashion: not telling a lie but not revealing the whole truth either. She mentioned that she was a native of Antioch and that she was now living in a house on the Aventine Hill. (The letter she had taken to Pliny's friend, Caecilius Macrinus, had prompted an immediate response. That very afternoon, he had shown her a small, charming house two blocks from his own. The rent he charged was unbelievably small although, unknown to her, Pliny had promised in his note to make up the difference between what Caecilius charged Lorcis and the normal rent for the house.)

The only awkward moment came when someone commented on her depth of knowledge of Martial's poetry and asked if she knew him personally. When Lorcis hesitated and reddened, Pliny put in, "Lorcis is, or rather was, Martial's . . . wife."

Eyebrows were raised; no one in Rome had known about this relationship. It was better, Martial had assured Lorcis, that people assume he was single to allow him greater freedom of movement as he cultivated wealthy patrons. "We were never actually married," Lorcis blurted out, thinking that would somehow improve the situation. The silence only left her more embarrassed.

"Whatever his marital status," Macedo gallantly observed, "he is a fine poet," and with that, the pace of the conversation gradually resumed. Lorcis couldn't help wishing, however, that the whole subject had never come up.

The next fortnight brought a dizzying round of dinners, afternoons in the baths, and visits to the Circus Maximus to watch the chariot races. The contacts made through Pliny were quickly extended to friends of Pliny's friends. One or two of them seemed to think they knew her, and she knew they had probably hired her from Regulus, but she could honestly say she did not remember meeting them before if she had. She realized that eventually she would have to face her past, but she hoped to establish herself securely before that happened.

For the present, her life could not have been better. There were lonely moments, especially in the mornings when she could not suppress memories of Erotion, but her frenetic social pace kept her from dwelling on the past. She even worked up the nerve to sell her flutes, the one link to her days as a slave. A dealer in ivory, jade, and other precious commodities gave her a decent, though not generous, price for them. "Too bad they're inscribed like that," he said. "That lowers the value considerably."

She had made her break with slavery and was now living her own life; no one controlled her. She had a house of her own and a maid and a cook. Her new friends were generous, none more so than Pliny. At first she felt uneasy about accepting gifts, especially money, but she soon convinced herself that it was all due her as partial repayment for the things people like this had subjected her to.

Early one afternoon her maid, Fortunata, came to her room somewhat agitated. "Madam, there is a man here to see you."

Lorcis thought this peculiar because most men were finishing their day's work and heading for the baths at this hour. It was not normally a time for social calls.

"What's his name?" Lorcis asked.

"He wouldn't tell me, madam. His only message was 'The poet wishes to see his lady.' "

Lorcis stiffened and drew in her breath quickly. Martial!

"All right, Fortunata. Thank you," she replied in a daze. "Tell him I will see him in a moment." She was already dressed and could have gone out to see him at once, but she needed to steady herself for what she knew would be a traumatic encounter.

She walked from her room to the atrium as slowly as someone who had been bedridden for days; her mind frantically searched for the right opening to disarm him at the very beginning of the conversation. As she turned the last corner and entered the atrium, however, she still had no idea what she was going to say.

He stood by the pool admiring a small statue on a pedestal, one of a set depicting the seasons that stood at each corner of the pool. He looked up when he heard her footsteps but said nothing.

"You wanted to see me?" was the best Lorcis could offer.

She could not read his expression, but his reply was the kind of sarcastic civility so characteristic of him. "Actually, I just wanted to see if the new social sensation, Lorcis who lives on the Aventine, is the same Lorcis as the former slave of Regulus and former wife of Martial." He paused. "Are you the same person?"

"No," Lorcis replied coldly. "The woman you describe died along with her child several months ago. She was last seen reading the pretty little epitaph you wrote for Erotion's tombstone. Her life has been all but forgotten."

"Well, then, it's a good thing we have her writings to remember her by. My own favorite is her farewell epistle."

Lorcis blushed. "I was in such a state then that I knew I couldn't confront you. Besides, I didn't think you cared much anymore what I did."

"Didn't care? You were my wife!"

"Be honest with yourself, at least," Lorcis shot back. "You never married me. I think you took me home with you after I was freed just because you couldn't think of any graceful way out of it. I sat out there in Nomentum, faithfully raising your child, but you never even mentioned marriage. Perhaps you didn't have time to think about it since you were too busy playing around in Rome with your friends."

"I told you that my social position made it awkward for me to be married. But I considered you my wife, and I love you," Martial protested.

"Not as often as you love a lot of women in Rome—and a few boys, too, I hear. Xanthippe came to see me occasionally, you know, and brought me quite a bit of news. And now I hear the same things for myself."

Martial looked hurt, surprised, like a man in a battle who is unaware that he is injured until he happens to glance down at his own body. "You never said anything when we were together. You seemed happy."

"I was," Lorcis conceded. "At first I was disappointed. You see, I had this ideal that you should be as loyal to me as I was to you. But I soon realized that loyalty was easy for me—I had no opportunity to be unfaithful. You had plenty of chances and took them, mostly in the name of 'cultivating the right people,' and I don't blame you for that. I was happy with Erotion. But then she was gone, and you took even her body away from me. You burned her! And suddenly I could barely stand the sight of you. I don't think you loved me anymore, and you found Erotion an inconvenience, something better kept a secret from your friends in the city."

"That's a lie! I loved her dearly."

He moved toward her, and she backed away from him. Like gladiators in the ring, they circled slowly.

"You doted on her, the way some people in Rome dote on their lapdogs, but I don't think you really loved her. Where were you when she was sick?" Lorcis' voice rose as the long pent-up anger surged toward its target. "She had a fever that morning, remember? But you went on to Rome all the same. 'Important business' you said. She'd be all right. I stood over her for two days—helpless! By the time you got back she was almost dead."

Martial stopped and raised his hands to her. "I couldn't have changed that, even if I had stood over her bed the whole time. I took her illness too lightly, I admit, but what could I do?"

"You could have cried!" Lorcis screamed.

For a moment, silence hung between them. Martial looked at the floor and finally whispered, "I'll never be able to convince you that I did care, will I? That I still do care."

Lorcis shook her head. "You are an intense, passionate man," she replied. "I've known that since our first meeting. But your poetry—which is just an extension of yourself—is always going to be your first love. Perhaps poets must be egotists, to have the courage to offer their work to the public, but that just means that no person can ever hope to hold more than second place in a poet's heart. I was that for a time to you, but your passion for me has burned itself out."

"Do you hate me so much?" he asked, slumping onto a bench by the pool.

"No, I don't hate you, Martial," Lorcis said softly, taking a step toward him. "I resent that you could never give yourself totally to Erotion and me. You always had to come back to Rome. I'd have been perfectly happy to have you stay on the farm with us and work the place. But that wouldn't have been you. I understand now what kind of man you are, and I cannot love you as I once believed I could."

"I wish I could understand you," Martial sighed. "I've given myself to you as completely as I could, but you're not satisfied. What do you want?"

"Something you can't supply," Lorcis answered. "You helped me gain my freedom, and I'll always be indebted to you for that. But now, for the first time, I'm in control of my own destiny. I'm not just passively accepting whatever happens to me. I'll always treasure the good parts of our life together, Martial, but it's time for us to take separate paths."

She stepped back from him and turned away, making it clear that she considered the discussion at an end. "I have to finish dressing for tonight's dinner," she told him. "I'm going to the palace," she added with undisguised pride.

Martial's mouth sagged open in horror, not in amazement. "Please don't go there," he begged.

Lorcis was more irritated than surprised by his reaction, which she attributed to jealousy. "This is the opportunity I've hoped for," she replied indignantly, glancing over her shoulder at him. "I hadn't dared dream it would come so soon."

"But you don't understand," Martial interrupted. "You don't know Domitian. He's not like Titus or Vespasian."

"I know," she said flippantly. "Everybody says he's much more fun."

Martial persisted. "Listen! The best way I can describe Domitian is to say that Regulus, who wasn't even admitted to the palace when Vespasian was emperor, is a close friend of Domitian's." He could see he had made an impression on her. "But you say you're in control of your own life now, so I guess nothing I can say will change your mind." What had begun as a statement ended almost as a question.

"No, it won't," Lorcis replied, but not without hesitation. Actually frightened, she still had no intention of admitting it, least of all to Martial.

He bowed his head slightly. "Well, thank you for your time, my lady. I hope your evening at the palace is truly memorable."

Lorcis nodded as he turned to leave. She watched him approach the door, hoping against her better judgment that he would stop and come back to her. He was a terribly difficult man to love, but she did love him. Could she have been so wrong about her feelings for him? Could she just let him walk out of her life? She raised her hand and opened her mouth, but the door closed behind him.

CHAPTER XXIII

In the days of Augustus, the first Roman emperor, the imperial residence had been an aristocrat's relatively modest house on the Palatine Hill. Each successive emperor, especially Caligula and Nero, had added on to it until it now sprawled all over the top of the hill. It was so large a complex of wings and additions that a visitor could hardly comprehend it. It was easier on the senses just to concentrate on the particular area or room one was visiting and trust a guide to know the way out of the labyrinth.

Lorcis and Quadratus, who had invited her to accompany him, were escorted along a maze of halls to a smaller triclinium, one which could accommodate only a hundred and twenty or so guests. At first Lorcis tried to keep track of turns and directions, but she was quickly and hopelessly confused. She tried to note landmarks, using the artworks they were passing. The statues and mosaics were magnificent, but there were so many along each corridor that they only heightened her disorientation.

The triclinium was about half full when they arrived and the slave guiding them announced their names. That was the only time Lorcis was ever uncomfortable in the presence of these people. Her name sounded so obviously foreign, and it was only a single word, whereas most Roman aristocratic women had adopted the fashion of taking two names, one from their father and one from their husband—or from a grandfather, if they were not married. The women seemed to reason that since they had wealth and social standing equal to many men, they ought to have men's names. Thus, if a Cornelia, the daughter of Cornelius Rufus, married Metellus Celer, she became Cornelia Metella, instead of merely retaining her single name as had been customary under the Republic. There were always stares and a few smiles when Lorcis was announced at a dinner—which simply made her more determined to rise above the status to which her name consigned her. She did not want to change her name; she intended to make others accept and respect it.

She and Quadratus were shown to their places on a couch by a slave with the seating list. Their table was almost full. Quadratus introduced Lorcis to the people he knew, and those unknown to him introduced themselves.

The last to give his name was a middle-aged man reclining by himself on the other side of Lorcis. He spoke Greek with something of an accent, a Semitic accent, she realized. Then his name, which had meant nothing at first, registered: Flavius Josephus. This Jewish priest and military leader had surrendered to the Romans early in the war and then helped Vespasian and Titus during the remainder of the campaign. His own people despised him as a traitor, and his history of the war, written from the Roman viewpoint, had completed his separation from his origins.

What made him significant for Lorcis was that this man had been responsible for Jacob being sold into slavery instead of being put to death in the arena.

Resisting the urge to ask direct questions about Jacob, thus giving away her own background, she struck up a conversation on the basis of their common Eastern origins. She admitted that her father had been a Jew but quickly added that she did not follow that faith.

"What was your father's name?" Josephus asked, showing genuine interest in the conversation for the first time.

"Lazarus," Lorcis replied. "He lived in Bethany just outside Jerusalem and later moved to Antioch."

"Oh, yes. I know Bethany well."

Lorcis sensed a note of suspicion in his voice.

"You say you don't follow the Jewish faith. Are you a devotee of any other?"

"No," Lorcis replied, "none in particular. One god is as good as another, as far as I'm concerned. Or, to put it more precisely, no god is any better than another."

"There are those who would object to such indifference,"

Josephus observed. Lorcis became uneasy. What did he mean? Was he driving at something? trying to trap her?

"Your father, for instance," Josephus continued in his carefully modulated voice. "He did not follow Judaism in the latter part of his life either. He became prominent among a group of fanatics known as Christians."

"How do you know so much about my father?" Lorcis asked. "I didn't realize he was ever an important person."

"Oh, my dear, yes. I'm researching a work on the history of the Jews from their beginnings to the onset of the war with the Romans, which I feel marks the end of Judaism. I am well acquainted with all sorts of people no one else ever heard of. And any man who claims to have been raised from the dead inevitably gains a certain notoriety. When one has as many witnesses as Lazarus had, even a skeptical historian like myself cannot entirely ignore the evidence. What really puzzles me, though, is the lack of precise information about him after his resurrection—or perhaps I should say, alleged resurrection. I'd like to know where he went, what he did. Can you tell me anything?"

Before Lorcis could reply, a brilliant chord from the musicians announced the arrival of the emperor and his party, and Lorcis turned with everyone else to face the door. She was probably the only person in the room who had never actually seen Domitian, even from a distance, so she was more excited than the rest. She caught only a glimpse of him, enough to see a tall, reasonably handsome man in his mid-thirties, whose looks were flawed only by his incipient baldness. Her gaze then fell on the man walking behind the emperor's right elbow: Regulus!

Once the initial shock passed, Lorcis had time to study her former master. She hoped she had not aged as much in six years as he had. He had gained considerable weight and lost most of his hair. The fringe that remained was heavily flecked with gray. The diminutive young woman walking behind him, Lorcis concluded, must be the new wife she had heard so much about. Regulus had divorced Sempronia three years ago and married this Lepida, a distant cousin of Domitian's. They had surprised everyone by producing a son a little more than a year after the wedding. Regulus' ecstasy over this proof of his virility had known no bounds. Since his wife was related to the emperor, no one even dared hint that there might be some doubt about the child's paternity. He was already pampering the boy and refusing to discipline him at all or to allow anyone else to do so. From what Lorcis had heard, she was doubly glad she was no longer in his household.

When the imperial party took their places on the raised dais, the dinner began. There was a great deal of entertainment, the conversation at all the tables was lively, and Lorcis' hope that Regulus would not notice her was realized until late in the evening. She and Josephus engaged in some further conversation, but he seemed reluctant to say much more about the Christians. He was willing to talk about Jewish customs—to disparage them, actually—but he turned aside any questions about the Christians, dismissing them as misguided but harmless fanatics. Lorcis finally surmised that one of the latecomers to their table must be a spy of Domitian's. No doubt there was at least one at every table.

When the conversation turned to gladiators and charioteers, especially to Domitian's innovation of adding two teams—the Gold and the Purple—to the long established four racing teams, Lorcis saw Regulus get up from his couch. She assumed he was merely going to relieve himself, but instead, he turned toward her table. Their eyes met and, held by her horror of him, she could not turn away.

Lumbering over to her couch, he sat down at her feet. "By the gods! It is! It is Lorcis!" he laughed stupidly.

Lorcis smiled faintly and nodded. The only words that came to her mind were "Yes, my lord," but she managed to keep them bottled up.

"I will admit I was stunned when I heard you had recovered," he went on. "I would never have let you go if I had thought there was any chance of that." He shook his head ruefully. "You're too beautiful and talented just to throw away."

Lorcis struggled to keep her composure by reminding herself that she was utterly free of this despicable man. He could not touch her. "But that was all a long time ago, wasn't it," she managed to say coolly.

"Yes, it certainly was," Regulus nodded. "Five years?"

"Six."

"Yes, of course. Your little girl's birthday was just a few weeks ago." Although he intended that statement to hurt her, he had no idea just how much it actually tortured her. He paused and looked at her more soberly. "I fully expected you to try to get her back, but I'm so glad you didn't. She's inherited a full measure of your special talent."

Remaining calm at that moment was the most difficult thing Lorcis had ever done. In that moment, too, she realized what a true Roman she had become, able to dissemble her feelings behind a curtain of ambiguous words. She managed a resigned lowering of her eyes as she said, "I have accepted the loss of my child. It is something beyond my control. A . . . that is, someone in my position learns to look at life fatalistically."

"You are a remarkable woman," Regulus said with sudden drunken honesty. "May I present you to the emperor?"

This was the moment Lorcis had begun planning for during that night beside Erotion's grave. She had never dreamed it would arrive so soon, and with such an ironic twist to it: Regulus himself introducing her to him. Her smile only faintly reflected her satisfaction.

She asked Quadratus to excuse her, but he was so drunk he hardly seemed aware that she was speaking to him. As she stood and straightened her gown, Regulus offered her his arm. She had never voluntarily touched him, but this gesture, though technically only an invitation, was also a command—and she obeyed.

They did not speak to each other as they crossed the triclinium. Domitian, joking with those around him, did not notice them until they stood by his couch.

"My lord," Regulus intoned with a respectful bow, "may I present an old . . . friend of mine, Lorcis of Antioch."

Seen up close, Domitian was not particularly attractive and by no means imperial. His complexion was too ruddy and his eyes bulged. He tried to hide his thinning hair, as Julius Caesar had done, by wearing a crown of laurel leaves decreed to him by the senate in honor of his dubious victories over some impoverished, disease-ravaged German tribes north of the Danube. The effect of the laurels, however, was comic. He looked more like a drunken Bacchus than the emperor of Rome.

"Lorcis? the flute player?" were his first words to her. She flinched inwardly. Regulus must have noticed her earlier in the evening and revealed everything to him in the grossest detail, no doubt. She tried to make the best of it.

"Yes, my lord," she smiled as she bowed. "That is one of my talents." She knew as soon as she said it that it had not come out the way she intended.

"You've also written a few poems, I hear."

"You flatter my humble efforts, my lord," Lorcis said with another slight bow. She had written some poetry and read it to appreciative audiences at a dinner party or two. His awareness of this minor accomplishment emphasized to her the truth in the rumor that everything that happened in Rome eventually got back to the palace.

"It's not flattery at all," Domitian said with apparent boredom. "I am merely reporting table gossip. I myself detest poetry. I've considered making it illegal for anyone to sell writing materials to a poet unless he intends to write poems praising me and my achievements."

Lorcis wondered if he was joking, but no one at the table smiled. Before she could reply, he moved over on the couch.

"Please join me. Regulus has told me that you have other talents which even an unpoetic soul such as myself might appreciate. Do you still have your flutes?"

"No, my lord. I sold them."

"Well, perhaps we could find an instrument around here for you to play."

Lorcis' heart sank as she lay down next to him. She thought she had come so far, but it seemed now that all she had done was to remove a slave bracelet from her wrist. Her place in this society, people's expectations of her, had not changed at all.

But she forced herself to be witty and jovial, partly because she would not give Regulus the satisfaction of seeing her humiliated again and partly because she still hoped to salvage something from the situation. At least she was known to the emperor; she was reclining on a couch next to him, with his body snuggled closer to hers than was necessary. She would not be the first woman of her class to charm an emperor. Claudius, in spite of three noble wives at various times, had remained loyal to the prostitute Calpurnia. Nero had almost married the freedwoman Acte. His mother, Agrippina, had allegedly offered herself to her son to distract him from the woman he loved. Was it utterly unthinkable that Lorcis, whose beauty men openly admired and whose erotic expertise had been the talk of Rome a few years ago, might assume a similar role in Domitian's life?

She was allowing herself such a fantasy as the dinner party began to disperse. Domitian turned to her and said, "Do you think Quadratus would mind going home alone tonight?"

"That was what I had intended for him to do all along," Lorcis replied a bit wickedly.

"Poor Quadratus!" Domitian chortled. "Very well, then. So be it. The emperor so orders it! I would like to have a chance to become better acquainted with you in more private circumstances. Would you be my guest for the rest of the evening?"

"My lord, I would be delighted."

CHAPTER XXIV

As Lorcis regained consciousness, she felt wet; she was lying on something wet, messy, and hard—stones, the street. The messiness came from the filth and garbage people had thrown from their windows, the wetness from the rain that was falling intermittently.

She tried to sit up, but even slight movement caused excruciating pain in her ribs. Grabbing her sides, she discovered she was naked. She tried to look at herself, but it was still dark—and her right eye was swollen shut. She licked her lips and discovered that the lower one was split.

She was still half sitting, half reclining, trying to force her mind to work and her body to obey its commands, when she heard someone coming. Apparently there were several people, though they were walking quietly. She was sure they were bandits; no one else would be out at this time of night.

Impending danger cleared her mind. Knowing they would kill her, or worse, she tried to get up and move. But her body would not respond to her mind's urgency. She managed to crawl only a few painful feet when the group rounded the bend in the street and saw her.

She was ready to plead with them, but realized they were not rushing to attack her. Instead, they stood in a circle of light cast by a torch one of them was carrying. After studying her for a moment, one member of the group walked slowly toward her.

"Please don't be frightened, my dear," a woman's voice assured her. "We will not harm you." Her voice was soft, her gestures slow and reassuring.

Lorcis drew away apprehensively, but the woman calmly unfastened her hooded cloak, stooped down, and wrapped it around the battered young woman. She then stood back up and said to the three men with her, "She's been injured and needs our help. Take her to my house."

The man with the torch stayed back while the other two approached Lorcis. One remained standing, glancing around anxiously, while the other, a tall, powerful man, knelt beside her. "Can you stand up?" he asked with a gentleness that belied his size.

Lorcis shook her head and tried to say, "I don't think so," but the words were indistinct.

"I'm going to pick you up," the man said. "It will probably hurt, but we've got to get you out of the street."

As he put his arms around her shoulders and under her knees, Lorcis thought, *Why do they have to get me out of the street? They don't even know me. Who are they?* At least they did not seem to want to hurt her, and if she remained where she was, she would certainly die. Besides, she ruefully conceded, she could do very little to stop them, whatever they had in mind.

They did not walk far, though the jostling of her battered body made the journey seem interminable. As they entered the house, Lorcis had the impression they were still very near the palace. *This woman must belong to a very wealthy family,* she thought.

"Take her to the blue bedroom," the woman said. "I'll get some things and be there soon."

A few minutes later Lorcis was lying on a bed with a blanket over her. The man who had carried her left as soon as he saw she was comfortable.

"You won't be able to get a bath for a few days," the woman said when she entered the room with a bowl of water and a towel, "but for now I can at least wash you off. That should make you feel better."

Lorcis lay back and relished the sensation of the warm water and the soft towel on her face, neck, hands, and arms. She flinched occasionally, but a sense of well-being settled over her. Though her vision was somewhat blurred, she could see that the woman tending to her was small, with delicate but not frail features. Her brown hair was gathered into a single braid and coiled around her head. She wore no makeup or jewelry, unusual for an aristocratic woman, but after all, Lorcis reminded herself, it was the middle of the night.

"You've been brutally mistreated," the woman commiserated, shaking her head in disbelief.

Lorcis turned her face away. The horror of the evening was still too vivid and, besides, she did not want the woman to ask who had done this to her. No one would believe that Domitian himself had tied her down, alternately raped and beaten her, and then had her dumped out into the street.

Then again, maybe someone *would* believe her. Martial had warned her not to go to the palace. Had he known something? Lorcis raised herself on one elbow and tried to speak to the woman, who was rinsing the towel and preparing to leave. But she could not form coherent words. Her swollen lips would not shape themselves and her jaw ached with every attempted sound.

The woman tenderly coaxed her back down onto the bed. "I'll make a poultice for your lip, then you need some sleep. Perhaps you'll be able to talk a bit when you've rested. You're quite safe here in my house," she said with a smile. "My name is Domitilla."

Domitian's niece!

For the next few days, Lorcis alternated between periods of restless sleep and wakeful anxiety. In her dreams she was tormented by visions of the horrible things Domitian had inflicted on her in his bedroom. She once woke up to find herself lying spread-eagled, acting out her nightmare. When she was awake, she lay tensely waiting for the heavy treads of Roman soldiers Domitilla summoned to take her back to the palace. It made no difference that there were no charges on which she could be arrested. What plagued her was the realization that Domitian had intended to kill her. She did not think he would want her left alive to spread stories of what went on in the inner chambers of the palace.

But the only people who came to her room were Domitilla and her soft-spoken, tender-hearted slaves.

These slaves seemed odd to Lorcis. In her own experience, slaves worked sullenly and listlessly unless directly supervised. They groused and gossiped behind their masters' backs and stole or consumed as much of his property as they could get away with. But Domitilla's slaves seemed to love her and carried out her orders—which were given in the tone of one friend asking a favor of another—promptly and meticulously.

Under their care, the pain in various parts of her body slowly subsided. By the end of the first week of her recuperation, the greatest discomfort she experienced was the rawness where Domitian had shaved her body hair. When Domitilla was bathing Lorcis, she noticed the disfigurement and the roughness with which it had obviously been inflicted. She said nothing about it, but her eyes had sought out Lorcis', and they had communicated all that was necessary without using words.

By this time, Lorcis was frantic to contact Fortunata and let her know she was all right. She also wanted to let Martial know her situation. They were the only two people in the vast population of Rome who would care in the least where she was—except for Jacob, of course. Even after their bitter parting, she knew he would still try to help her, but she did not see how he could: receiving a message from her might endanger him. Association, however tenuous, with an enemy of the emperor was a crime which obviated the necessity of trial or proof.

Saying more than a few words at a time was still difficult for her, so she asked for writing materials. When a stylus and wax tablet were brought, she quickly scratched a message to Fortunata, handed it to Domitilla, and croaked out, "Send this, please?" When Domitilla read the note, she shook her head. Lorcis panicked. *Now it comes out*, she thought. *I'm trapped.*

But Domitilla went on to explain her refusal. "You're better off if everyone presumes you're dead or just left Rome suddenly. No one asks questions these days when a person disappears. My uncle is a depraved monster who rules under the guise of an enlightened monarch. He cannot allow a survivor of his depravities to make them known. You're safe only as long as he believes you're dead."

She could see the alarm in Lorcis' eyes and took her hand to calm her. "I share only a family name with my uncle. I detest everything he stands for. I can't undo the great evil he does as emperor, but I try to make small differences where I can. You can stay here as long as you need to. Then we'll figure out some place away from Rome where you can live safely."

The days turned hot and the nights were hardly any cooler. Lorcis felt well enough that she began to get restless. She remembered the late summer months spent in the cool of Regulus' estate north of Rome and reflected that Jacob and the other people she had known in the house had probably escaped the heat and were enjoying that retreat. Even at her modest farm on the outskirts of the city, August had not been this oppressive. She felt if she could just get out of the stifling room into the garden she would feel better, but movement still caused enough pain that she did no more than she had to. One night, ten days after her encounter with Domitian, she simply could not sleep. She decided to make her way to the relative coolness of the garden, whatever the cost in discomfort to her aching body.

The garden was large, and it wasn't until she had made her way painfully to the middle of it, where there would be the best chance for a breeze, that she heard a murmur of voices. She couldn't imagine what a group of people would be doing in this part of the house so late at night. Her first suspicion was that a group of slaves, in spite of their superficial happiness, might be plotting something against Domitilla. She decided to find out what was afoot.

Moving from bush to column to avoid detection, she crept close to an open door. Inside the dimly lit room she could see a group of fifteen or more people. This was the largest room in the house, but it must have been stifling in the evening heat; the sweat on the brows of the people sitting closest to the door testified to that.

But what were they doing? Who were they? Why were they here at this hour? She recognized a couple of Domitilla's servants, but there were other people there whom she did not know. A nighttime meeting, seemingly secret, was highly unusual, even suspect. The Roman government, extremely sensitive to plots, had long forbidden groups to meet at night without a permit. Domitilla had mentioned opposing Domitian; was this a conspiracy in the making?

After one person briefly spoke, his words indistinct, the entire group began to sing. Lorcis could not make out all they were saying, but the repetition of the words "Jesus Christus" was clear enough. These people were Christians!

Her first instinct was to return to her room and pretend she had heard nothing. Something held her to that spot, however, and when the singing stopped, another voice began to speak. Although the cadence was slower than Lorcis remembered, the dignity and grace that had marked Jacob's speech were undiminished by age.

Lorcis moved around to the side of the column nearest the door. She had hoped to observe Jacob without being seen, but the arrangement of the room made that impossible; her vision of him was blocked by the open door. Did she dare go in? What would they do to her when they realized that she knew them to be Christians? They hadn't done anything to her the whole time she had been here, but would they hurt her now?

She wanted to stand at the back of the room and remain unnoticed long enough to glimpse Jacob. Her first glance at the interior, however, revealed a much larger crowd than she would have imagined possible. Several of the men wore on their tunics the broad purple stripe which identified them as senators. But they were mixed in at random with slaves and freedmen. One senator was even sitting on the floor next to a slave or freedman who was sitting on a stool. Under Roman law, that simple arrangement would result in death for the slave.

An apprehensive murmur shot around the room when the crowd noticed Lorcis. No one moved to expel her, but people glanced uncertainly at one another. Jacob looked at her, smiled, and raised his open arms to her.

"It's all right," he said to the group. "I know Lorcis. She is not fully one of us yet, but God has his eye on her."

There was that damnable 'God has a plan for you' business again, Lorcis thought. But the love and warmth radiating from the old man held her, prevented her from turning to leave, and finally drew her into his arms.

Holding her with an arm around her shoulders, Jacob addressed the group again. "Though she is not one of us, Lorcis has a special connection to this church. Her father was Lazarus, the very Lazarus Jesus raised from the dead."

There was an appreciative gasp and a buzz of conversation before Jacob continued. "Some of you are recent converts and may not have heard this story." He motioned for quiet. "Even those who know it can profit once more from hearing this remarkable testimony to the power of God."

He looked expectantly at Lorcis. "Will you stay with us, my child? Even you haven't heard the entire story."

Lorcis nodded and was helped to a seat beside one of the senators in the group. Looking around the room, she saw pleasant faces which fairly glowed with contentment, an expression that seldom graced the scowling Roman countenance. She would have thought these people foreigners had she not seen the obvious signs of their Romanness, such as the senatorial stripes and the gold rings that several wealthy members of the equestrian order wore.

When everyone was settled again, Jacob began to tell the story, and his listeners turned their faces up toward him like a group of children gathered around their grandfather to listen to some favorite old tale.

"Three of Jesus' closest friends," Jacob began quietly, "were Lazarus and his older sisters Mary and Martha. They lived together in Bethany, a small village outside Jerusalem. One day Lazarus, who was about twenty, was taken ill. His sisters sent word to Jesus, hoping he would come and heal his friend just as he had healed so many others, even strangers and foreigners. But Jesus seemed in no hurry to respond to their plea. He didn't even turn his face toward Bethany until he received word that Lazarus was dead, and he didn't arrive in the village until four days later. Now, that's important. Under Jewish law, revival of the dead is considered possible until the end of the third day. But by the fourth day the process of decay is deemed irreversible.

"Mary and Martha met Jesus as he walked up to the house, berating him for not coming sooner. Jesus didn't say a word, although an eyewitness has told me that he was weeping silently. He strode out to the burial ground and stood in front of Lazarus' tomb, ordering some of the men who had accompanied him to remove the stone that covered the entrance. Those who were there tell me that he raised his face to heaven, closed his eyes, and clenched his fists as though concentrating God's power into himself. Then, in a voice that nearly deafened those around him, he commanded 'Lazarus, come forth!' "

Jacob paused and slowly surveyed the half circle of upturned faces, stopping on Lorcis'. "There was a moment of silence, then a grey figure slowly emerged from the darkness of the tomb. Lazarus walked slowly into the sunlight and struggled a bit with the grave clothes which still wrapped him." Jacob's happiness and excitement were as fresh as though he were telling the story for the first time, and he infected his hearers.

"Nobody knew quite what to say or do," he stated with a smile. "What would you do if a friend of yours walked out of his grave?" Everyone chuckled and nodded their heads. "All Jesus said was 'Give him something to eat.' Jesus was really a very practical man."

Jacob now turned deliberately, even reverently, to a table holding a bottle of wine and a loaf of bread and picked up Lorcis' medallion, now framed in silver to hold the three pieces together. "This picture of our Lord was painted by Lazarus after his resurrection—and he became the father of Lorcis after his resurrection, too. So you can see, he was alive in every sense of the word."

Someone behind Lorcis asked, "Elder Jacob, what happened to Lazarus after that?"

"I regret that I do not know," Jacob replied with a shrug. "He did flee to Antioch during the persecution of the church in Judaea that followed the stoning of Stephen. There was already a strong church in Antioch, and many Judaean Christians settled there, including Peter. I know the legend that, once having been raised from the dead, he could not die again. But I do not believe that. God raised Lazarus to show his power to all men, not to grant immortality to one person. There is already a dangerous tendency afoot among some Christians to read too much into Jesus' actions and words. It's not surprising that we have no record of Lazarus' death. Those were chaotic times for the church, and record-keeping is a luxury when one's survival is in doubt."

Domitilla raised her hand tentatively to indicate that she would like to speak. Lorcis was marveling over the novelty of an aristocrat asking a slave—not a lower class free person or even a freedman, but a slave—for permission to speak when she realized that Domitilla was addressing her. "Your father, Lorcis, do you know anything about him?"

"Unfortunately, no," Lorcis replied diffidently. "My mother told me that he died when I was a few months old. She remarried, and my stepfather sold me when I was five."

"What a pity," Domitilla said with gentle compassion. "To be so close to a link to Jesus, then to have it broken by the inhuman act of selling a child into slavery." Her voice took on added fervor as she turned toward Jacob. "I would give anything just to have had a glimpse of Jesus as you did, Elder Jacob."

"Now, now, my sister," Jacob scolded her kindly. "Remember Jesus' words to the apostle Thomas who would not believe in the resurrection until he had seen Jesus himself. Our Lord said,

'Have you believed because you have seen me? Blessed are those who have not seen and yet believe.' " Domitilla shook her head slowly as tears ran down her cheeks. "I believe, Lord!" she moaned. "Help my unbelief."

Jacob replaced the medallion on the table behind the wine and bread. Turning to face the group once again, he spoke with a new solemnity. "The resurrection of Lazarus was a significant event in itself. It had a deeper meaning, however; it foreshadowed the resurrection of Jesus. And it is that resurrection which gives us our hope. These common table elements are signs of that hope, given new meaning by Jesus himself on the night before he died."

He stopped and raised his arms, spreading his sleeves as if to hide the table from view. "We have come to that point in our worship where those who have been baptized according to the commandment of the Lord will share in the meal which he shared with his disciples. Those who have not yet been baptized will be asked to leave until the completion of this eucharist."

A half dozen people rose and made their way to the door. Helped by the senator sitting at her feet, Lorcis joined the small group sitting in the garden. Because she did not know what to say to any of them, this seemed the logical time to go to her room and escape the necessity of returning to the meeting. Jacob, though, would be disappointed, and she sensed that the others in the group wanted her back. And somehow, she felt eager to go back.

She sat with her back toward the others and watched the door intently, partly because she was anxious for it to open and partly to avoid having to join in any conversation with these strangers—strangers not just in the sense that she did not know their names, but because their whole manner of life was contrary to everything normal.

Absorbed in such thoughts, she was startled by a hand placed on her shoulder. Turning and looking up, she found a handsome young man staring at her. Something about him was familiar, but she could not recall where she might have met him.

"Forgive my boldness," he apologized, "but I feel I know you, if only slightly. I am Zosimus, a slave of your friend Pliny."

"Yes, of course," Lorcis smiled in relief. "I have enjoyed hearing you read and sing at several dinner parties. And Pliny has nothing but the highest praise for you."

"I am fortunate," Zosimus replied, "to have so humane a master. Jacob—and you also, I understand—have not fared so well."

"No, we haven't," Lorcis said ruefully. "I'm lucky enough to have escaped. Poor Jacob has had to serve so many long years under that monster. But he seems able to endure anything," she added, recalling the horror of his family's destruction in the siege of Jerusalem.

"He lives his faith," Zosimus said with admiration. "He's an example to us all."

"Does Pliny know you're a Christian?" Lorcis asked impulsively.

"No," Zosimus replied. "I doubt he would approve. It's not truly Roman to be a Christian, you see, and my master is nothing if not truly Roman."

"But if you're out here now you're not fully a Christian yet, I take it."

"That's right," Zosimus said. "I am what we call a catechumen, one who is being instructed in the faith. Soon I'll be baptized and will become a full member," he added proudly.

"What are they doing in there?" Lorcis asked with a jerk of her head toward the room.

Zosimus hesitated, glancing toward the door as if it could give him guidance.

"Are the rumors true?" Lorcis pounced. "Are they really drinking blood and eating someone's body?" She could not believe for a moment that Jacob would do such things.

"No, no," Zosimus laughed knowingly. "I hesitate to answer because you aren't even a catechumen, and I'm reluctant to reveal too much to an outsider. But I see you have some knowledge of the charges against us, and Jacob vouches for you, so I suppose it will do no harm. They are re-enacting the last meal which Jesus ate with his disciples. They share the bread and wine, which recalls his broken body and shed blood, then repeat words which he said on that occasion. And finally, they sing a hymn in his honor."

"And that's all?"

"That's all. Our enemies, of course, have spread all sorts of outlandish lies. They accuse us of cannibalism, even of kidnapping children and devouring them. You didn't see any dead children in there, did you?" Zosimus joked.

Lorcis knew that he did not intend to hurt her, but she could see only one dead child in her mind. Closing her eyes, she bowed her head. Would that wound never heal? She needed to change the subject.

"Everyone's so respectful to Jacob," she observed. "What is his position in this group?"

"He's our presiding officer and teacher. This is a new community which he's helping to start. His own group meets on the Caelian Hill in a house near Regulus'. We'll soon be large enough, though, to choose our own elder, probably Flavius, though that's not a foregone conclusion."

The door opened at that moment and one of the women in the room invited the catechumens and Lorcis back in for a final hymn and a farewell blessing. Jacob prayed for God's care of each person by name and then walked over to where Domitilla was sitting. Taking both her hands between his, he kissed her lightly on each cheek and said, "The peace of God go with you, my sister."

Domitilla then turned to the slave sitting next to her and passed the blessing along in the same fashion. As it went around the room, Lorcis marveled at the joy and, yes, peace on the face of every person in the room and felt herself caught up in the beauty of the moment. When Zosimus turned to take her hands, however, she drew away. He hesitated only briefly, then reached across her to the man on her left and passed the blessing on to him.

Lorcis could not keep back her tears nor could she explain them. These people, these good people, loved Jesus in a way she had never known anyone to love a god. Greeks and Romans worshiped their gods basically out of fear. Their worship was a contract: the god provided protection if the worshiper provided enough sacrifices. Such a religion had no effect on a devotee's relationships with other people, even others who practiced the same cult. But these Christians loved their God, and that love made them love one another.

Could she love Jesus? No—not until she could blot out the vision of Erotion's fever-racked face. To her, Jesus was still the one whose image had hung over that bed, powerless or—more damning yet—unwilling to save her child. Until that injustice could be explained—it could never be made right—she could not, would not, love Jesus. Even if he had raised her father from the dead and thus, however indirectly, given her life, he had taken that gift back when Erotion died. She could not yet forgive him for that. She wondered if she ever would.

Another week passed, and Lorcis felt strong enough to get out on her own. The worst of her aches and bruises were barely noticeable, but Domitian had taken his toll. In spite of Domitilla's tender care, Lorcis now bore a scar on her lower lip and several less obvious marks on her arms and torso. Her left hip had been dislocated, leaving her with a slight limp. Any hope of charming Roman society had vanished along with her beauty. Lorcis saw herself as a disfigured cripple and even bathed quickly, loath to look at herself any longer than necessary. Without Domitilla's encouragement, she would have even given up fixing her hair and face.

Since she was ten, her life had centered around her physical beauty. She had put her intelligence and musical talents to good use, but it was her beauty which had gained her the attention necessary to capitalize on those other aspects of her personality. It had been her entree to any society—but that was now gone. How would she live? What did she have to make herself desirable to other people? *Martial would never have looked at me twice if I had looked like this when I bought his silly book,* she reflected disconsolately.

So there was the problem of what to do with her—not that Domitilla or anyone else phrased it quite so bluntly. But Lorcis felt a tension building within herself to stop temporizing and to begin whatever new phase of her life was about to unfold. No options seemed left to her in or around Rome. Domitilla was right: the emperor would not allow her to resume her old life as though nothing had happened. Too many people had seen her leave the party with him. Lorcis suggested that Domitilla tell her uncle to circulate the story that she'd been beaten by a gang of hoodlums on her way home that night.

"That might work for a time," Domitilla replied, "just because the emperor and I are the ones telling the story. But no one will really believe it, and Domitian would soon resent that he was being blackmailed. Then you—and Flavius and I—would be worse off than ever. No, you must leave Rome and its environs entirely."

Lorcis knew Domitilla was right; besides, she had no real desire to stay in the capital in her present condition. "But where can I go?" she almost moaned. "A single woman, deformed, with no money?"

"You make yourself sound absolutely hopeless," Domitilla protested. "You have your own remarkable instinct for survival, the love of a number of friends, and the watchful care of God, whether you acknowledge it or not," she added as Lorcis shook her head.

Taking a deep breath, Domitilla went on. "There is one possibility that we haven't talked about, Lorcis. The place may not be ideal, but it is secure and out of the public eye—and quite comfortable, as a matter of fact."

Lorcis raised her head hopefully as Domitilla took her hand.

"We have an estate near Milan," the older woman continued, "a lovely place, really."

Lorcis winced and lowered her head. So it had come to this. Roman nobles frequently sent elderly or disabled servants to their country estates when they had no more use for them and put them to picking grapes or feeding pigs. She had not expected such treatment from Domitilla.

"The overseer on this estate, a man named Junicus, lost his wife several months ago when she gave birth to a little girl. He has not been able to find a woman there to care for his daughter in a manner that suits him."

Lorcis' heart beat faster.

"I realize you lost a child of your own and that this may be too much to ask of you, but to Flavius and me it seems to be the best option. Junicus is an older man, in his mid-forties, a Christian, and he would not make any demands of you. He needs a mother for his child, he says, not necessarily a wife. Will you do it?"

BOOK V

August - September, A.D. 96

CHAPTER XXV

The dust of a vehicle racing up the road toward the house caused Lorcis to stop splitting wood and raise a hand to shade her eyes against the late afternoon sun. The small hill on which the overseer's modest house sat gave her a clear view of the road which led from where she was standing, past the gate of Domitilla and Flavius' villa several hundred yards to the north, then curved and ran another quarter of a mile until it joined the Via Aemiliana, the paved highway between Rome and Milan. As the carriage shot past the villa, Lorcis recognized it as belonging to her patrons. There was only one person in it besides the driver, which ordinarily meant that a messenger was coming to get the place ready for a visit from Domitilla and Flavius. But they had made their annual visit to the estate two months ago, and they never came in August except for special occasions, such as Lorcis' wedding to Junicus seven years earlier. Why would they send someone now? Was there a problem with their last report on the harvest and the financial condition of the estate? some trouble in Rome?

Well, no use speculating, Lorcis reminded herself. *One thing's for certain. There'll be two more mouths to feed at supper.* "Maria," she called into the house, "put two more plates out for supper."

"Yes, mama," her nine-year-old stepdaughter replied.

Assuming that the messenger would want to see her husband, she slammed her axe into the stump she had been using as a chopping block and turned toward the stable. She found Junicus there working with one of the slaves on a broken harness.

"There's a carriage coming up the road, Junicus," she said. "You'd better see what they want." She then headed for the house to get supper ready.

"They always ask to see him," she muttered to herself. "Don't they realize that I practically run the place now?" Not that Junicus was incompetent or even particularly stupid. He was a German, captured as a boy during Civilis' unsuccessful revolt on the northern frontier some thirty years earlier. He was several inches taller than the average Roman, with broad shoulders, large hands, and reddish-orange hair which he had passed on to Maria.

Junicus was really not an ignorant man—it was his lack of education that hampered him. Of necessity he had learned a serviceable Latin but he often fell into German sentence patterns which made his speech seem quaint to those who loved him and uncouth to those who did not. He could not read or write until Lorcis came to the estate. She had taught him, partly to allay her boredom and partly because she did not want the burden of preparing the reports they had to send to Stephanus, Domitilla's chief steward at Rome. Within six months of her arrival, Junicus was proudly signing his own name to the documents. A year later he could write out the complete report himself, albeit slowly. No, he was not ignorant, but he was unimaginative and indecisive. The estate had barely made a profit under his management, but with Lorcis making suggestions, it was now Domitilla and Flavius' most profitable business venture.

"Yet, they still ask for Junicus every time they send a messenger," she groused, "just because his name's on the report."

Maria had the table set and was chopping vegetables for a stew. Lorcis smiled at her and ran a hand through the girl's long, silky hair.

"That looks like plenty," she said. "Get me a bucket of water now while I get the kettle set up."

"Yes, mama."

She watched contentedly as her daughter—technically her stepdaughter, but hers in every real sense—hurried to the well. Only infrequently now did memories of Erotion haunt her. Not that Maria replaced Erotion in her affection; they were entirely different little girls. But she had found room in her heart for both of them. Her deepest regret in life was that she had been unable to bear Junicus a child. Twice she had been pregnant, but both times she lost the baby after only a few months. She blamed Domitian for that.

Junicus stuck his head in the back door. "Lorcis, this man brings a message for you."

The messenger wanted her? That was as remarkable as his untimely arrival. Lorcis went to the door where the man stood patiently behind Junicus. In the background, the driver led his tired horses to the stable, Maria walking with him, deluging him with questions about Rome, no doubt. The young girl had never seen a town larger than Milan, which was no more than a good-sized village, and Lorcis' painful memories made her reluctant to talk much about the capital. So the child seized any visitors and plied them for information.

"What news do you have for me?" Lorcis asked the messenger.

He stepped forward, uncertain how to address her. Was her status the same as his or should she be addressed as a superior? Finally, he resolved his quandry by adopting a very formal tone as though he were reading a document.

"I am Nereus, freedman of Domitilla. My lady has asked me to inform you that your friend Jacob is perilously ill. He insists he will recover, but my lady Domitilla is not so confident. She thinks you might want to see him once more. If you wish to go to Rome, I am instructed to take you there tomorrow."

It was not surprising that a seventy-five-year old man should be ill, but Lorcis had begun to believe Jacob's oft-repeated prophecy that he would die in the arena, though that had begun to seem unlikely. His fortunes had improved in recent years. He had been living in Domitilla's house since she purchased him from Regulus, who considered him too old and slow to manage his affairs any longer. Domitilla had assured Regulus that her household was not nearly so magnificent as his and that an experienced steward like Nestor could be of service to her own steward, Stephanus. She had privately given Jacob his freedom, and he had devoted the past two years to preaching about Jesus and furthering the work of the church. He had written to Lorcis several times.

"What's wrong with him?" she asked.

"It's his stomach. He can't keep any food down and has severe pains," Nereus replied. "The doctors have prescribed cold lettuce compresses, but the problem persists."

Lorcis pursed her lips and touched her clasped hands to her mouth. "My husband and I will need to discuss the matter," she said. "You will have your answer at supper."

"Very well," Nereus nodded. "I'll attend to the horses and carriage until then." He bowed, but only slightly, and turned toward the stable.

Junicus waited until the messenger was out of earshot, then smiled and said, "You don't need to talk to me about it. If your friend is sick, you should go to him. We'll manage without you for a few days."

"Are you saying you don't need me?" Lorcis teased.

Junicus took her hands, one of his rare spontaneous gestures of affection. "I can't imagine life without you," he said urgently. "All the years of my life before you came along were meaningless, hardly life at all."

"You sound like I'm leaving you for good," Lorcis replied, trying to lighten a suddenly serious moment.

"I know it's only temporary," Junicus shrugged, "but it will be the first time we've been separated since we were married. Waiting for your return will seem like forever."

Lorcis patted his hand tenderly. How ironic. After years of searching for happiness and trying to fall in love with a handsome, witty young man, she had discovered profound contentment in a pragmatic marriage with an older, gruff, poorly educated man she did not love—at least, not in the way she had always defined love. Could there be a plan behind it all, as Jacob believed? "It's just chance," she said softly, not realizing she had spoken aloud.

"What?" Junicus asked, squinting as though it would help him to hear.

"I mean, there's a chance I might be gone for several days, a week perhaps," Lorcis said, snapping out of her reverie. "Jacob is a hardy old character, and he won't give up without a fight. I personally doubt that he's ready to die yet." She didn't mention his prophecy about the arena—there was no sense in disturbing Junicus.

"Well, stay as long as you need to," Junicus said paternally as he got up to see that their guests had everything they needed for their horses.

During supper Junicus was silent, studying his plate as though he needed to identify every piece of food he ate. The conversation focused exclusively on Rome, a place Junicus had never seen but thoroughly despised. In spite of herself, Lorcis could not help being interested in Nereus' news about people she had known and, in some cases, loved.

Martial was the city's new poet laureate, the unchallenged master of the epigram. His poems, especially the scurrilous ones, were on everybody's lips. To be mentioned by name in one of them, even in ridicule, was the height of social distinction.

Pliny was the most famous lawyer in Rome, compared even to the great Cicero. He walked a difficult road, daring to voice his opposition to Domitian on occasion but also receiving important appointments from the emperor, who seemed to respect his honesty.

But most honest men had to be content with the emperor's admiration at arm's length because the man who had his ear was Regulus. His insinuations and innuendos were enflaming the young emperor's naturally suspicious nature into paranoia. Arrests for treason, on even the most specious charges, were daily occurrences. Even an elderly imperial secretary, Epaphroditus, had been executed because as a young man obeying his emperor's order, he had steadied the sword on which Nero had hurled himself to commit suicide. Domitian did not want it said that a man could kill an emperor and live unpunished. That would set a bad precedent.

"Things are tense," Nereus concluded. "Our lord and lady are secure because of their relationship to the emperor. He has even adopted their two sons and designated them as his heirs since he has no children of his own."

And likely will not have, Lorcis thought, touching the scar on her lip thoughtfully as she wiped her mouth after a bite of stew. *Women don't often get pregnant when treated in the fashion he likes—or survive to give birth.*

"Two weeks ago," Nereus continued proudly, "he even invited the boys to come live in the palace for a time."

"Did Domitilla and Flavius let them go?" Lorcis asked uneasily.

"Yes. Why?"

"Oh, well, I . . . just think it is important . . . that young children be with their parents," Lorcis stammered. The thought that had prompted her question was that Domitian had actually taken the children hostage or was removing them in preparation for action against Flavius and Domitilla. But it was an intuition supported only by her hatred of the man.

Nereus resumed his report. "At least the work of the church is prospering. Under Jacob's leadership the congregation in our house has grown so large it has split and another group, led by the former consul Glabrio, has been formed."

"Very impressive," Lorcis nodded, hoping she sounded polite, but not wanting to encourage this train of conversation. The whole subject of Christianity still raised her hackles. When Junicus had finally stopped pressing her to become a catechumen, she had agreed to let him give Maria instruction in the faith and to remain silent about her own doubts. They seldom discussed the matter, but Lorcis knew her husband was disappointed in her refusal to share his faith.

Junicus suddenly cleared his throat and everyone turned to the end of the table where, virtually forgotten, he had been munching like some great ox amidst the gabble. Even with all eyes fixed expectantly on him, he still waited before saying anything. This habit had given him a reputation for wisdom in and around Milan, but Lorcis knew he was, as he himself put it, just getting his words into proper Roman order so they would not come rushing out like a tribe of Germans barging across the frontier.

"You said that senators' slaves, even some senators themselves, have become members of the church?"

"Yes," Nereus replied cautiously, uncertain whether Junicus was asking a question or making an accusation.

"Have any of them been arrested for treason yet?"

"None, so far as I know. Why do you ask?"

"Well, in all this prosperity you've been describing, we seem to forget that it's against the law to be a Christian. In the eyes of the emperor, our faith is a crime punishable by death, an unspeakable death in the arena. The emperor hasn't been much interested in us recently, so it's been kind of easy to be a Christian—exciting even. We have secret meetings, signals passed to other Christians in public. It's become a game. But if Domitian should arrest some senator for treason and find out he's a Christian, then he'll suddenly have a new whipping boy."

Nereus squirmed, more in irritation than in fear, but Junicus went on. "That's what happened with Nero and the great fire. He didn't plan to blame it on the Christians, but when he got to arresting people and trying to find some group of bandits or thugs to use as scapegoats, he found us."

"I'm too young to remember that era personally," Nereus said condescendingly.

Junicus glared at him. "That's precisely my point," he growled, thumping the table with his index finger on every word. "You're all too young! So you talk about the glorious martyrs and pretend you want to be like them. Have you ever seen someone die in the arena?"

"No," Nereus admitted. "Christians don't go to the games."

"Well, I have, right here in Milan," Junicus replied. "And they don't just die, my friend. They scream in agony and mess all over themselves. And they bleed. God, do they bleed!"

"Junicus, please!" Lorcis yelled, putting her arms around Maria and drawing the child's head to her breast.

"I don't see what all this has to do with us," Nereus said agitatedly.

"Domitian may not have arrested a Christian senator yet," Junicus intoned, shaking his finger like a prophet, "but if he keeps up what he's doing, he's bound to get one of us. And when he finds a Christian senator 'plotting' against him, all Christians will stand accused of the same crime."

Supper was finished with a minimum of conversation and then Junicus escorted Nereus and the driver to the villa where they would spend the night. As she and Maria cleaned up the kitchen, Lorcis went over the things the young girl would need to do over the next few days. There was the vegetable garden to weed, chickens to feed, and eggs to gather. Some of the tasks were the girl's regular responsibilities, but Lorcis couldn't refrain from being a mother. She might never have the chance again.

"There's one more thing. The day after tomorrow is Aunt Xanthippe's birthday. Can you make the offerings at her grave? I know your father won't approve, but maybe while he's working you could slip out there and leave a small cake and pour out some wine. It's not really a religious observance, you know. I don't believe in the old gods any more than your father does. It's just a way to acknowledge that she was important to us."

"I will, mama," Maria promised, and started off to bed.

"Give me a hug, young lady," Lorcis called after her, pretending to scold. "You're not that big yet."

With her daughter tended to, Lorcis turned her attention to preparing for the trip. Jacob sick, Xanthippe dead; the memories flooded over her. She wanted to do what she could for Jacob just as she had tried to do for Xanthippe. Once she felt secure and settled on the estate, she had asked Domitilla to have one of her financial agents check around in Masillia to see if he could find Xanthippe. When they located her, Domitilla had been quite willing to buy her freedom—old, drunken, abused prostitutes didn't cost much—and allow her to live on the estate with Lorcis. Xanthippe had not been well for most of the four years she'd spent there, but at least Lorcis had made her comfortable and provided her a decent funeral. It was little enough to do for a friend.

She had almost finished packing when Junicus returned. He sat on the bed watching her, saying nothing.

"You don't want me to go to Rome, do you," Lorcis asked, stopping in the midst of folding a stola.

"Maybe I worry too much about things that won't ever happen," he replied. "At the moment, there's no danger to you in Rome—at least, no more than usual," he added, running a finger lightly over one of the scars Domitian had left on her arm. "Your good friend is very sick. If you feel you have to go, then you have to go. It's not mine to permit or forbid you anything. It never has been," he added with a smile. "You are my wife, not my slave."

"I'll be eternally grateful to you for saying that," Lorcis replied, "and for believing it."

She bent down to kiss him. As their lips met, she lost her balance and they tumbled over onto the bed, laughing. Their lovemaking was passionate, as it always was, but more prolonged and skillful than it had been seven years ago.

Afterwards, Junicus held her in his arms as she slept. The prospect of her departure troubled him intensely. In nine years he had come to rely on her, to adore her. He'd had two earlier wives—and a dozen or so other women, he admitted to himself with a blush—but no woman had ever possessed him the way Lorcis did. She had civilized him, giving him literacy and whatever social graces he now boasted. She had taught him to make love instead of merely copulating.

He shook his head as he recalled their wedding night. He had approached her with all the tenderness of a rutting animal. No one had ever taught him anything about the finer points of making love. He had learned the basic facts from watching animals mate on the farm where he had first been enslaved. The slave girls and prostitutes he had known as a young man had only been interested in finishing quickly to avoid detection or to collect their money. Consequently, he had grown accustomed to dealing with all women that way.

Lorcis was the first woman in his experience who wanted him to slow down, to give her time to enjoy what they were doing. Junicus was surprised to learn that she could experience a sensation similar to his own if he took time to kiss and caress her in the ways she taught him. And she knew ways to please him that he had never dreamed possible.

At first he had been put off by her behavior in bed. To his way of thinking, only whores knew such perverse things. But she was a good wife and a fine mother. He knew enough of her background to understand why she had a certain sexual expertise, and once he stopped worrying about how many men she had done a particular thing with, he began to experience physical delights he had thought only emperors could know.

Lorcis stirred and whimpered, her face wincing. She did that too often, Junicus thought, wondering what unpleasant incident from her past was disturbing her sleep this time. He stroked her hair with a gentleness he would not have been capable of a few years ago.

"She'll only be gone for a few days," he assured himself, "and she's taught Maria to be a real help around here. So we'll be all right till she gets back. We'll be all right . . ." he muttered as he dozed off.

It was not fully daylight the next morning when Lorcis poured water from a bucket into a shallow kettle on the hearth and began to wash herself by the light of the fire. There was no sense taking a full bath now; the trip would be dusty and she would need to bathe upon arriving in Rome.

As she laved herself, she noticed how much of a country woman she had become. She had gained no weight—the work was too hard for that—and her body was strong, sinewy. Her skin, brown from the sun, would look like leather next to the soft white complexions of Roman noblewomen who prided themselves on avoiding the sun and any work which had to be performed in it. Those with naturally darker skin resorted to bleaching creams and heavy white powder to achieve the pale, languid look so in vogue among the upper classes.

And her hands. The hands that had once run so gracefully up and down a flute were now accustomed to wielding an axe or a meat cleaver. Looking at them, she became conscious of the callouses and the roughness of the skin against the smoother parts of her body. Perhaps she could keep them folded in her lap while she was in Rome.

She smiled ruefully, anticipating how out of place she would be among the people she had once dreamed of dominating with her beauty and wit. "But I'm not going to see those people," she reminded herself. "This is just a short visit to see Jacob. I probably won't even get outside the house."

CHAPTER XXVI

Pliny took the letter which his scribes had just finished copying and read it over for mistakes, to be certain it expressed exactly what he intended:

Gaius Plinius to his friend Attius, greetings.

Regulus has lost his son, a tragedy which even he did not deserve. The boy was intelligent but erratic. He might have been a decent sort of young man had he not taken so strongly after his father. Regulus now grieves extravagantly. The boy had a regular menagerie of pets: horses, dogs, and birds of all kinds. Regulus had them all slaughtered around the funeral pyre. That, I submit, was not grief but a display of grief.

It is unbelievable how he is surrounded by people who despise him and yet crowd around him as though they admire him, even love him. He does not seem to notice that they are courting him by his own methods. He keeps to his gardens across the Tiber, where he has buried acres and acres of land under huge porticoes and cluttered the riverbank with statuary. He is extravagant, for all his greed, and proud of his reputation, bad though it is. Thus he keeps the city in a turmoil and consoles himself by irritating everyone else.

He even says he wants to get married again, and he is as perverse on this subject as he is in everything else. You will soon hear that this old codger is taking a wife, probably still wearing his mourning garments. How can I predict this? Not from what Regulus says (nothing could be less reliable), but because it is certain that Regulus will do whatever he ought not to.

Farewell.

"Too sarcastic?" he asked himself, then shook his head in reply. Being childless himself at thirty-five, after two marriages, he did feel a twinge of sympathy for his old enemy. A child was a man's hope of immortality. But this was not, strictly speaking, a man. This was Regulus, and with Regulus there was no such thing as too much sarcasm.

He placed the letter on the table and folded down a flap beginning a quarter of the way down from the top and a similar flap coming up from the bottom. Taking a stick of wax he softened the end of it over his lamp and pressed it onto the papyrus where the two flaps met, sealing the letter. He then pressed into the wax his signet ring with its unique design of a boy and a dolphin swimming together. Every Roman with any pretensions to social standing had such a ring with his own distinctive design on it. Worn on the right index finger, it served as a man's signature, almost a fingerprint. A document sealed in this fashion could not be opened without destroying the seal and leaving evidence of the tampering.

Writing Attius' name on the outside, Pliny placed the letter in a small box with three others to be delivered by a servant traveling to his estate at Ticinum, south of Milan. All were just chatty little notes, none dealing with anything weightier than the death of Regulus' son. Pliny longed to write the real news to someone, but it was too early to know how the issue would be resolved, and he did not want to commit himself to one side or the other, even in a letter to a friend.

The real news had spread across Rome like Nero's fire: Glabrio, former consul and member of the senate, had been arrested just before dawn on treason charges. Almost a dozen of his slaves and freedmen had been seized along with him. Glabrio was a senior member of the senate, one of Domitian's chief advisors, the highest-ranking nobleman thus far arrested in Domitian's purge. What alarmed everyone in Pliny's circle was that his arrest made it clear that no one was immune from suspicion.

"Perhaps he'll be found innocent," his friend Tacitus had offered when Pliny told him the news. "He's just been arrested.

He's not been tried or condemned yet."

"Open your eyes!" Pliny had remonstrated. "How many people have been found innocent thus far?"

"None," Tacitus had conceded glumly.

"Even if those who've been condemned were actually guilty, Domitian's got little to worry about," Pliny added sarcastically. "We're such an inept pack of conspirators. If the whole senate is involved, as Domitian suspects, there are four hundred of us, and he's still alive. It took only sixty senators to do in Julius Caesar."

He and Tacitus had exchanged despairing glances. Had anyone overheard them? Could Pliny trust Tacitus not to report his statement? Repeated in Domitian's ear, that comment could be Pliny's death warrant—and Tacitus', too, if he did not report it and someone else informed Domitian that Tacitus had heard it and had done nothing.

But no one had come to arrest him during the day so perhaps he had escaped. Now, as evening darkened the city, Pliny rubbed his hands over his eyes. The left one was acting up again, a bit pussy, sensitive to light. Mustn't show any change of behavior or life-style, though. Someone would interpret it as sinister. "Oh, gods, how long can this go on!" he muttered.

The carriage bearing Nereus and Lorcis reached Rome as the sun went down and the ban on vehicular traffic was lifted for the night. The streets were lightly traveled by a few weary souls getting home late for supper. The carriage entered the Flaminian Gate on the northwest side of the city and followed the Via Lata through the section known as the Campus Martius, originally a flat plain between the Tiber and the edge of the city kept open for military training. As the population had grown, however, buildings had crept into it. The first had been raised by Pompey and Julius Caesar. Then Augustus' general Agrippa had put up a huge bath and a temple—the Pantheon, or temple of all the gods—and apartment houses soon crowded around them. Gradually, it had become as densely inhabited as any other part of Rome. The buildings were newer and the streets a bit broader and straighter, but it was as dirty and as dangerous by night as any other sector. Being relatively far from the center of town, it remained a less desirable and less expensive district, drawing people who could not afford to live in the better areas.

As they neared the heart of Rome, they skirted the base of the Capitoline Hill and turned onto the Via Sacra, which led along the edge of the Forum at the foot of the Palatine Hill. An unnamed side road took them halfway up the Palatine, then the driver turned into an alley that led to the stable at the back of Flavius and Domitilla's house.

The relatively small house sat just below the walls of Domitian's newly enlarged—or engorged, as Pliny silently considered it—palace. The last private dwellings on the top of the hill had been demolished to make room for the expansion. The only houses left on the east side of the hill belonged to members of the imperial family and their favorites. The steeper western side formed part of the Circus Maximus, and Domitian, as mad about chariots as any plebeian, had built his own private entrance leading from the palace directly to the imperial box in the stands above the race course. In fact, still not sated with the races, he had built a smaller stadium atop the Palatine, within the palace walls, where the best drivers raced before the emperor and his privileged guests.

By the time the carriage stopped before a door, it had grown completely dark. The driver got down and pulled a leather thong that rang a bell inside the house. When no one answered promptly, he rang again. After yet another delay, he rang more vigorously and pounded on the door. A peephole in the door finally opened and an eye peered out at them. "Open up!" the driver bellowed. "Don't leave us standing out here like unexpected company!"

The servant, opening the door to the stable yard, seemed agitated, checking to see if anyone was in the street as he closed and locked the gate. He quickly guided the horses to the center of the area.

Nereus jumped down from the carriage and laid a hand on the servant's arm with concern. "What's wrong, brother?" he asked, lapsing into Christian terminology now that they were safe within their own walls.

"Glabrio's been arrested!" the servant blurted out.

"Glabrio! When?" There was no need to ask why.

"This morning, just about dawn. We've heard nothing, and we're all on the verge of panic."

Lorcis shared the feeling immediately, but she knew one person in the house who would not. "Take me to Jacob, please."

"Oh, yes, of course," Nereus stammered. "He's upstairs."

He led her through a back gate into the garden where a small knot of people gathered around a column beside which someone was sitting; it was too dark to recognize anyone. Several of the group gasped when the gate opened and were still cowering when Lorcis and Nereus came into view. Flavius recognized them and stepped forward to greet them, his face ashen in the torchlight but his voice reasonably calm.

"Dear Lorcis, welcome. I'm afraid we've brought you into some serious trouble. We just received word that some of our friends in the palace have been arrested."

"You mean there are Christians right in the palace?" Lorcis asked in amazement.

"Some of Domitian's own slaves," Flavius replied, managing a tight smile. "But this means that Glabrio's slaves have broken under torture and told all they know. It's just a matter of time, now, until the soldiers come for us."

"Why don't you run while there's still time?" Lorcis implored.

A voice from the knot of people behind Flavius answered for him. "Where would we go?" The others stepped aside and Lorcis saw Jacob propped up on pillows, lying on a litter, the sort used to carry noblemen through the streets. His face was drawn with pain, but his expression was suffused with an enthusiasm Lorcis could not comprehend.

"Where can anyone go that the might of Rome cannot find him?" Jacob asked. "A commoner like me might hide in some hole for a time, but the emperor's niece?"

"But if you run," Lorcis argued urgently, "there's always the chance you could get away. If you just sit here, you're giving up all hope." Several voices murmured in agreement.

"No!" Jacob weakly insisted. "We give up all hope if we run. Our only hope is the mercy of God." The exertion caused him pain, and everyone fell silent waiting for him to recover. When he could speak easily again, he called them close, holding out his arms to gather them around him as though they were his children and he would embrace them all.

When they were still he said, "We cannot control what happens to us, nor can we know whether any particular crisis will be resolved for good or ill. It may be that we are under no suspicion at all. If we flee, we confess that we have done something wrong. Remember, we are not criminals; we are Christians. And we must make everyone realize that we are no threat to them or their society if we or our children are ever to live in peace in this world."

"But they might kill us," one frightened voice cried out. Lorcis recalled Junicus' vivid description of the arena and her own brief exposure to it.

"We will only be with Christ that much sooner," Jacob replied calmly. "I know you're frightened, my children, and that's normal. Even Jesus, on the night he was arrested, went into a garden and prayed, 'Father, if it be possible, let this cup pass from me. Nonetheless, not my will but yours be done.' Then he calmly met those sent to arrest him and refused to let his disciples defend him by force. We have tried to live like Jesus in all else. Let us follow his example especially now, at this supreme moment."

Raising one hand in a gesture of blessing, he intoned fervently, "Our Father, who are in heaven, may your name be kept holy." His fellow believers repeated the phrases after him, but he put his own peculiar emphasis in certain places. "May *your* kingdom come, *your will be done,* on earth as it is in heaven. Give us this day our daily bread and forgive us our sins as *we forgive* those who sin against us. Lead us not into temptation, but *deliver us* from evil. Amen."

They remained silent for a moment after the prayer, then Jacob touched the heads of those closest to him. "Go on, now," he smiled. "Get some sleep. It's late."

Someone offered to move his litter, but he declined. "I'd like to sit here a bit longer and talk to my dear child who has come so far to see me," he said with a nod toward Lorcis. When everyone had left, he shifted his feet to make room for her to sit on the couch.

"I'm very pleased to see you, Lorcis," he said as she settled herself beside him, "though I regret that you're here under such difficult circumstances. I hope Nereus made it clear that Domitilla sent for you. If I had been convinced I was dying, I would have asked to see you, but two days ago when Nereus left, I did not feel death was my destiny yet."

"But now it looks like you might get your glorious martyr's death after all," Lorcis replied edgily, "and I'll have to watch you dragged away."

Jacob eyed her sternly. "I imagine you'll get a much closer view than that, my child."

As his full meaning dawned on her, Lorcis protested, "I'm not a Christian! Why should they arrest me?"

"You're in a house full of Christians," Jacob pointed out. "Saying you're not one of us is like claiming you're the only virgin in a whorehouse."

"I might as well be a Christian then," Lorcis shrugged. "Isn't that what you want?"

"I have always wanted you to believe in the Lord," Jacob answered. "Your refusal to commit yourself to him when he has so obviously been working in your life has been the one disappointment in my own ministry. I've led so many people to Christ, but I have been unable to lead a person I've known so long and loved so dearly."

"Well, if it means that much to you . . ."

"No," Jacob barked. "Don't even finish that thought! The Lord wants no half-hearted allegiance. A Roman god would be satisfied with a bit of incense and a few ritualistic prayers, but not the one true God. Give him all of yourself and give it wholeheartedly or give him nothing."

Their conversation was stilled by a steady clinking and rattling coming from outside the house, while muffled voices came from various points around them. Lorcis looked at Jacob questioningly but said nothing for fear of missing some crucial sound.

"That would be the praetorian guards surrounding the house," Jacob said in the same tone he might use to announce the arrival of guests.

There was a moment of silence followed by the sharp bark of an order. Rams thudded against the front and rear doors simultaneously. After only two blows, the rear door splintered; the front stood up to four. Two companies of praetorians—the emperor's handpicked bodyguards and the only armed troops allowed in the city—advanced methodically through the house, searching every room and herding everyone they found into the garden.

Lorcis had expected running and shouting and mayhem, but the soldiers were businesslike. They worked in pairs, one holding a torch while the other checked a room. Several of them carried short sticks with enlarged blunt ends which they used to test for secret rooms or passageways behind walls and under floors.

As the group of Christians in the garden grew larger, some of the weaker ones began to break. The sight of one or two of their friends resisting arrest and being clubbed by the soldiers prompted an outburst of weeping. "Please don't kill us!" several cried out, falling to their knees. "We've done nothing wrong!"

The centurion commanding the squad raised a hand for silence. "We've not come here to kill nobody," he assured them in a rough Latin that betrayed his provincial origins. "Our orders are to arrest anybody found in the house and bring the lot back to the palace. You'll make it easier on y'selfs if you cooperate."

"Please, my children," Jacob implored in his most soothing tone, "don't resist. Remember the commandment of Jesus: 'If anyone strikes you on the right cheek, turn to him the other also.' "

The centurion patted his left palm with the small rod which was his symbol of office. "Well," he muttered to a subordinate, "at least we know we're in the right place."

The soldiers had perfected their search techniques and made quick work of it in a house no larger than Flavius and Domitilla's. As the last few members of the household were found, tension rose in the garden. While Jacob continued to urge passivity and to encourage his flock to look heavenward, most prayed and embraced one another. Many wept.

One of the last to be discovered was a recent convert, a young Greek cook named Telemachus. He had been in the household slightly more than a year and had converted to Christianity only within the last three months. Among the slaves he had a reputation as a complainer and slacker, but Domitilla had great hopes for him and refused to let Flavius take any meaningful disciplinary action against him.

The soldier who was escorting him was trying to shut him up. "All right, I said I'd let you talk to the centurion, and I will." He came to a halt at the edge of the garden. "Stand right here," he ordered, leaving him separated from the others. After a whispered conversation with the centurion, the soldier motioned for Telemachus to approach them.

"Macrinus tells me you claim not to be a Christian," the centurion said suspiciously.

"That's right, sir," Telemachus responded quickly.

The centurion turned to Jacob. "Is he one of you?"

"He's what we call a catechumen. He's receiving instruction

in our faith and would've been baptized within a month or so."

"Has he been attending your meetings?"

"Yes."

The centurion glowered at Telemachus. "It sounds to me like you be a Christian, son," he accused in his broken Latin.

"But I had to pretend to join them," Telemachus whined. "They'd kill me if I didn't and use my blood for their rituals. They drink it—you know that?"

"You got no proof you were pretending," the centurion said. "You looked like a Christian to them."

"Here, I'll show you," Telemachus said frantically, jumping in front of the centurion as he started to turn away to other business. "I'll curse Christ. Damn Christ! Damn him to hell!" There was a gasp from the knot of Christians. "See! None of them will do that. I'll sacrifice to the gods!"

"I'm not the judge," the centurion said. "I'll tell the emperor about you. He'll have to decide. Now get on over there with the rest of them."

"No! They'll kill me now that they know I'm not one of them."

"Keep quiet, Telemachus," Jacob said tiredly. "You've told enough lies already. You know we won't harm you. We will only shun you. Do you not remember Jesus' words: 'If any man confesses me before men, I will confess him before my Father who is in heaven. But whoever denies me before men, him will I deny before my Father.' You've made your choice, Telemachus. You have damned not Christ but yourself."

The centurion disgustedly waved a hand at the whole group as though trying to get rid of an offensive smell and turned to supervise the search for the two remaining members of the household: Flavius and Domitilla.

"All right, lads," he addressed his soldiers, "let's give this some thought. They've not left the house, we know that. And they're not in any of the most obvious places. So we'll just have to think of some less likely hiding holes. Let's start at the top."

He scanned the second story of the house. From the garden he could see the back wall of the slaves' quarters. Each room had a small window, now shuttered against the unseasonable cool nights. "Albinus," he said to the tribune standing nearest him, "take a couple of men and some torches and search those rooms again."

"But, sir," Albinus protested mildly, "we looked through every one of those rooms. And that's the last place you'd find the master of the house hiding, I should think."

"You took the words right out of my mouth," the centurion replied. "Now get moving!"

Stomping up the narrow stairs, the soldiers began to search the slaves' rooms. Light flickered through the chinks in the wooden shutters, tracing their progress down the hall. They reached the next-to-last window, but then the light disappeared momentarily. When it became visible again its movement revealed that the men were returning down the hall to the stairs.

"Ho, Albinus!" the centurion called up to the second floor.

The lights stopped, a shutter flew open, and the tribune stuck his head out the window. "What is it?"

"You missed the last room on the east end," the centurion snapped.

"No, sir. We went in every room up here."

"I didn't see no light in that last window."

The tribune screwed up his face in confusion. "On the east end? There ain't no window in that room."

"Albinus, I've traveled all over the empire in my years of duty," the centurion said sarcastically, "and I never did see anybody put up shutters where there's no window."

"Beggin' pardon, sir," the tribune replied in all sincerity, "but it must be a peculiar window, 'cause it don't open onto the inside."

"Oh, but I'll bet it does," the centurion chortled with a childlike glee in his discovery. "Was there anybody in that room when you searched it?"

"Yes, sir, two slaves."

"And when you found them, I'll bet you didn't check for any hiding places, did you?"

Albinus pondered a minute, withdrew his head to consult with the other soldiers, then reported, "No, sir. The two that was caught in there made quite a ruckus and we had to drag 'em downstairs."

The centurion's every suspicion was confirmed. "Gather your men down at that end of the hall, Albinus. I'll be right there."

He maintained his dignity by walking across the garden with normal military strides, but once out of sight he took the stairs two at a time. His commander made it clear that if Flavius and Domitilla escaped, he might as well not come back. But now he was sure he had them!

The room on the east end was Jacob's. Though no longer a slave, he preferred the less pretentious accommodations he had known for so many years. The most trusted Christian slaves in the household shared this wing, and all of them knew about the false wall in the room.

Flavius and a few of the slaves had built it a year earlier during some routine household renovations. All but a handful of the slaves had been sent to one or another of the family's estates while the work was in progress. During the evenings Flavius and those few remaining slaves used some of the construction materials to put up the wall and repaint the entire hall to cover up the work. They had wanted to tear out the window and brick up the hole but decided it was not only beyond their skills but impossible to do without attracting attention. They had settled for boarding up the window from the inside and plastering the chinks so that a lit candle in the room could not be observed from the outside. Since the room was Jacob's and because he was revered so highly in the house, it had not been difficult to keep other slaves out. A lock had also been fitted on the door, a privilege befitting Jacob's status as a freedman.

With his sword drawn, the centurion led his men into the room. It contained a bed, a small table and a chair, a shelf of books, and against the false wall, a large chest. The back of the chest was hinged and served as a door to the chamber behind the wall. The centurion, however, had little patience for such niceties. "Shove it aside!" he ordered, and the soldiers quickly carried out the command.

A low opening had been left in the wall, scarcely half the height of an average person. Above it was written "The eye of the needle."

"That mean anything to you?" the centurion asked Albinus. The tribune shook his head.

"Well, make a note of it and we'll ask the old man when we get back downstairs."

He knelt and peered into the small chamber but did not put his head through the opening. There might be some trickery here. A soft light flickered but there was no sound or perceptible movement.

"Ho, you in there! The game's up," he said forcefully. "We'd prefer you come on out so we don't have to come in after you, but we will if you make us."

There was no reply. Were they waiting to attack? Not likely, considering how the rest of this bunch had behaved. Did they prefer to die here rather than face what they knew would be a ghastly fate at Domitian's hands? He had known some of these aristocrats to take that course, preferring to deny the emperor the satisfaction of witnessing their deaths and to retain some dignity in their last moments.

Holding his sword at the ready in front of him, he squatted and crawled through the opening. The dim light revealed a room about four feet by six. Against the wall to his left was a table. Flavius and Domitilla were standing there, facing the east, their hands raised in prayer.

The centurion surprised himself with his own reluctance as he approached the couple and almost gently invited the two out of the room. "My lord and lady, it's time to go."

"Yes, it is, isn't it, my Lord," Flavius said, not to the centurion but to an unseen Presence. He turned and clasped Domitilla's hands.

The centurion sheathed his sword. "This, I take it," he said, "is your cult room." He glanced around and seemed disappointed at the barrenness of it. There were no wall decorations. On the table was a candlestick beside which lay Lorcis' medallion. The centurion picked it up and examined it, turning it over several times.

"So now we know what your leader looks like," he said. "Be a feather in my cap to nab him."

Domitilla could not help but smile. "Somebody's already beaten you to it, but they couldn't hold him."

"Slippery weasel, is he, huh? We might just have to pin him down," he grinned, patting the handle of his sword.

Domitilla wanted to say more, to explain about the resurrection of Jesus, but the centurion ordered them out of the chamber. The soldiers surrounded them for the walk back to the garden.

When they joined the others in the garden, Jacob raised up on one elbow to greet them. "I'm sorry we weren't clever enough," he said softly. "I was hoping you would be left to carry on the work."

"We didn't hope to escape," Flavius replied. "The emperor

would've torn the house down around us before he would have given up the search. We only wanted a few moments to pray. The work will go on though. It is God's, not ours."

"Let's move!" the centurion barked. Several of the slaves started to pick up Jacob's couch and carry it, but the centurion stopped them. "No extra baggage," he said roughly. "Everybody walks."

"But he's an old man, and sick," Lorcis broke in.

"We got our orders. Nobody carries anything. If he can't walk, we kill him right here."

"If I may be allowed to lean on a friend," Jacob interjected, "I'll try to walk."

"Lean on anyone you like, old man," the centurion replied, "as long as you keeps moving."

Jacob got up slowly, bending almost double from the pain in his stomach. One of the other Christians moved to help him, but Lorcis got to him first. "This is for me to do," she said firmly as she put one of Jacob's arms around her shoulder and slipped her left arm around his waist.

"You look less and less like a virgin," he quipped.

The fifty-yard march to the nearest gate of the palace was quiet; the street was empty. The only illumination came from the soldiers' torches. Since Roman houses had few, if any, windows on the street, there were no witnesses to that reluctant pilgrimage. No one saw the serenity with which Flavius escorted Domitilla, her arm slipped lightly through his. No one noticed how easily Lorcis, flute player turned farm woman, supported old Jacob on that climb up his own personal Calvary. Nor did anyone mark the quiet courage with which these leaders imbued the others in the group.

Once inside the palace, they were herded along gloomy, unpainted corridors and down steps that became increasingly dank and slippery until they were brought to a stop in a large vaulted chamber. Lorcis was no longer frightened by the idea that she was soon to die; she had quickly accepted that fact with surprising equanimity. What distressed her was not knowing what was to happen at each step of the way. Where were they now? Would the soldiers torture them? lock them in dark, vermin-infested cells? That latter possibility frightened her the most..

The centurion singled out several of his men. "Get chains on these two," he ordered, pointing to Flavius and Domitilla, "and let's see, the old fellow there seems to be some sort of priest or holy man. At least he does most of the talking. The wench holding him up will have to come along, too, I suppose, so shackle her, too."

The soldiers pulled Flavius' arms roughly behind his back and clapped heavy manacles on his wrists. Another fetter fastened around his neck had a chain dangling from it by which a prisoner could be led.

Domitilla was shackled in the same fashion, but not without a good deal of fondling by the soldiers and some coarse speculation about the merits of aristocratic women compared with the girls in the brothel near their barracks.

"Have you ever had a *real* man?" one soldier sneered, grabbing Domitilla by the back of the neck and forcing a hard kiss on her.

Flavius lunged at him, but another soldier cuffed him across the face, striking him with his leather wristband embossed with brass studs. A gash on Flavius' chin trickled blood as he staggered to his knees. Without his hands to brace himself he toppled forward onto his face. The soldiers laughed raucously. The man who had struck him leaned down and waved a fist in Flavius' face. "I believe I heard you say something earlier, my lord, about turning the other cheek." He drew back his hand to slap him again.

"Stop it!" the centurion yelled. "We're not supposed to harm anyone, just truss 'em up and deliver 'em to the emperor. Be about your business." Two soldiers lifted Flavius to his feet roughly. "Oh, and get this one ready, too," the centurion added, pushing Telemachus toward the pile of chains. "I think the emperor will find him interesting."

"Sir, we do have one problem," the soldier standing next to Lorcis offered.

"What's that?"

"Well, if we fix her up like the others, with her hands chained too, she won't be able to support the old goat."

The centurion studied the possibilities. "Shackle her feet and put one on her neck," he said. "I'll stand by her with my sword drawn and hold her chain when we go in to see the emperor." He left to report to his commander that the prisoners were ready.

"Why are you chaining us now that we're in the palace?" Lorcis asked the soldier who was fastening manacles on her and

Jacob. "You brought us all the way here without these things and we didn't try to escape. Do you seriously think we'd try now?"

"Well, miss, the emperor is, shall we say, a bit edgy these days," the soldier replied dryly, "what with all these plots against him. So when he questions prisoners he likes to be sure they can't make any last desperate attempts on his life."

A door opened on the far side of the chamber, and the light from the room on the other side shone out like the sun peering through afternoon clouds. A soldier stepped out and announced, "The emperor is ready to interrogate the prisoners."

"Let's go," a tribune growled as the soldiers jerked their captives into motion. Lorcis' fetters had only a short chain between them so she had difficulty staying beside Jacob, who tried to keep up the pace demanded by his captor. Her ankles were quickly rubbed raw.

They were towed into a room of moderate size but elaborately decorated. At the opposite end near another door which, Lorcis guessed, opened to a passageway leading directly to the emperor's quarters, sat Domitian on a magistrate's chair made of gold. His back was against the wall and three praetorian guards stood on either side of him. The prisoners were halted about ten feet in front of him, with the soldiers retaining a firm grip on their chains.

Nine years of unchecked indulgence of his power had left their mark on the emperor. Even the purple and gold cloak he was wrapped in could not disguise how bloated he had become. His complexion, never very good, was now horribly splotchy. He sat hunched up, his eyes darting around the room. He inspected each prisoner briefly, showing no sign of recognition when his eyes met Lorcis'.

"All right, centurion," he said in a shaky voice, "let's begin with the little fish."

"Yes, my lord," the centurion replied snappily. "You, Telemachus, step forward!" The cowering slave stepped closer to the emperor, who took his chain from the guard.

"This man, my lord, claims not to be a Christian," the centurion explained. "He says he was forced into the cult by threat of death, so he only pretended to be one of them."

"Is there any evidence of coercion?" Domitian asked.

"None, my lord. These Christians are a remarkably passive lot."

"But they threatened me, I tell you!" Telemachus pleaded.

"We have a witness who, I believe, can clarify this point," Domitian said smugly. "Stephanus!"

Flavius and Domitilla looked at each other in disbelief and dismay. Their trusted steward, a spy!

Stephanus entered the room through the door to Domitian's right. He was wearing expensive new clothes and a gold ring signifying his overnight promotion to the wealthy equestrian order.

"Stephanus, my friend," Domitian gloated, "Telemachus here claims that he was forced to join the Christians. Is that true?"

Stephanus spoke softly, slowly, with little enthusiasm. "No, my lord. Christians do not coerce anyone. Telemachus appeared to me to be a most enthusiastic convert."

"It seems, Telemachus," Domitian said, trying to rivet his somewhat bleary eyes on the slave, "that you are not a man at all, but a chameleon: a Christian when it is advantageous to be a Christian, a Roman when you want to blend into a Roman background. In short, you are totally untrustworthy, a born liar. You have no convictions, no moral fiber! A typical Greek, I might even say. The world, I think, would be just that much better if you were removed from it."

He nodded, and before Telemachus could open his mouth the soldier standing behind him whipped out his sword and stabbed the slave in the back with such force that the point protruded through his stomach. Telemachus gasped, "Oh, Jesus!" and fell to the stone floor, twitching a few times as he died.

Domitian handed the chain to the soldier. "Perhaps he was a Christian after all," he said disinterestedly. "Get him out of here." The soldier used the chain to haul Telemachus' body across the smooth floor and back into the large chamber. The outcry from the prisoners waiting there could be heard before the door closed.

"Who's the old man?" Domitian asked Stephanus. "He seems vaguely familiar."

"I am Jacob ben Malak, a servant of Christ," replied Jacob before Stephanus could say anything. "You must recognize me as Nestor, once the chief steward of Marcus Aquilius Regulus."

"Yes, of course," Domitian said, nodding his head. "So now you are someone else's slave?"

"No," Jacob replied, deliberately omitting the honorific "my lord," a term the Christians reserved for God. "In the eyes of your law I am a freedman, thanks to the generosity of my sister in Christ, Domitilla."

Domitian half rose out of his chair. "You dare to call my niece your sister?"

"We are all sisters and brothers in Christ," Jacob said forcefully. "We draw no distinction between slave and free, rich and poor, male and female."

"Then you are truly as mad as I've heard," the emperor said disdainfully. He sat back down and leaned forward, resting his elbows on the arms of the chair and clasping his hands together as if about to have a talk with a difficult child. "How could the world exist without such distinctions?"

"In peace, perhaps," Jacob replied.

"You idealists just cannot learn from the mistakes of others, can you?" Domitian countered. "Plato thought philosophers should be kings or, failing that, that kings should be philosophers. Dionysius of Syracuse invited him there to set up his utopia. After three months that damnable Athenian meddler was sent packing."

"He failed because . . . " Jacob started, but Domitian cut him off.

"It makes no difference," he said irritably. "I was simply drawing an analogy, the sort of thing my insufferable tutors used to make me do for hours preparing for just this occasion, no doubt," he added with a sarcastic smile. He leaned back in the chair. "There are only two questions before us right now. First, do you acknowledge the gods of Rome and reject Christ? Second, will you show your allegiance to Rome and to me by doing homage to the images of the gods and to my image?" He looked straight at Jacob. "What is your answer?"

"To both questions I must answer no," Jacob calmly replied at once. "The gods of Rome . . . "

"I need no explanations," Domitian broke in. "I asked for an answer and I have it. You are a self-confessed member of an illicit, treasonous cult. I sentence you to die in the arena three days from now when the next games are given."

Only Lorcis, who was still supporting Jacob, was aware of the tension which gripped him as Domitian pronounced the sentence. Was it fear, she wondered, or perhaps a strange kind of elation. She did not have time to do more than pose the question to herself because Domitian next focused his attention on her.

"Who is she?" he asked Stephanus.

"I do not know her, my lord."

"Centurion?"

"I don't know her name, my lord. She was in the house and volunteered to assist the old man, who's too sick to stand alone."

"I see," Domitian muttered. "Who are you, my dear, and how do you explain your presence among this pack of atheists and traitors?"

"My name is Lorcis," she replied and paused to see if it had any impact on him.

"Oh, yes," Stephanus blurted out. "She's a freedwoman who lives on one of their estates near Milan. I have received reports from her but had never seen her. I do know the name, though."

"So do I," Domitian said slowly. "There was . . . a woman a few years ago, but I . . . "

"No, you just thought you killed me," she shot back. "You came close, but I was picked up out of the streets by these 'atheists and traitors' and nursed back to health."

"Are you one of them, then?"

"I haven't been baptized or formally instructed in their doctrines."

"I want direct answers!" Domitian stormed. "Are you a Christian?"

What good would denial do? Telemachus had recanted and all that was left of him was a smear of blood across the floor. Jacob had admitted it, and he was doomed to die. Well, if her answer made no difference to Domitian, at least she could be honest with herself.

"No," she answered. She felt Jacob sag against her as she said the word.

"To prove that you are not, you must curse Christ and worship the images of the gods and myself," Domitian demanded. "Will you curse Christ?"

Lorcis hesitated. She noticed Jacob's head down and his lips moving in prayer. She remembered a time in what seemed like another life when she had cursed Christ, had used the very words Domitian wanted her to use now, and had meant them. But at this time, in this life, it seemed perfectly natural to answer "No."

"Then you stand condemned!" Domitian shouted, slapping

his hands on the arms of his chair. "You will die also, and this time I'll make certain of it. You'll regret that you did not die in the street that night."

Now he turned to Flavius and Domitilla. "So, Flavius," he said with unconcealed hatred, "my childhood friend, my comrade in battle. This is my reward for the trust I placed in you."

"If we are to speak of misplaced trust," Flavius said bitterly, "let's not forget Stephanus. Or perhaps Judas would be a more appropriate name."

Stephanus blushed and hung his head.

"What does he mean by that?" Domitian asked, looking from one to the other suspiciously.

"Judas was one of the early followers of Jesus, my lord," Stephanus explained, "but he betrayed him and turned him over to the authorities."

"Well, then, don't take it as an insult," Domitian reprimanded him. "You did what a loyal Roman ought to have done, and you'll be well rewarded."

"So was Judas," Stephanus replied glumly.

"What?"

"I mean, thank you, my lord," Stephanus said more clearly, taking a deep breath and raising his head again.

"Flavius," Domitian continued, "I'm deeply hurt and quite bewildered that a man such as yourself could get mixed up with a bunch of Eastern riffraff and then drag my niece, whom I entrusted to you in marriage, into it."

"No, uncle," Domitilla interrupted. "It was I who first became a Christian and then brought my dear husband to the Lord."

"The fact of the matter, however, is that you both admit to being Christians. Is that not so?" Domitian demanded.

"We proudly profess the name," Flavius replied. Domitilla nodded briskly and held her head erect.

"Even though that profession implicates you in a plot against my life?" Domitian challenged.

"I have no plan, nor even a wish, to kill you," Flavius said sincerely.

"But Glabrio's slaves confessed under torture to a conspiracy," Domitian informed him, "and Stephanus has been reporting that Glabrio regularly attends your Christian meetings, which, I might add, are illegal and held at the most suspicious hours."

"Glabrio attends our meetings because he is a Christian," Flavius protested, "not to plot an attempt on your life. What proof have you that I intended to kill you?"

"You are a member of a secret, illegal sect which refuses to worship our gods or pay homage to me. Either of these is, in itself, an act of treason punishable by death. You consort with a man who has been implicated in a plot against me, a man who is a member of your sect. The conclusion is inescapable."

"In the face of such logic, I cannot hope to defend myself," Flavius replied with a sarcasm that was lost on the demented emperor.

"Then you admit you were planning to kill me!" Domitian crowed, clapping his hands together like a child who has finally solved a difficult puzzle.

"No, I profess that I am a Christian. You will make of that whatever you wish, I'm sure," Flavius said tiredly.

Domitian addressed his soldiers morosely. "My comrades-in-arms, I, like all emperors, am of necessity wretched, for only my assassination will convince the public that the conspiracies against my life are real."

He then drew himself up with what little imperial dignity he had left. "Flavius Clemens, I find you guilty of atheism and treason. Under Roman law either of those crimes is punishable by death. Since you are a nobleman, the law requires that you be put to death out of public view, by beheading with a sword. So it shall be done. The law further provides that all your property be confiscated by the state and that your wife be sent into exile. These provisions of the law will be carried out."

He slumped back in his chair and sighed raspily. "Now, get them out of here! Lock them up and we'll dispose of them in a day or two. That rabble in the outer hall can be packed off to the arena on Friday as well."

"Uncle!" Domitilla cried. "What will become of our children?"

"They seem unaffected by your perverse doctrines. Their youth, I suppose, has saved them from its influence. They will be raised as true Romans."

As he finished speaking, he stood up somewhat laboriously. On a signal his guards surrounded him and escorted him from the room. The centurion remained to take charge of the prisoners, and Stephanus stood transfixed, hardly aware that Domitian had left. He glanced from Flavius to Domitilla, afraid to say anything that the soldiers might interpret as remorse for his actions or sympathy for those he had betrayed.

He longed to be able to explain his dilemma: a deep affection for his master and mistress, genuine gratitude for receiving his freedom from them, but a profound and sincere suspicion of their religion. From his observation he had concluded that it was a purely emotional faith which relied too strongly on the individual's feelings or state of mind. Lacking verifiable doctrines, even priding itself on being paradoxical and irrational, it offered nothing to the intellect, as his own Epicurean beliefs did. In its own way, Christianity seemed as dangerous to him as the orgiastic cult of Bacchus, which Rome had also tried to ban. If he could only make them understand that his decision to inform on them had been a hard one, based on his convictions, not on greed or personal enmity.

As the guards jerked on their chains to lead them out of the room, Domitilla looked up at Stephanus. "We forgive you," she said.

CHAPTER XXVII

Once back in the main hall, the prisoners were unshackled and herded into a single large cell. The centurion, however, instructed two of the guards to take Flavius and Domitilla to the "guest room" on the upper level. "We ain't supposed to mix noble folks with commoners," he explained.

"We would rather be with our friends," Domitilla pleaded. "Can't you let us spend a few last hours with those we love?" she added softly, touching the centurion's arm.

"I got my orders, my lady," he said obdurately, then stopped. "Hell, I don't see what difference it makes." He opened the door and motioned for the two of them to enter. "I don't imagine the lice and fleas will care either," he joked, trying to regain the hard exterior which he had temporarily dropped.

The little congregation huddled together around Jacob, hardly daring to examine their wretched surroundings. Roman jails were designed solely for short periods of imprisonment, until a prisoner's fine had been paid or he was led away to be executed. Lengthy incarceration was not viewed as suitable punishment. Most prisoners spent no more than a day or two in a cell awaiting resolution of their cases, so there was no need for niceties.

The Christians found themselves in a cell which was completely dark except for light which came from the outer chamber through a small barred opening in the door. There were no seats, only dirty, damp straw which could be scraped up into a bug-infested bed. Lorcis gathered a pile of reasonably dry straw and Domitilla and Flavius spread their cloaks across it. The three then helped Jacob get down onto the straw and made him as comfortable as possible.

A large bucket on one side of the door served as a latrine. "If you gotta go, go in the bucket," the guard warned. "If you mess up the floor, we'll make you clean it up in a very unpleasant way." On the other side of the door hung a smaller bucket which supplied drinking water.

Once everyone was still and quiet, Lorcis became aware that she had not had a drink of anything since late afternoon when she and Nereus had stopped to eat twenty miles or so north of Rome. Stepping carefully over and around several people, she worked her way to the water bucket. Even as she raised the wooden ladle to her lips, however, she began to have second thoughts about slaking her thirst. It was too dark to see the water in the ladle clearly, but its stale odor caused her to hesitate. While living on the farm she had grown accustomed to pure, cold spring water. Even water that was fresh by Roman standards was warm and tasteless after its trip through one of the long aqueducts which tried to keep pace with the city's unquenchable demand for drinking and bathing. But the liquid in the bucket hardly deserved to be called water.

Lorcis dropped the ladle back into the bucket. "I hope I never get thirsty enough to have to drink that stuff," she muttered in disgust. Returning to her place beside Jacob, she sat down, held his hand, and leaned back against the clammy wall.

I'm going to die, she thought. *It's just a matter of waiting*.

She had come close before, she reflected, but had never had the opportunity to anticipate it. She was surprised at her own calm. Was that because her life had had no meaning and was just as well ended? Surely not. Martial, Erotion, Xanthippe, Junicus, Maria; if her life was without meaning, then they meant nothing either. And that was unacceptable.

I reject the notion that my life has had no meaning, she told herself. *So I must accept the proposition that it has been meaningful. Perhaps I've believed that all along without realizing it. That might be why I've fought to keep myself and my loved ones alive*.

But what was that meaning? Was it in the striving itself? That seemed futile. Was there a plan she was unaware of, a plan designed by someone else? Was she like one piece of a huge mosaic, not really knowing whether she was part of a nose or a flower petal, yet playing her part in creating a beautiful whole? Did it matter if she knew what the entire picture was, or even her own corner, as long as she did her part as well as possible?

Domitilla was moving quietly from one person to the next, saying an encouraging word, touching an arm, wiping a tear. As she passed Lorcis, she paused and placed a hand on her knee.

"I'm sorry that my message has gotten you into this," she said with compassionate regret. "If I had thought it could possibly come to this, I would never have sent for you."

"It may surprise you to hear me say this," Lorcis replied. "It surprises me, too. But I think God planned for me to be here."

Jacob squeezed her hand, unable to speak through his tears.

"For whatever reason," Lorcis went on, "I don't regret being here. I would have come to see Jacob if I had been told that the soldiers were surrounding the house at that very moment."

Domitilla smiled, embraced her, then moved away to minister to the others.

With considerable effort Jacob raised himself slightly. "Do you believe what you just said or were you saying it just to please me? Or perhaps you've given up hope?"

"No," Lorcis said. "I've thought many times about our conversations, and I've been sitting here working some things through. I can see how God could have been working to achieve a certain result in things I didn't comprehend. And, as you pointed out that night in the worship service, he has raised me from the dead twice already . . . with the help of others, of course."

Jacob's smile was barely visible in the gloom. "God must always work through us, imperfect implements though we may be," he struggled to point out. "The tool, not the plan, is the cause of most of the unhappiness in this world. Not even the most skilled carpenter can build a straight wall if his square is out of line."

Lorcis picked up a piece of straw and twisted it aimlessly. "He makes it so difficult to believe in him though."

"If faith were easy, Lorcis, it would not be worth having. You have seen God's power. Do you believe he can raise you again, one last time, even after your body is truly dead?"

"Yes, I do," Lorcis replied without hesitation.

"Do you want to profess your faith and be baptized?" Jacob asked hopefully.

In the dim light, Lorcis turned to face him squarely.

"There's one thing I still would like an answer for. I think I can accept it now, but I would feel better if someone—if you—could explain it to me."

"You're going to ask me why Erotion died, aren't you?"

Lorcis nodded, her words blocked by the lump in her throat. The memory of the beloved face, livid with fever, was still too strong.

"I don't know why," Jacob said, "any more than I know why my own dear daughter died. Neither of them deserved it. I think I can tell you how you can live with it, though. At least it satisfies me to think of it in this way."

Lorcis clung to his every word like a child awaiting the answer to a difficult riddle.

"I've tried to tell you before how you might deal with this, but you've never given me a chance to finish," Jacob chided her, and she blushed to remember how she had thrown him out of her house.

"I was awful to you, wasn't I," she admitted.

"You were distraught," Jacob said. "It was understandable, and I may have been too authoritarian, lacking in sympathy. But I wanted to tell you that God's purposes aren't always revealed to us as fully as we would like. He is God; we are only human.

"Think of him as our father, as Jesus taught us to do, and ourselves as his children. He is the most loving father we can imagine, desiring only good for his children. But even the most loving parent cannot explain to his children everything he does. Children cannot even conceive of an adult's thought processes or the contingencies with which he must cope. Does that make sense so far?"

Lorcis nodded. With much effort, Jacob painfully shifted his weight and pinched at a few fleas.

"Now, as the child grows older he or she understands more of the parent's plan. The love behind it, behind the discipline and denials, becomes clear. God is our loving father; he is doing what is best for us. If we could live long enough, I suppose we would understand it all, but we must believe that he is working for our best interests."

Lorcis was silent for a moment and Jacob looked at her, waiting for some kind of response. Finally she said, "Sometimes parents don't act in the child's best interest. My stepfather sold me into slavery. And other parents have sold their own flesh and blood. Surely you don't think that is a loving act."

"You don't know what motives they have. Perhaps they sell one child to keep the others from starving. But that isn't the best example of parenthood we could find. Being a parent is more than a biological accident. Aren't you Maria's real mother because you love and nurture her?"

Lorcis nodded. "You're right, of course. I think I've felt that way for several years, but I've just been throwing up defenses, trying to keep myself from seeing what is so obvious."

"Do you see, at least to some degree, the path your life has been following? One of our martyrs, a man named Paul, wrote that we sometimes see 'through a glass, darkly,' but have you come to understand why certain things happened to you?" Jacob was becoming more earnest now.

"Yes," Lorcis replied confidently. "I don't actually accuse God of killing Erotion anymore. She died of a fever, just as thousands of other people have. I see that God used that experience to prepare me for other things in my life. I couldn't have been a very good mother to Maria if I hadn't had Erotion first."

"The beginning of wisdom . . . " Jacob said joyously.

"It's been too much to figure out," Lorcis said tiredly. "I want to know everything, but I'm not sure I would know what to do with the knowledge if I had it."

"That thirst for knowledge was the original sin," Jacob pointed out. "Satan said to Eve, 'Eat the fruit from the tree of knowledge and you shall be as God, knowing good and evil.' But such things belong in God's hands."

Lorcis opened her mouth to respond, but the words were cut off by the creaking of the cell's door hinges. Had Domitian changed his mind? Were they to be executed immediately? Or had the guards come to take the women out? Under Roman law a virgin could not be executed. The guards made sure that technicality was taken care of before any woman was taken to the arena. No one required them to do it; it was an example of their devotion to duty.

But only the centurion entered the cell. Looking around until he found Domitilla, he approached her and stood respectfully until she looked up and acknowledged him. "My lady, I thought you might like to have this." He handed her the Jesus medallion.

"Thank you, my friend," Domitilla said. "You are doing a greater thing than you realize."

The centurion saluted. "I don't rightly understand all of this, my lady, but I know I don't like what I'm doing. And I guess I'd better not say any more than that."

"God bless you, my friend," Flavius said, offering his hand. The centurion shook it, then left quickly.

"This is rightfully yours," Domitilla said, handing the medallion to Lorcis.

She had thought never to see it again and yet here it was in her hands, as if it had pursued her across the years. She had rejected it and the power it symbolized, but it had never let go of her.

"Jacob," she said impulsively, "I want to be baptized!"

"Oh, my child, I have longed for so many years to hear you say those words! But how am I to baptize you? There is no pool here, no way to perform the rite properly."

Domitilla stood up excitedly. "Don't you remember the story of Philip and the Ethiopian eunuch? When the eunuch was ready to be baptized, he said, 'Here is water. What prevents me from being baptized?' The only thing preventing Lorcis is our lack of imagination. Baptism represents cleansing, washing away the old life. Couldn't we pour the water over her? The symbol would still be true if her heart were convinced."

Jacob pondered the matter. "Our Lord is no legalistic Pharisee," he finally pronounced. "I believe he will acknowledge what we are about to do."

Domitilla fetched the bucket of drinking water while everyone gathered around Jacob and Lorcis. The old man struggled to his feet in spite of Flavius' protestations. "I will do this much of it as I am accustomed," he asserted vigorously.

Lorcis knelt in front of him and looked up expectantly. "Baptize me, father Jacob," she wept. "Cleanse me."

"My dear Lorcis, you are cleansed in your heart by your belief in Christ. Through this baptism, you acknowledge his lordship and become one body with all who follow his Way. So I joyfully baptize you in the name of Jesus Christ."

With Flavius' help he raised the bucket and began to pour the water onto Lorcis' head. As it ran down her face and touched her lips it seemed to her the sweetest liquid she had ever tasted.

CHAPTER XXVIII

Junicus stopped in a doorway across the street from Flavius and Domitilla's house. The soldiers on guard there paid no particular attention to him. People were going about their early morning business, glancing only briefly at the barricaded house. It would not do to show too much interest in what was going on there.

"So the fellow was right," Junicus muttered to himself in German. One of Pliny's slaves, a fellow Christian, had stopped by the estate on his way to Ticinum to deliver some messages and had let Junicus know what was happening. But he did not know if the arrests had been made before or after Lorcis arrived. Leaving Maria in the care of a trusted freedwoman, Junicus had taken Flavius' best horse and ridden it mercilessly, trying to get to Rome in time to . . . what? What could he do against the might of Rome? He was powerless against even the few soldiers across the street. Nor could he admit that he knew Flavius and Domitilla or ask questions about them, or he'd be in irons along with them. If he was to do anything he needed an ally, someone who knew his way around Rome.

But who in Rome would open their door to him? He knew no one himself. Thinking over the names of people Lorcis had mentioned, he eliminated Pliny. An aristocrat such as he would not likely endanger himself to help a former slave he hadn't seen for years, no matter how close a friend she might have been.

There was that fellow Martial. He certainly had been close to Lorcis, but would he still feel any obligation to her? And how could he be found? He wrote books, so a bookshop might be the best place to start. No sense standing here gawking any longer in any case, he reasoned with himself. The soldiers would notice. There would probably be a bookshop somewhere around the Forum at the bottom of the hill where he could ask a few questions without arousing suspicion.

During the night, the second night since their arrest, Lorcis, Jacob, and the others were moved from the palace cells to cells under the floor of the Colosseum. Flavius and Domitilla had been taken off by themselves when the others were moved. The tears shed at their departure had been quiet, and the centurion allowed them ample time to say their farewells.

Under the arena the cells were small, foul smelling, and poorly lighted. The rumbles of the big cats echoing along the passageways added to the terrifying unreality. Watching the others weeping and trying to comfort one another, Lorcis realized that death in the arena could hardly be worse than the dread of the experience. Death itself, at least, would be over in a moment or two. The anticipation of it seemed to have been going on forever.

She checked to see that Jacob, who was sleeping next to her, was comfortable. They had hardly left each other's side since the arrest. Any movement was painful for him, and she had virtually carried him from the palace to the Colosseum. The soldiers could have killed him with one quick thrust either in Flavius and Domitilla's house or in the cell in the palace. But Jacob wanted the martyr's death in the arena which he felt had been denied him so many years ago. Perhaps, he had pointed out to Lorcis as they labored down the Palatine Hill and across the dark Forum, she had been brought back to Rome as part of God's plan to deliver him to his death in the arena. None of the others in the household were physically capable of assisting him as steadfastly as Lorcis had been doing. They were household slaves, accustomed only to light work.

"Perhaps that's so," she had replied, "but then, maybe this is my destiny, too. I'd like to think I'm more than just an animated crutch."

Jacob had smiled and patted her hand. "You don't know how very much you've meant to so many people, myself most of all. That's one of the frustrations of life. We seldom know the impact we have on other people, nor do we recognize the influence of others on us until it's too late to acknowledge them. I'm happy to have had the chance to tell you what a blessing you've been to me, Lorcis."

As Lorcis smoothed his grimy, matted hair, the old man moved slightly in his sleep, like a child. From the noises made by the guards and the animal handlers as they greeted each other and chatted casually, she guessed it was morning, the last morning of her life. It would have been nice to see the sun come up one last time. That had been one of the rewards of the hard work on the farm—being up and outside in time to watch the beautiful sunrises. With their promise of a new start, they thrilled her more than the sunsets, which the poets and artists always seemed drawn to.

The growls of the big cats mingled with the voices of the animal handlers in what almost seemed a conversation. For these men it was another working day and the cats were their colaborers; the condemned were merely the raw material. The finished product would be the delighted crowd in the stands. Their voices betrayed no hint of sympathy as they called to the cats by name and jeered at the anonymous victims.

Lorcis clutched the Jesus medallion hanging around her neck on a piece of cloth torn from Domitilla's gown. The Christians often prayed, "Even so, Lord Jesus, come quickly!" That cry echoed in her heart. "If not," she added to herself, "at least let death come quickly."

Martial listened patiently as the big German finished his plea. "Do you realize what you're suggesting?" he asked in a low voice. "How can you hope to get a prisoner out of the arena? It's impossible! You're endangering both of us by even talking about such a thing." He looked around cautiously. He had worked hard to climb to even the lower echelons of the upper class. His staff of slaves was small and he thought he could trust them, but this conversation was making him nervous nonetheless. If so much as a word of it got to the wrong ears. . . .

"As I recall the story, it seemed impossible to get your daughter out of Regulus' house," Junicus countered.

"The odds were considerably better in that case. We merely had to sneak around behind a fat, sleepy toad. We weren't charging into the lair of a monster that's heavily armed and constantly on the lookout for troublemakers. Even Regulus proved difficult when his suspicions were aroused. It was Jacob's inspiration that saved us. We can't go into something like this just counting on luck."

"Well, my lord, I cannot sit back and let Lorcis die without making an effort to save her. I love her too much for that. I never thought I would hope that another man loved my wife, but I was praying that you did." He turned to leave, but Martial called after him.

"Wait! You're right, of course. I do love her. I always have, even though she wouldn't believe me." He sighed and shrugged his shoulders. "I have no earthly idea what we might do, but at least let's go down to the arena."

"Maybe we'll think of something by the time we get there," Junicus said hopefully. He had planned nothing beyond getting to Rome and finding someone to help him. Having accomplished that, he was ready to turn the thinking over to someone else.

The midday sun had driven Pliny to the shade of a portico. As much as he loved his seaside villa, he did find the bright sunlight troublesome to his inflamed eye, a chronic problem which occasionally left him all but blind on the left side. He would have preferred to read the letter which he had dictated, to actually see it on the page, but that was too difficult at the moment. He asked the scribe to read the letter back to him. The man cleared his throat, then read:

Gaius Plinius to his friend Minicius, greetings.

It's amazing how, if you take a single day spent in Rome, you can give a fairly accurate account of it, but hardly any account at all of several days put together. If you ask someone to recall what he did on a particular day, the answer might be, 'I attended a coming-of-age ceremony, a betrothal, or a wedding. I was asked to witness a will, to speak for someone in court, or to act as a judge.' This all seems important when it's happening, but quite inane when you consider that you do the same sorts of things every day. If you start thinking about it when you're out of town, then the utter futility of the whole business overwhelms you.

I am reminded of this especially when I'm here at Laurentum, reading and writing and taking time for the physical activity which clears my mind for what I must do. I hear or say nothing which I regret later, no one poisons my ear with vicious gossip, and I have only myself to blame when writing doesn't come easily. I am not torn between hope and fear, and my time is not frittered away in speculative talk. Only my writing book knows my thoughts. It is a good life, a pleasant exile, certainly more rewarding than anything going on in Rome. The sea and my piece of the shore are a source of inspiration.

Take the first opportunity to leave the meaningless bustle and business of the city and devote yourself to the more serious pursuit of literature. Our friend Atilius was wise and witty when he said that it is better to have nothing to do than to be doing nothing.

Farewell.

"Thank you, Zosimus," Pliny said. "That will be all for now." He took the letter in his hand. It sounded innocent enough, he was sure; just one senator's paeon for the country life. Here, far enough from Rome to be out of Domitian's immediate grasp—though no spot within the bounds of the empire was out of his reach forever—he could actually relax without trembling at the first knock on the door. His most dreaded visitor here would be a peasant farmer on the estate come to complain about the condition of his roof.

But if the letter fell into any hands but Minicius', would its real message be too obvious? "Only my writing book knows my thoughts" was Pliny's way of telling Minicius that they need not fear eavesdropping slaves who would report whatever they heard to the palace. "Take the first opportunity to leave . . . the city" was a request for Minicius to come to the villa as soon as possible so they could discuss further their plan to overthrow Domitian.

Pliny had initiated the plot in desperation. With Glabrio and Flavius arrested, he saw no reason to hope that he would survive much longer. Domitian had obviously decided to eliminate the most prominent people in public life, no matter who they were. Regulus had surely poisoned the emperor's mind against him by now and his only chance lay in striking first.

But the group he had gathered thus far was small and dispirited. The fate of Flavius and his family had spread terror through aristocratic circles, just as the emperor had intended. If even his own niece was not immune from punishment, then who would be? But now that a bold man like Atilius had decided to join them, Pliny's optimism was renewed. If all went well, within the week Rome would be rid of its latest despot and would be governed again by its rightful rulers, the senate. If all did not go as planned . . . *Well, I won't be around to worry about it,* he consoled himself.

A breeze had sprung up and Pliny found it too cool in the shade. He gathered up his writing materials and was about to go back into the house when a servant came out.

"Forgive the intrusion, my lord, but there is a man here to see you."

"At this hour?" Pliny said anxiously. "Who is it?"

The slave hesitated as though reluctant to reveal bad news. "It's Stephanus, my lord," he said in a tone which made it clear he was as mystified as his master. Since the arrest of Flavius and Domitilla, Stephanus had been made Domitian's steward and given elaborate gifts, including a fourth of Flavius and Domitilla's property. In this manner, Domitian hoped to encourage other servants to keep their ears open. But Stephanus had also earned the undying enmity of most of the other aristocrats in Rome.

"What in the name of all the gods is he doing here?" Pliny wondered aloud.

"I'm trying to save your life and mine," a voice answered from the doorway, "and perhaps atone to some extent for what I've done." Stephanus stepped out of the shadows. He was dusty from his ride and appeared extremely agitated, holding one hand in the other and glancing around nervously at the slightest noise.

Pliny knew he could not betray any knowledge of a threat to himself. That would be tantamount to admitting guilt. Why would he be afraid, the Roman mentality would reason, unless he had something to hide?

"What makes you think I'm in any danger?" he said as lightly as possible. Surely Domitian couldn't know about the plot. There were only five men involved, and they'd only been planning for two days.

"You're harboring Christians," Stephanus replied.

"Christians?" Pliny snorted. "Preposterous—and the emperor knows it! I've been a priest of Jupiter, I've conducted sacrifices, and now you think I have Christians in my house?" He was immensely relieved that that was all the emperor was concerned about. The charge, though serious, could be dealt with.

"I have known it for some time, though I did not inform the emperor. One of Domitilla's servants broke under torture and revealed that Zosimus is a member of their group. I used to see him regularly myself at their worship."

"Zosimus! That scoundrel! After all I've done for him. Well, I'll certainly have him whipped!" To think that he could have spent the entire morning sitting not five feet from a Christian and not have known it!

"My lord, you have more serious problems at the moment. Because you have a Christian in your house, the emperor suspects you of being involved in Flavius and Glabrio's plot against him."

"But there was no plot. How could I be involved?"

"The emperor's mind doesn't work that way. Both men were convicted of a plot. Therefore, there was a plot. And surely, he will reason, you must know one of your most trusted slaves is a Christian. He needs only a few more days to gather a witness or two and any written evidence he can find or manufacture, and he'll be ready to act against you."

Pliny put his hand to his head. "Why did you come all this way to warn me? I'm no friend of yours."

"I have no friends, I know. Even Domitian mistrusts me. He has accused me of embezzling money from Flavius' estate before the division was made. I came here because you are one of the few decent men left in Rome. I realize now that by informing on Flavius and Glabrio I killed two of the finest men Rome has seen in recent years."

"Why did you do it?"

"I thought they were corrupting Rome with this new faith and that if we made an example of them we might turn people back to the old ways. But I see now that all I've done is weaken Rome and give the Christians new determination to hold on to their faith. If something like this appeals to the really good people in our society, I've concluded, then there must be something good in it. And if Domitian, Regulus, and their sort uphold the old ways, then the old ways aren't worth maintaining."

"I don't share your viewpoint, but I do agree that something must be done. Let's go to my study and talk."

"There's very little time left for talking, my lord."

"There is never any time for rash action," Pliny lectured him, "especially against an enemy as powerful as Domitian."

He took his visitor by the arm to lead him to the study, but Stephanus winced and drew back, suddenly growing pale.

"What's wrong with your arm?"

"My horse threw me shortly after I started out. I hurt my hand and arm when I hit the ground."

"Let me have my doctor clean it and put a bandage on it, then we can talk."

"Could we walk along the shore while we talk," Stephanus suggested, "just to be safe?"

Realizing that he did not know his slaves as well as he thought, Pliny hesitated. "I understand your reasoning, but the bright sunlight is unbearable with my eye acting up."

Lorcis squinted as she emerged from the dark tunnel into the arena. Even with the awning in place, the light was too bright for her eyes to tolerate after several days of subterranean gloom. She and Jacob stopped to get their bearings and let their eyes adjust, but the guard prodded them with his spear.

"Keep moving!" he said roughly. "Can't keep the people waiting." His shove sent them stumbling out toward the center of the arena. Lorcis looked around at the mass of people and heard the angry rumble that greeted the appearance of the Christians, but the only thought she was conscious of was how hot the sand felt under her bare feet.

Once the Christians were herded together in the middle of the arena, the consul who was sponsoring the games drove out in a chariot with several attendants marching along on either side of him. He motioned for quiet, and when the crowd had given him its attention he called out, "Noble Romans, fellow citizens!" At the sound of his voice Lorcis strained to see him. Yes, it was Regulus!

"My friends," he went on, using all his oratorical training to make himself heard by the majority of the people in the stands, "you see before you a herd of Christians—a congregation they call themselves, a term derived from our word for herd. It seems appropriate, doesn't it, from the appearance of them? For their refusal to do homage to our gods and our beloved emperor, they've been convicted of atheism and treason."

The crowd made angry noises.

"It is well that you vent your wrath on them, for they attack the very foundation of our society. What good Roman would refuse simple acts of piety and patriotism? And they are criminals of long standing. Even in Nero's time they were found guilty of starting the fire that destroyed a large part of Rome."

The crowd booed and shouted insults at the pathetic little knot of twenty or thirty people huddled together in the center of the arena.

"Not only are they notorious criminals, but their private behavior is also reprehensible. It is well known that they commit the grossest acts in their secret rites, even eating human flesh and drinking human blood."

A buzz ran around the arena.

"The peculiar thing about these Christians is that, as dangerous as they are, they put up a facade of pacifism, refusing to fight when attacked." He dismounted from his chariot, walked over to one of the women, and struck her in the face. She held her gaze steadily on him and offered him the other side of her face. Regulus laughed in disbelief and motioned for one of his attendants to strike her with his rod, the symbol of Regulus' office. The woman dropped to her knees from the force of the blow.

With a sneer, Regulus addressed the crowd again. "You probably couldn't hear her, but the wench's only response to that was to mutter, 'Father, forgive them for they know not what they do.' You swine, I know exactly what I'm doing." He kicked the woman in the mouth, sending her sprawling on her back.

"Their leader was crucified," Regulus went on, straightening his toga, "in Palestine when Tiberius was emperor. Crucified, mind you, like any common criminal. But they claim he was a god and that he rose from the dead! Yes, they think a dead man can rise again! Well, let's test their theory."

A squad of soldiers brought out the pieces for six crosses and laid them out around the edge of the arena at different points so everyone in the stands could clearly see at least one victim.

"Now, I don't suppose it matters . . . " Regulus said cheerfully. He tapped three men and three women on the shoulders. "Crucify them!" he ordered.

There were a few wails of despair from the huddled Christians, but Jacob touched as many of them as he could before the soldiers dragged them away. "You are going to God. Do not be afraid," he exhorted them.

When Regulus noticed him blessing the others, he forced his way through the group to stand in front of Jacob and Lorcis. "By the gods! You two! Still thick as thieves, I see. Nestor, I named you well. You threaten to outlive us all, but we'll put a stop to that this afternoon. And you, Lorcis. Every time I think I've seen the last of you, you pop up again. I daresay if I crucified you we could make sure you would stay dead."

Lorcis gasped. She thought she could endure almost any form of death so long as it was quick. Death on the cross could take hours and inflict untold pain on the victim. The death actually resulted from suffocation as body fluids accumulated in the chest cavity and crushed the lungs.

Regulus smiled his evil smile. "I have something else planned, though, and it turns out to be even more appropriate than I could have hoped. There will be a delicious irony to it, though you may find it difficult to appreciate."

He returned to his chariot and was helped back into it by the driver. He then looked around at the crowd. "Another form of punishment in Palestine—one inflicted on some of the early Christians—is stoning. This seems a fitting punishment for people who accept everything so passively. They don't even provide decent entertainment in the games, we've found, because they just stand there like so many lumps. To demonstrate just what sort of spirit animates these people, I have invited my daughter, Aquilia, and the children of some other noble families to join in stoning to death this bunch of rabble."

Gates in the walls of the arena swung open allowing soldiers to wheel out carts laden with small, fist-sized rocks. The creaking of the carts' axles partially drowned out the cries of those Christians being fastened to the crosses. The real pain came, Lorcis had heard one of the guards say, when the cross was hoisted and dropped into the hole in the ground where it was to stand. Her prayers were with her unfortunate friends, but she focused her attention on the people moving toward her.

Beside and behind the carts walked several dozen youngsters, most in their early teens. Lorcis had no difficulty guessing which one was Regulus' Erotion. Her dress was the most elegant, her bearing the haughtiest. Even though she wasn't Regulus' daughter, she had picked up some of his characteristics along with the adoptive name he'd given her. "I'm to blame for that," Lorcis thought. "I'm the one who gave that child to him. But maybe Xanthippe was right. Her life wouldn't have been any more pleasant if she had grown up with her own parents."

Lorcis could see that Regulus was going to enjoy this. He had no doubt debased the girl in every way imaginable already. Now he stood beside her proudly, about to teach her to kill—and he thought the child was going to kill her own mother. Lorcis wished she could tell him the truth, just to rob him of that satisfaction, but she had to content herself with her own knowledge that he was a misguided fool.

The children hesitated, none quite willing to begin. This whole business, which had seemed such a lark when they talked and laughed about it beforehand, felt so different out in front of all these people. Sensing their reluctance, Jacob hobbled forward. Only the children and a few senators in the front rows could hear him when he spoke.

"A woman caught in adultery was once brought before Jesus. The law required that she be stoned to death, and the Jewish priests asked Jesus whether he thought the penalty should be carried out. But Jesus merely replied, 'Let the one who is without sin cast the first stone.' "

A rock thudded into his shoulder, and he cringed. "Shut up, old man!" Aquilia screeched. "My father says you always did talk too much."

Another child also grabbed a rock from a cart and flung it into the group, aiming at no one in particular, but it grazed a man's head, drawing blood. The crowd cheered and encouraged the other children to participate. "Show us you're Romans!" someone shouted.

A rock struck Lorcis on the arm and she turned her head in pain. Then in rapid succession another hit her in the neck and a third in the head. She collapsed and Jacob fell on top of her.

Junicus left his seat as soon as he recognized Lorcis, but Martial stayed until the rocks started flying thick and fast, almost burying the Christians as they killed them. When the two men found each other in a passageway under the seats, they embraced and wept. Lorcis was beyond their help. Perhaps she had been all along, if they had faced the truth.

"I want to give her a decent burial," Junicus finally said. "Is there any way we can get her body out of here?"

"You don't give up, do you," Martial said, shaking his head in disbelief. "I don't know why I don't just walk away right now. What more can you hope to accomplish?"

"To show my love for my wife."

"Damn! You've always got an answer." He looked around, as though formulating a plan. "Come on. They take the dead bodies out through the south gate. Let's go down there and see if there's anything we can do."

Fending off prostitutes and food vendors, they worked their way around the arena under the seats until they could see slaves carrying bodies out and dropping them at the head of a ramp to a lower level under the stadium. Other slaves then rolled the bodies down the ramp.

A guard blocked their progress with his spear. "And what would you gents be wanting down here?"

Martial assumed his most foppish air, seeming to take the guard into his confidence. "My friend here has never made love to a woman who is, shall we say, totally passive. I thought we might find a suitable subject for such an experiment here." He smiled sickeningly. It was easy after watching the people around him do it for so many years.

"Well, these folks is marked for feeding the cats, my lord," the guard replied. "Meat for those critters is mighty expensive, if you take my meaning."

"Oh, indeed I do," Martial said, pulling a fistful of coins out of his money pouch and slipping them to the soldier.

"Be quick about it," the guard said.

Junicus and Martial separated and scanned the faces of the dead bodies, which were stacked up like firewood. Martial went down the ramp, then called, "Here she is!"

Junicus rushed down to join him and found him trying to move several bodies which were piled on top of Lorcis. "Damn! I can't get her out," he cried in frustration. Junicus tenderly lifted the two bodies on top and laid them down as though he were putting the children to bed. Martial dragged one more body out of the way, then Junicus picked Lorcis up. He brushed her hair out of her face and tried to wipe some of the blood off.

"Never mind that now," Martial urged him. "Here, wrap her in my cloak and let's get out of here. If anybody says anything to you, just tell them she passed out from the excitement."

When they came back up the ramp the guard spotted them. "There's several in this lot prettier than her," he said. "Might as well get your money's worth."

"Well, there's something about this one that appeals to both of us," Martial replied. "Now, what's the least conspicuous route out of here?"

The guard pointed to a passageway opening to their left. "Follow that and take the second right turn. That'll take you to the animal trainers' entrance. Not likely there'll be anybody coming in there this time of day."

"Thanks," Martial said, handing him a couple of more coins. The guard took them with a smirk. "A pleasure to be of service, my lord."

Small torches did little to illuminate the dank passageway where Junicus and Martial had to walk. At first they were afraid the guard had tricked them, but after making the right turn they saw a patch of daylight ahead. Suddenly Junicus cried, "Oh, my God!"

Martial, who was leading the way, whirled around, expecting an attack from soldiers, animals, anything. But he saw and heard nothing. "What's wrong with you?" he demanded.

"She's breathing!" Junicus almost shouted.

"Well, shut up about it and let's get out of here!"

EPILOGUE

From Suetonius' *Life of Domitian,* chapter 17:

Not much is known about the assassination of Domitian. Stephanus, formerly the steward of the emperor's niece Domitilla, was accused of embezzlement. He approached a band of conspirators and offered them his services, which were gladly accepted. To allay suspicion, Stephanus pretended he had injured his arm and for several days wore bandages with a dagger concealed in them. Finally he told Parthenius, Domitian's personal attendant, that he had information about a plot. Having been admitted to the emperor's bedroom, he produced a list of names. While Domitian was reading it, Stephanus stabbed him. The wound was not fatal, and Domitian fought back, struggling to reach a dagger which he kept under his pillow. But his dagger proved to have no blade. Domitian fell on top of Stephanus and cut his own hand attempting to wrest the knife away from him. He clawed at Stephanus' eyes and almost overcame his assailant before several other conspirators rushed in. Domitian succumbed to seven stab wounds.